DEVIL SENT THE RAIN

Music and Writing in
Desperate America

TOM PIAZZA

HARPER  PERENNIAL

NEW YORK • LONDON • TORONTO • SYDNEY • NEW DELHI • AUCKLAND

HARPER ● PERENNIAL

HarperCollins books may be purchased for educational, business, or sales promotional use. For information please write: Special Markets Department, HarperCollins Publishers, 10 East 53rd Street, New York, NY 10022.

FIRST EDITION

Designed by Michael P. Correy

Library of Congress Cataloging-in-Publication Data is available upon request.

ISBN 978-0-06-200822-0

11 12 13 14 15   OV/RRD   10 9 8 7 6 5 4 3 2 1

DEVIL SENT THE RAIN

Also by Tom Piazza

Fiction

City of Refuge

My Cold War

Blues And Trouble: Twelve Stories

Nonfiction

Why New Orleans Matters

Understanding Jazz: Ways to Listen

True Adventures with the King of Bluegrass

Blues Up and Down: Jazz in Our Time

The Guide to Classic Recorded Jazz

Setting the Tempo: Fifty Years of Great Jazz Liner Notes (editor)

To Mary, of course

ACKNOWLEDGMENTS

My gratitude to the editors who helped to refine and shape many of these pieces, especially Eric Banks at *Bookforum*, Marc Smirnoff at the *Oxford American*, Fletcher Roberts and Peter Keepnews at the *New York Times*, and James Marcus at the *Columbia Journalism Review*.

For encouragement, friendship, and various forms of aid during the composition of these pieces, thanks to Jeff Rosen, David Gates, Elvis Costello, Eric Overmyer, Benjamin Hedin, Jeffrey Gaskill, Peter Guralnick, Mary Gaitskill, Terri Troncali, Wyatt Mason, Harry Shearer, Roy Sekoff, J. Michael Lennon, Phillip Sipiora, Ed Newman, Robert Birnbaum, Jeff Martin, Bob Dylan, Sven Birkerts, Lillian Piazza, and the late and badly missed Jean Howell. Thanks to Yaddo, the MacDowell Colony, and the Virginia Center for the Creative Arts for time and space.

And special thanks to my colleagues and friends in the writers' room of HBO's *Treme*: David Simon, Eric Overmyer, Lolis Eric Elie, George Pelecanos, the late David Mills, Mari Kornhauser, James Yoshimura, and Anthony Bourdain.

For my longtime editor and friend Cal Morgan, no praise or thanks will suffice. Much gratitude to Carrie Kania at Harper Perennial for her meaningful and gracious support, and to my patient and loyal agent and friend, Amy Williams. Thanks, too, to Brittany Hamblin of HarperCollins for a hundred favors, large and small.

This book is in memory of Mike Seeger, David Mills, Barry Hannah, Clara Park, Michael P. Smith, and Herman Leonard.

And as always, my biggest thanks to my only one and only, Mary Howell.

Poor naked wretches, whereso'er you are,
That bide the pelting of this pitiless storm,
How shall your houseless heads and unfed sides,
Your loop'd and window'd raggedness, defend you
From seasons such as these?

—William Shakespeare, *King Lear*

Lord sent the sunshine,
Devil, he sent the rain.

—Charley Patton

CONTENTS

INTRODUCTION

Devil Sent the Rain contains articles and essays I wrote in the years between when I moved to New Orleans, in 1994, and the present. The first section, about musicians who interest me and whose work I love, is made up of articles (with one exception) written and published before Hurricane Katrina slammed into the Gulf Coast in 2005. Part Two contains pieces written after that disaster; they are concerned mainly with New Orleans and its fate, although the last few shift the focus to literary matters. Part Three is a coda, consisting of an essay about fiction writing—a kind of post-post-Katrina stocktaking—and a very short column, written before the storm, about things that endure.

The pieces have been selected to form a narrative arc, or perhaps a fever chart, of the past fifteen years. Concerns and themes that percolate under the surface of the music writings in Part One were brought to a boil during the George W. Bush presidency and then were forced out into the open, and into the national consciousness, by Hurricane Katrina. The sense of vitality and pluralism embodied in the work of Jimmie Rodgers, Charley Patton, Bob Dylan, Carl Perkins, Gillian Welch, and the others represented here point toward a set of possibilities for both personal and societal transformation and growth that came under direct threat during the Bush years.

The destruction that followed Katrina tore roofs and walls off houses and scattered people's most personal belongings, usually broken and waterlogged, randomly into public view. It sent American citizens from their ruined homes in New Orleans to strange places, and brought people from very different backgrounds into close contact in ways they had perhaps never anticipated. It exposed a degree of governmental ineptitude that was shocking and frightening to most who paid attention. A landscape of poverty and pain was lit up for all to see, and with it, most surprisingly to some, an extraordinary spirit, a will not just to exist but to return, with all that implies.

If there is a single factor most responsible for the extraordinary distance New Orleans has traveled in the years since its near-death experience, it is the city's culture. Not only the city's music, dance, funeral traditions, cuisine, and architecture—its look and its smell and its feel and its sense of humor—but the interaction among all those factors, their coordination, is what makes the city live, what makes it *alive*, in its unique way. The elements that give American music its vitality—the sense of disparate cultures brought together and finding a way to dance, to make something that did not exist before—is also the animating spark of the spiritual exaltation at the heart of New Orleans culture. French, Spanish, African, Caribbean, German, Irish, and Italian traditions all cook together here in endless permutations, and it provides a sense of joy and possibility, along with obvious challenges. That had always been the promise of American culture at large.

The nation got a new new deal in the fall of 2008 with the election of its first African-American president. And in 2010 New Orleans chose a new mayor, one who inspired hope and confidence, just a day before the New Orleans Saints won the Super Bowl. People were also ready to swear that they had seen pigs fly. It was an exhilarating time, especially if you didn't look too closely at the fine print.

The pieces on music in Part One express, for the most part, a kind of optimism about the basic template of American possibility, for the reasons suggested above. After the September 11 attacks in 2001, and the Bush administration's hideous series of blunders that followed, culminating in the Iraq War, that very sense of possibility itself, and the implicit entitlement that always seemed to be lingering nearby, began to feel questionable in a new and more painful way. The divisions that were being wedged more and more deeply into the national dialogue were psychological, even mythological. What were once differences of policy and even philosophy had become coated with magic and superstition, manipulations cunningly crafted to bypass the reasoning faculty and go right to the heart of the fear and uncertainty that were there under the crust, like rich oil reserves that could be tapped to fuel a brutal expansion.

The question became whether there was an opposing magic to counteract the enormous undertow of all that imagery, all that appeal to easy, comforting answers. The pieces in Part Two and Part Three are, in their oblique ways, a series of raids on this question. Some concern themselves directly with issues around the rebuilding of New Orleans. The two pieces on music—one about Jelly Roll Morton and one about jump blues maestro Joe Liggins—are really pieces about New Orleans and its peculiar spiritual qualities, as well. Two essays look at the work and persona of Norman Mailer, a writer who always faced into the relations between the inner life of the individual and the fate of the society at large, and who was also a friend of mine.

Hurricane Katrina forced itself into the foreground of my consciousness and life and stayed there for five long years. During that time I wrote about the disaster in two books—the nonfiction *Why New Orleans Matters* and the novel *City of Refuge*—as well as in two seasons (so far) of the HBO dramatic series *Treme*. After the publication of *City of Refuge*, in 2008, I began work on a new novel, not about New Orleans, but set partly in New York City and partly in the American Midwest, just after the U.S. invasion of Iraq in 2003. I badly needed to begin thinking about something else after three years of writing about, rebuilding in, and advocating for New Orleans. And yet I found that I had changed as a fiction writer as a result of what I saw and experienced during and after Katrina. The essay "The Devil and Gustave Flaubert," in Part Three, addresses this; it is a kind of ground-clearing operation, perhaps.

As of this writing, the notion that the written word is doomed, or doomed to irrelevance at least, because of the power and immediacy and omnipresence of electronic media, is so widespread that it has become almost axiomatic. But it is not true, unless you measure relevance strictly in terms of quantity and size, as opposed to sharpness and penetration. The written word is not simply a less efficient delivery system for information or opinion. In the private space shared by the writer and the reader, one individual soul encounters another and a spell is cast, created by both of them. That set of conditions cannot be approached or even approximated by any other medium. Even when the marching band declaring an end to all private vision comes triumphantly through town, those words, direct from one mind to another mind, will be there to stretch the strings taut between the private consciousness and the public drama and play a tune, or a symphony.

—*Tom Piazza, New Orleans, March 2011*

One

From 1997 until 2001, I was the Southern Music columnist for the Oxford American, *which meant that in each issue I had absolute freedom to write about whatever I wanted. I also wrote a longer piece for each of the magazine's annual music issues, where the following two pieces appeared.*

The two subjects—Jimmie Rodgers, often referred to as the "Father of Country Music," and Charley Patton, sometimes called the "King of the Delta Blues"—began their recording careers at a time (the second half of the 1920s) when the indigenous music of various parts of the American South was first becoming easily available to the rest of the country via recordings. It was also a time when the popular music of the rest of the country was making its way, via recordings and radio, into the farthest reaches of rural America. Rodgers and Patton, both of whom were born in the final decade of the nineteenth century and died in the deepest trough of the Great Depression (Rodgers in 1933 and Patton a year later), are emblematic figures of that cultural moment, for reasons that I hope the articles make clear.

JIMMIE RODGERS DIED FOR YOUR SINS

He was not the boy next door. Or maybe he was. There is that high school graduation picture of him—the jacket, the bow tie, hair neatly combed, head slightly tilted, the eyes looking directly into the camera, a hint of baby fat still clinging to the cheeks. Hard to locate, in those eyes, the legendary railroad brakeman dying by degrees of tuberculosis, making his last recordings over a long five days in New York City, far from his family and friends, resting desperately on a cot between takes, dying of a massive hemorrhage two days after recording his last song in May 1933. Or maybe it was right there in those eyes all along, the mixture of curiosity and trust, shyness and self-assertion, an enigma to match the surge of adolescent self-confidence and insecurity that was America's in the wake of World War One. We were a world power. But who were we?

In photos from the 1920s you get a sense of him casting repeatedly into the river of possibility for an identity. Even before he was famous, and he became famous on a scale unprecedented—unimagined, really—for a man with a guitar, he looks different in almost every picture. Here he wears round, Harold Lloyd horn-rim glasses, slicked-back hair, and a suit—an insurance man or a Wall Street broker, smiling and playing a Hawaiian guitar. Here he wears a grease monkey's jumpsuit at a service station, surrounded by his buddies, just a good old boy. Here he's squinting meanly and challengingly into the camera, his eyes insufficiently shaded by a straw boater, hands in pockets, a small-town slicker, on the make, thinking about Bigger Things.

Once he became famous, the chameleon-like quality only became more expertly managed; the photos were taken by professionals, the smile was more practiced, more genial. He looks like a man who has stepped out his front door into a spring morning of possibility. Jimmie Rodgers, the Singing Brakeman, dressed in full railroad brakeman's outfit, giving the double thumbs-up. Jimmie Rodgers, America's Blue Yodeler, in a nice striped suit, playing his guitar thoughtfully, the country gentleman. Jimmie Rodgers, the . . . well, we'll figure it out later; first take the shots . . . dressed in full cowboy garb, complete with leather chaps and spurs, smiling and smoking a cigarette. . .

Ordinarily one would say *Skip it; pay attention to the music.* But the music seems to be a reflection of these shifts. Rodgers was both a one-man summation of the nineteenth century and an avatar of the Media Age, pointing, like all truly epochal figures, both backward and forward. He sang of rural nostalgia, cabins in the pines, Mother and Daddy waiting at home (or no longer waiting at home), freight trains, mean brakemen, rough barrooms, policemen, jail cells, long nights away from home, springtime again and work in the fields, courtship . . .

He assembled, in a sense, a personification of the growing nation itself, and he involved the individual listener in that drama of growing up: the tension between the lust for change and travel, adventure, mobility for its own sake, violence even, and at the same time a profound and occasionally corrosive sense of nostalgia for The Way Things Were Back Home—either back in the cabin, or Down South below the Mason-Dixon Line—somewhere back, back, before it all got industrialized and built up, before the innocence was lost. The endless American dynamic: Strain at the leash, transform yourself into something unrecognizable, burn off the old, claim every possibility for yourself— contain, as Whitman suggested, multitudes—then memorialize the past that you have killed to pay for all that possibility. The more resolutely you have murdered it, in fact, the more sentimental you will be about it.

Rodgers was born in 1897 in a railroad town, Meridian, Mississippi, to a railroad-man father. When he was barely in his teens he ran away a couple of times with traveling shows, before starting to work on the railroads in earnest at the age of fourteen. At some point in there he contracted the tuberculosis that would kill him. The 1920s were for him a mix of railroad work and various lunges at a show business career. He had a wife and child to support. In 1927 he left Meridian for Asheville, North Carolina, where he started hooking up with several groups of musicians, trying on different kinds of musical situations for size, everything from Tin Pan Alley to what was already being called "hillbilly" music.

Then the important thing happened: Ralph Peer came to Bristol, a town on the Virginia-Tennessee border. Peer, a key figure in the recording industry of the 1920s, arrived in the summer of 1927 and advertised open auditions in the hopes of finding rural performers worth recording for the Victor label. (The two-disc set *The Bristol Sessions*, put out by the Country Music Foundation, documents the extraordinary recordings made that summer.)

Along with dozens of others—old-time fiddlers, family musical groups (including the Carter Family, who made their first recordings that summer), blind singers, religious singers—Rodgers smelled something cooking and made the trek to Bristol. He went with a group of musicians, but before they got to the auditions they parted ways in a quarrel over billing. The band recorded separately, under the name the Tenneva Ramblers, and Rodgers cut two sides accompanied only by his own guitar. These two recordings sold well enough for him to be asked to follow up. The second pairing contained his first "Blue Yodel," sometimes known as "T for Texas." A loosely strung collection of outlaw lyrics sung in a jaunty, sly manner, interspersed with what was to become his trademark yodel, it made Rodgers a star.

Rodgers was really the first white performer to sing the blues convincingly on recordings; he got the essence of it. Blues is, among other things, an antidote to sentimentality, and in singing them Rodgers didn't exaggerate or caricature or force anything. He found a part of himself there, obviously, and the exhilaration in his "Blue Yodels," as well as things like "No Hard Times" and "The Brakeman's Blues," is unmistakable. Although Rodgers preceded them into the recording studio, a number of white performers (among them Darby and Tarlton, the Allen Brothers, Dick Justice, and Gene Autry) did sing the blues very well around the same time. Even Jimmie Davis, years before he wrote "You Are My Sunshine"—and decades before he became the gentleman segregationist governor of Louisiana—made a specialty of singing some very authentic-sounding blues. If you want a good demonstration of what the same material sounds like in the hands of a talented singer without the gift for blues, get Lefty Frizzell's tribute album, *Songs of Jimmie Rodgers*. Frizzell was, of course, one of the very greatest country singers, but he wouldn't have known the blues if it hit him over the head with a plate. Merle Haggard, on the other hand, knew exactly what to do with this kind of material, and his Rodgers tribute album, *Same Train, A Different Time*, is one of the best things he has ever recorded.

The flip side of Rodgers's way with the blues is his body of recordings in which Mother and home, dear old Daddy, and the little cabin, are all extolled with a dewy-eyed sentimentality that has remained part of country music:

> *There's a little red house on top of a hill*
> *Not very far from an old syrup mill . . .*
>
> ("Down the Old Road to Home")

On sides like these, Rodgers was nothing if not a one-man syrup mill. Still, there's no overwrought, throbbing, grabbing of the listener's heart strings; Rodgers could deliver such lines and then turn around and shout, "Hey, sweet Mama!" the way he does in, say, "Jimmie's Texas Blues."

In any case, Rodgers didn't represent the expression of a unique personality so much as he did the fluidity of identity. He didn't have a single easily defined image that took its place in a larger drama, the way Gene Autry did, or Johnny Cash, or Waylon Jennings, or Bob Wills. He was not a fixed personality who used the guitar and the songs as a vehicle. Rather than just being a man with a guitar, Rodgers became Man With A Guitar, an archetype. Singers of the most diametrically opposite types have always found plenty to work with in his songs. On the disc *The Songs of Jimmie Rodgers: A Tribute*, put together by Bob Dylan, singers as different as Willie Nelson, Van Morrison, Aaron Neville, Iris Dement, Dwight Yoakam, and Dylan himself perform songs either written by or associated with Rodgers, and the results are startlingly fresh and individualistic.

I doubt whether any other popular performer of his time recorded in as many widely spread-out places. Rodgers made records not just in Bristol, but in Dallas, Atlanta, New York City, New Orleans, Louisville, San Antonio, Los Angeles, and Camden, New Jersey. He recorded by himself, but he also recorded with country fiddlers, with slick studio jazz bands, with Hawaiian guitarists, pianists, banjo players, jug bands, and blues guitarists. Few white musicians in the jazz genre, where racial integration was not uncommon—let alone musicians who performed anything resembling "country" music—recorded as often with black musicians in the 1920s as Rodgers. Not least among these recording companions was Louis Armstrong, the closest thing Rodgers had to an opposite number in the jazz field (they teamed up for Rodgers's "Blue Yodel #9" in Los Angeles in 1930). But he also recorded with the excellent guitarist Clifford Gibson and with the Louisville Jug Band. In 1929 he even made what might be considered the first music video, entitled *The Singing Brakeman*, in which he sat in his brakeman's outfit on a stage set and sang three songs to two women, accompanied only by his own guitar.

Unlike just about every other major rural performer, though, black or white, Rodgers recorded almost no sacred material. To be precise, he recorded exactly one track: a duet with Sara Carter on "The Wonderful City." That is one song out of the 150 or so tracks included on the six-CD Bear Family box *Jimmie Rodgers: The Singing Brakeman*, which contains everything he did. Even blues musicians renowned for the most salacious kinds of material, including Blind Lemon Jefferson, Charley Patton, Blind Willie McTell, and Blind Boy Fuller, recorded gospel numbers here and there, although they customarily used pseudonyms to do so. Rare indeed were the white performers who ignored sacred material.

In some way Jimmie Rodgers seemed to represent a kind of mystery cult of his own. In his persona, as in his music, he united disparate elements in one being. People have the kind of reverence and affection for him that the devout reserve for saints. Bob Dylan, who has a way with an image, says that Rodgers's sound was like the smell of flowers. His voice, Dylan added (in the notes for the Rodgers tribute disc), "gives hope to the vanquished and humility to the mighty." Even though we're a thousand miles away from home, waiting for a train, that train will come, don't you see, and we'll be forgiven our rough and rowdy ways and shake hands with Mother and Father again.

Yet Rodgers delivered not just an echo of the redemption of the New Testament but the earthiness of primitive religion and fertility rites. According to blues authority Paul Oliver, as quoted in both major biographies of Rodgers, a tribe in East Africa called the Kipsigi, who were introduced to gramophone recordings sometime during the 1950s, developed an entire cult around the recordings of Jimmie Rodgers, whom they transformed into a deity they called Chemirocha. To them he seemed to be "a formidable player on their local *chepkong* lyre, and Kipsigi girls have come to believe that Jimmie Rodgers is a kind of centaur, half man, half antelope."

And, of course, there was always a strong element of the sacrificial in Rodgers's life. His time was not long, as he sang in one song, and he knew it. His entire six years of recording was carried out under what was at the time the almost certain death sentence of tuberculosis, which of course eats away at the very bellows that push the songs out—the seat of the spirit, the lungs. Repeatedly ordered by doctors to stay in bed, he never did. In the last three weeks of his life, he traveled by train, in the company of a private nurse, from San Antonio to Galveston, and then by boat to New York City for an epic series of recording sessions, so that his wife and daughter would have a backlog of material to help out financially after he was gone. He stayed at the Hotel Taft, and he took the time to look at a few songs by a couple of young songwriters, whom he received while in bed, propped up on pillows.

At the Victor recording studio on East Twenty-fourth Street, a cot was set up where Rodgers could lie down and regain his strength between takes. The first day, May 17, 1933, he recorded four tracks, an amazing effort under the circumstances; they included "I'm Free from the Chain Gang Now," a composition by one of the young songwriters who visited him at his hotel. The next day he recorded three tracks, including the beautiful "Dreaming with Tears in My Eyes," and a track released as "Jimmie Rodgers' Last Blue Yodel," sometimes known as "The Women Make a Fool out of Me." Rodgers skipped a day and went back in on May 20, but he was able to record only two songs before quitting.

He rested for three days. On May 24 the Victor people had set up a session with two other guitarists, and Rodgers, hanging on by a thread, recorded three songs with them. Then, solo, he recorded his last song, "Fifteen Years Ago Today," sometimes issued as "Years Ago."

The next day his nurse took him for a tour of Coney Island. He suffered a terrible attack of coughing and spasms and had to be brought back to the hotel, and in the deep morning hours of May 26 he died. Listening to the last recordings, if you know the story, is almost unbearably poignant. If you don't know the story, they are merely great records. You would never guess the circumstances.

After Rodgers died, a number of the best known country singers, including Gene Autry, Bradley Kincaid, W. Lee O'Daniel, and Ernest Tubb, recorded tribute songs. Most, if not all, of them are assembled on Bear Family's disc *Memories of Jimmie Rodgers*. Decades later, the list of major country performers who either recorded Rodgers's songs or did whole albums in tribute is not just long but nearly endless.

There is an inner poetry in Jimmie Rodgers's work that doesn't force itself on you, that reveals itself in its own time. It is very precious. It is tempting to say that they don't make them like that anymore, but maybe they do and we just don't know about them.

From the Oxford American's *Fourth
Annual Music Issue, Summer 2000*

A LIGHT WENT ON AND
HE SANG

It is always a shock to hear him again.

I first heard Charley Patton thirty years ago, on a two-LP compilation called *The Story of the Blues*, which I won in a contest. My adolescent ear was immediately sucked in by the mystery, the wit, the slyness, and the expressive variety of the performances by Blind Boy Fuller, Memphis Minnie, Texas Alexander, Leroy Carr, Barbecue Bob, Bessie Smith, Big Joe Turner, Blind Lemon Jefferson, Otis Spann, Blind Willie McTell, and the rest.

Nearly all the tracks, even one by a group of "Fra-Fra Tribesmen" from Ghana, felt somehow familiar to me. Each had some rhythmic or melodic or expressive handle to grab onto. But one track seemed nearly unlistenable: It was "Stone Pony Blues" by Charley Patton, recorded in 1934. It seemed almost to be an artifact from some lost world. Patton hollered and growled, rather than sang; he sounded like someone suddenly and belligerently addressing you from a nearby stool in a darkened bar. On top of that, his diction was nearly opaque. His vowels were stretched out, inflated from within; they expanded until they were all but unrecognizable. The words "stone pony" came out sounding like "doughboanayyyy." What I eventually recognized as "door" sounded like "duwowwwwahhhh." He added to the confusion by breaking words in half, and by choosing odd syllables to accent. All of this was delivered by a voice from which any trace of varnish had apparently been stripped.

Patton was too much for me, like the first time you taste really strong black coffee as a kid. He left an aftertaste that burned. And yet, exactly because his sound felt so repellent, I wanted to come to terms with it. It seemed, almost, to be daring me to recognize it as a human sound.

To this day listening to him can be like having a caged tiger in the middle of your floor. Something is a little too close for comfort. On any given afternoon you might prefer to hear Tommy Johnson, or the Mississippi Sheiks, or Son House, or Willie Brown, or any number of others. But Patton ultimately exerts a greater claim on the imagination, for me at least. Underneath the surface, once you learn how to breathe in the atmosphere Patton generates, there is humor, subtlety, pathos, braggadocio, wit, and, the more you listen, an extraordinary musical sophistication. But that quality of being part of a time and a world that are lost to us adheres to Patton's recordings in ways that remain palpable.

Charley Patton was probably born in 1891, of mixed black, white, and Native American ancestry, on a plantation near Edwards, Mississippi, midway between Vicksburg and Jackson. He was one of twelve children, only five of whom survived infancy. Before he was in his teens he had moved a hundred miles or so north with his family to the Mississippi Delta, to the now legendary Dockery plantation, on Route 8, near Ruleville.

His family was stable and even well-off by the standards of African-American Delta life in the early twentieth century. Patton's father worked hard and eventually owned some land and a drugstore. His sister Viola married the man who ran the plantation grocery store. Apparently Patton had some schooling; according to one of his nieces, Patton and Viola stayed in school through the ninth grade.

Beginning in the late 1910s and up to his death in 1934, Patton traveled all through the Delta, playing at house parties and in small makeshift barrelhouses for white and black audiences, and his songs are full of references to places and people and events of that world. The Mississippi Delta at that time was a backwater's backwater. It was a very circumscribed area through which few outsiders made their way. Nobody thought much about documenting black life there. People didn't have cameras; there are no snapshots of Patton hanging out on a porch with his friends or family, no pictures of dances where he played. By the time the WPA photographers and folklorists like the Lomaxes came through, Patton was dead. Except for a couple of trips north to make records, Patton almost never left the Delta.

There was no reason for anyone to think that the black Delta's people, landscape, and atmosphere would be immortalized. Other entertainers of the time—Bing Crosby, Maurice Chevalier, Fanny Brice, Rudy Vallee—came into homes by way of the Victrola or the gramophone. Jimmie Rodgers sang of the railroads and of traveling out West; Duke Ellington brought a new level of sophistication to African-American artistic expression. The medium of the phonograph was a road by which the Great Wide World was made available to the Local World. But it was also, as it turned out, a road by which news of the local, the idiosyncratic, and the personal made it out into the Great World. It was a two-way street, although people didn't realize it yet.

When Patton made his first recordings, in June 1929, he'd already been a well-known local musician for more than a decade. Citified, jazz- and vaudeville-influenced artists such as Ma Rainey and Bessie Smith had been making records with piano and jazz band accompaniment since the early 1920s. But in 1926 Blind Lemon Jefferson showed the companies that they could make money by recording solitary men, with guitars, singing the blues.

Patton's first records were issued in the late summer of 1929, a few months before the stock market crash, and he had a couple of regional hits with "Pony Blues" and "Down the Dirt Road Blues." Patton recorded much more than any of the other major first-generation Delta bluesmen—Son House, Tommy Johnson, Skip James, Ishman Bracey, Willie Brown, and the others. But as the Great Depression deepened, the entire industry was hurt. Records were a luxury item, and those that were issued after the crash tended to sell less and less, until, at the bottom of the Depression—from 1931 to 1933—very few records of any kind were selling anywhere, much less in the Mississippi Delta.

It is clear from the testimony of eyewitnesses that Patton was very much an entertainer. He would, apparently, do just about anything to get to an audience—play the guitar behind his back or around the back of his neck, stomp on the floor. He played blues, he played dance music, he played religious music, ragtime songs, sentimental ditties, and he recorded examples of all of it.

But it is, finally, his blues that sit at the center of his body of recorded work. They burn with a fierce bravado and deep emotion. His titles themselves are a kind of poetry: "Heart Like Railroad Steel," "Circle Round the Moon," "Devil Sent the Rain," "When Your Way Gets Dark," "Moon Going Down," "High Water Everywhere." His lyrics are full of the names of towns, and of the people who populated them: Natchez, Vicksburg, Clarksdale, Sunflower, and Belzoni; Sheriff Tom Rushing (spelled "Rushen" on the record label), Jim Lee, even Will Dockery, the owner of the plantation where he lived for most of his adult life.

If you figure in alternate takes and tracks on which he accompanied others, like the singer Bertha Lee and the fiddler Henry Sims, Patton made somewhere around sixty recordings. Certain lyrics and turns of phrase burn in the mind for keeps after you hear Patton sing them: "Lord, the smokestack is black, and the bell it shines like gold." "My baby's got a heart like a piece of railroad steel." "Where were you, now, baby, when the Clarksdale mill burned down?"

One reason that Patton's recordings are so intense is that several different layers of what you may as well call discourse are going on at once. On most of his recordings, Patton hollers out his lyrics while simultaneously using his guitar both to accompany and to comment upon the main vocal line. In addition, Patton frequently adds another layer by making spoken asides, interjections, and questions in a slightly different voice. So he sings a line such as "When your way gets dark, baby, turn your lights on high," and immediately uses his "other" voice to say, *"What's the matter with him?"*—as if he were standing there along with you, listening to himself. Sometimes this other voice addresses the singing voice directly. All the time this is happening Patton is playing chords, bass lines, or little repeated riffs on the guitar. The result is a kind of three-dimensional listening experience. Patton summons up not just his own persona, but an entire set of implicit dramatic relationships. A performance like "A Spoonful Blues" is practically an anthology of these devices, an amazing example of someone thinking and playing on several parallel lines simultaneously.

Some writers speak of Patton's "imprecise" diction, but the word "imprecise," with its implication of inadvertency, seems wrong. I would say that his diction often seems to be intentionally distorted. Words are broken in half for rhythmic effect; vowels, as mentioned, are stretched and pulled until they seem to be little more than sound for sound's sake. But what a sound they make. Patton's timing is staggeringly effective, his rhythm is elastic yet absolutely steady, and his intonation—for all the roughness in his voice—is perfect, and perfectly controlled.

His last records, made for Vocalion at the beginning of 1934 as the Depression was starting to be relieved by President Roosevelt's efforts, came along too late to do him any good; he died in April, before the records were issued. And anyway, by that time Patton was an anachronism. As the 1930s went on, the danceable, more urban sound of Peetie Wheatstraw, Sonny Boy Williamson, Tampa Red, and Big Maceo began to dominate the scene. There was little appetite anymore for Patton's kind of dark, rough, uncut sound. Robert Johnson's records of 1936 to 1937 were a kind of throwback, the last big explosion in the munitions dump of the Delta blues. The slightly later recordings of Tommy McClennan and Robert Petway were little more than a footnote to the classic era of Patton and the others.

In the very late 1950s and early 1960s, it began to occur to a handful of young record collectors that some of the men and women who made the super-rare 78 records they treasured might still be alive and living in the Delta and environs. Guitarist John Fahey, collectors Dick Spottswood, Gayle Dean Wardlow, and a number of others looked in phone books, accosted people on the street, followed leads, and encountered the singers' friends, cousins, nieces, sons, daughters and, occasionally, the singers themselves. In this way Skip James was found, and Son House, Bukka White, Ishman Bracey, and Mississippi John Hurt, all of whom had recorded around the same time as Patton. But Charley Patton, of course, was long gone.

From interviews with these sources, a very sketchy life story for Patton began to be pieced together. In the late 1960s Samuel B. Charters included some of this material in a chapter on Patton in his book *The Bluesmen*. In 1970 Fahey published a groundbreaking study of Patton, including lyric transcriptions, musical analysis of the songs, descriptions of instrumental techniques Patton used, and what biographical material he had access to at the time. It looked as though it would be quite a while before anything like a full-scale biography could be attempted, and now it appears that there never will be one. There just isn't enough documentation—no diaries, no letters, no logs of engagements, calendars, pay records, accountants' books. Researchers had to rely on the memories of a small handful of people who actually knew Patton and were articulate enough to convey some of what they remembered.

The closest thing we have to a biography is *King of the Delta Blues: The Life and Music of Charlie Patton*, by Stephen Calt and Gayle Wardlow. It is in some ways a valuable book and in other ways an unfortunate one. It gathers together a lot of information, but in a disorganized and sometimes nearly unreadable fashion. Calt, who has also written books on Skip James and Robert Johnson, and who seems to have done much of the actual writing here, has a style full of a puzzling mean-spiritedness and pomposity. For some reason the authors rely on Son House's negative evaluations of Patton's musical abilities, which were transparently motivated by professional jealousy. Calt's own musical analyses verge on gibberish. For example, he calls "When Your Way Gets Dark" a "12 and 1/4 bar" song that "begins with an amputated six beat vocal phrase that is followed by an unexpected instrumental measure. . . . An unorthodox eleven beat bottleneck figure, capped with a conventionally fretted six beat bridge, follows a repeating of the tonic riff." Huh? There is worthwhile material to be had in this book, just as there is nutriment to be had in a plate of fish that is filled with tiny bones. Eat carefully, and swallow nothing whole.

The good news is that the late John Fahey's remarkable record company, Revenant, which has put out landmark collections of Dock Boggs, Charlie Feathers, the Stanley Brothers, and others, has released a seven-CD set dedicated to Patton, entitled *Screamin' and Hollerin' the Blues: The Worlds of Charley Patton*; it includes every note Patton played, as well as recordings by his closest associates, recordings of interviews with those who knew him, a full reprint of Fahey's 1970 book, essays, lyric transcriptions, reproductions of ads for Patton's recordings, and photos of every

Patton record label. This set is the definitive word on Charley Patton and his surroundings.

The best single-disc collection, for both tune selection and sound quality, is Yazoo's *Founder of the Delta Blues*, which contains "Down the Dirt Road Blues," "A Spoonful Blues," "When Your Way Gets Dark," "Stone Pony Blues," "Devil Sent the Rain," "Moon Going Down," and twenty other tracks. Yazoo's other Patton CD, *King of the Delta Blues*, is not quite as consistent, containing several lesser tracks, as well as a few of his religious recordings. There's a nice 3-CD set from the British Catfish label, called *The Definitive Charley Patton*, which contains a handsome booklet and neat individual jackets for the CDs on which are reproduced old 78 sleeves. The Patton sets on the Wolf and Document labels, while better than nothing, are carelessly remastered.

A final remark: When you acquire Patton's music today on CD, you face an array of at least twenty tracks, back-to-back, ready to go. But putting the CD on and letting her rip may not be the best way of listening to these recordings.

The music of Patton's that we now have comes down to us not from pristine masters that have been sitting in a record company's vault; they have been transferred from extremely rare and worn old shellac discs, each of which once belonged to someone for whom that disc was a very important possession. These recordings were acquired mostly by very poor people at what was to them a significant cost, one by one, just as they were conceived and recorded. They meant so much to the original owners that they would often be played until the grooves disintegrated. We have these performances now because they were collected—one by one, and often from the original owners—by collectors who went out into neighborhoods and knocked on doors to find them.

The performances were not assembled digitally in a modern studio, with overdubbing and multitracking. Patton walked into a room and sat in a chair; a light went on, and he sang. Then the light went off. Charley Patton opened a window in time for himself. And the real meaning behind that voice and that guitar reveals itself only over time. Be glad.

From the Oxford American's *Fifth Annual Music Issue, Summer 2001*

In 2003 PBS presented a series of films, produced by Martin Scorsese, about the blues. Each film was auteured by a different director, among them Clint Eastwood, Wim Wenders, and Scorsese himself. A couple of different companies got together to produce a companion five-CD set, for which I wrote the accompanying essay, which won a Grammy Award for best album notes.

The physical award itself arrived at my New Orleans home, surrounded by perfectly fitted dense foam that filled a box the size of a small guitar amplifier. The box was retrieved from my house in the weeks following Katrina and brought to our temporary evacuation quarters in Missouri. It is presently in a witness protection program in a location we cannot disclose. Six years later, it is remarkable how many people still have not fully unpacked from their Katrina evacuation.

THE BLUES:
A MUSICAL JOURNEY

I.

The blues is a tangle of contradictions. It is sad and funny, personal and traditional, optimistic and fatalistic, dark and bright. The blues is, in fact, a way of holding such opposites in the mind, and the heart, simultaneously. It originated among people at the bottom of the American ladder, and it came to be treasured throughout the world.

And, of course, it is too big a subject to be covered completely in five thousand words. How could you do justice to a genre that includes Bessie Smith, Ma Rainey, Blind Lemon Jefferson, Charley Patton, Big Bill Broonzy, Robert Johnson, Blind Willie McTell, Jimmie Rodgers, Memphis Minnie, Muddy Waters, Howlin' Wolf, Bob Dylan, Eric Clapton, Cassandra Wilson, and the White Stripes? The blues has been played and sung by lone men and women with guitars and by full orchestras, by jug bands, rock and roll groups, jazz pianists, and cabaret singers. Its borders are porous, and its influence has seeped out into nearly everything surrounding it.

In fact it may be helpful to see the blues as a huge river through the middle of our culture. Almost every notable form of American music in the twentieth century is a city, or a village, along that river. Jazz, rock and roll, rhythm and blues, bluegrass, and even so-called serious or classical music, have all drawn strength, power, and refreshment from, and owe much of their character to, the blues.

2.

No one knows exactly where, when, or how the blues began. Blues as a specific musical form is at least one hundred years old as of this writing. But blues performance involves a body of expressive techniques, many of which are traceable back well into the nineteenth century, and some of which clearly go back to Africa.

Visitors to the antebellum South commonly reported hearing unusual vocalizing from slaves. The English actress Fanny Kemble, who in the 1830s spent time visiting a Georgia plantation, published a memoir that contained widely quoted references to "a music . . . extraordinarily wild and unaccountable." What she heard may very likely have resembled music that survived to be recorded by the Library of Congress in the 1930s and even later. The sound of the vocal line, based on the five-note "pentatonic" scale common in folk music the world over, contained a cry, or a holler; notes were bent, flattened, "worried" for expressive effect. The group singing relied heavily on call and response between leader and chorus, establishing a rhythmic element that was part of the melody and that helped set a tempo for heavy labor. These work songs and field hollers survived almost unchanged, apparently, in poor rural areas of the south well into the middle of the twentieth century.

Beyond the strictly musical elements, the blues implies a stance—you might, if you were feeling ambitious, call it a philosophy of life. It was and is a way of neutralizing hard luck, of gaining a purchase on the facts of life that would allow one to survive and even thrive with humor, resilience, and style. The subject matter often involved ironies, things that couldn't be spoken out loud, which would be couched in a kind of code that might sound like nonsense to an outsider. Often the songs were about men who had run off from an oppressive situation, finding better luck down the road, a theme that has proved to be one of the most enduring in the blues.

Formally, the blues most commonly consists of a line, a kind of proposition (*"The woman I love, got great long curly hair"*), which is then repeated over a slightly altered harmonic background. Then a rhymed answering third line arrives (*"She's a married woman; her husband don't 'low me there"*), and the effect is satisfying. But there are many variations on this basic form, and watching for those variations is one of the pleasures of listening to the blues.

The subject matter of the blues has a long literary pedigree, at least as old as Odysseus, wandering for years with a worried mind, trying to make his way home. Furry Lewis's existential question of whether to put an end to himself under an Illinois Central train—"Went to the IC station, lay my head on the IC track; saw the IC comin', Lawd, and I snatched it back"—is a variation on Hamlet's "To be or not to be" soliloquy, just funnier. Blues has its antecedents in the thirteenth-century Provençal troubadours, in Cervantes (himself an ex-slave), in the bawdy adventures in Chaucer and Boccaccio. To all this, the blues added a specific, overtly erotic urgency—an exultation in the body and sexuality, combined with a sense that it is an abiding source of trouble. Perhaps because of that, the spirit of the blues is often close to the spirit of the joke. When Rodney Dangerfield says, "My wife always wants to make love in the back seat of the car. While I'm driving," he's singing his own version of the blues. A piece of hard luck, but you laugh at it. Or you dance to it.

3.

The blues had been around for a while before anyone realized it was worth recording or trying to sell. The songwriter and bandleader W. C. Handy, himself an educated man and a schooled musician, was one of the first to see the commercial, and artistic, possibilities in the blues in the early years of the twentieth century. He had been playing show tunes and light classical music without much success, when he began noticing an appetite in both white and black audiences for more syncopated or overtly African-American music. His imagination was captured one evening in 1903 by an itinerant musician in a train station in Tutwiler, Mississippi. Playing guitar in what we would now call a bottleneck style, the man repeated the words,

I'm goin' where the Southern cross the Dog

—a reference to two railroads. The line haunted Handy, who got the man's name and transcribed the lyric, which later found its way into one of Handy's own formal blues, "The Yellow Dog Blues."

Handy had heard something there that he knew might be useful, and he set to work writing a series of songs that became some of the best-known blues—"St. Louis Blues," "Joe Turner Blues," "Memphis Blues," "Beale Street Blues," and a long string of others. These were regarded at the time as novelty tunes. He made his headquarters in Memphis, a city that was to play a huge role in the spread of the blues.

His early blues became hits, performed by singers, pianists, jazz bands, and even military bands. Following in his wake came a procession of other songwriters, black and white, hoping to capitalize on Handy's success. Much of what they wrote had little to do with what we think of as the blues, being more like minstrel-influenced Tin Pan Alley material, with titles like "Farmyard Blues," "War Bride Blues," and "Prairie Blues." It is worth mentioning, too, that from the beginning the blues as a form—as well as the bent notes and call-and-response techniques we associate with it—was an element in jazz music. In fact the very first issued jazz record, made in 1917 by a group from New Orleans called the Original Dixieland Jazz Band, was the "Livery Stable Blues."

Had it stopped there, the blues might have come to be regarded as another caricature of African-American expression, like the "coon song" of minstrel days. But in 1920 something happened that made all the difference. The record companies had been slow to record black talent (despite the success of a handful of minstrel-based recording artists, like the great stage performer Bert Williams), fearing that there might not be a market for it. But through the efforts of the pioneering songwriter Perry Bradford, in 1920 a young black singer named Mamie Smith recorded a song called "Crazy Blues." The success of that record—it sold more than 75,000 copies in the first month alone—told the companies that there was a lot of money to be made from black music.

They began signing up and recording a string of black "comediennes"—theater singers with vaudeville experience on the black circuit—who would sing the bluesy pop songs with something close to an African-American sound. The great Ma Rainey—a seasoned vaudeville performer—was one of the best of these, a flamboyant performer who wore a necklace of gold pieces and was often accompanied by the best jazz musicians of the time. But she was preceded into the studio by almost a year by the greatest of all the women blues singers, Bessie Smith.

Bessie Smith had the talent to make what had been regarded as a novelty into a serious art, and she raised the bar for everyone who followed. Her sound was heavy and powerful, yet full of subtle expressive detail. She had a way of inhabiting the lyrics—even the occasionally inane ones that she was called on to record—and investing them with a meaning and commitment that was beyond anything anyone had heard on records. Called the "Empress of the Blues" by Columbia Records publicity, Smith garnered unprecedented financial success and popularity. She recorded vaudeville material and pop tunes as well as blues, but she brought her blues sensibility to everything she did, and became a major influence on many who followed her, including Billie Holiday and, much later, Janis Joplin. Behind her came a long line of talented singers in the same vein, such as Clara Smith, Trixie Smith, Ida Cox, Alberta Hunter, Sippie Wallace, the irrepressible Victoria Spivey, and many others.

4.

The recordings of these so-called classic blues singers sold very well in the early 1920s. But, partly because of the new competing medium of radio, the record companies were under constant pressure to find something new to sell their established customers— or, better still, to find entirely new markets. Very often they would take chances on things with no idea what they were doing, trying to find something that would lure customers. A lot of good music got recorded in this almost accidental way, including much of the best early white country, pioneering Cajun, and other ethnic and regional music of all types.

And in this spirit, in 1926, a Wisconsin-based company called Paramount, which had been recording Ma Rainey and Ida Cox and many of the classic blues singers, recorded two sides by a street singer from Texas named Blind Lemon Jefferson. These were much rawer and closer to the rural sound of the field holler than anything that had ever been put on record. Jefferson was a great singer, and the wailing melodic lines of his high tenor voice were supported by a constant and extraordinarily inventive commentary from his guitar. The recordings sold extremely well, and Paramount lost no time in getting Jefferson into the studio again, to be followed by a series of others: a trickle at first, then a deluge, of men (and a handful of women) with guitars who could sing what came to be called the country blues.

There was an apparently insatiable appetite for this kind of expression among black audiences, to whom these discs were exclusively marketed as "race records." Most record companies got involved in recording for this market, often setting up specially numbered series to distinguish the "race" discs from others in their catalogues. The companies made field trips into the South, to cities like Atlanta, New Orleans, Dallas, and Memphis, to record local talent; in many cases they would bring favored artists north to recording facilities in Wisconsin, Indiana, Chicago, or New York.

And what music and poetry they found waiting out there for them. It was like discovering a lost continent, or a parallel universe that had been there all along, hidden in plain sight. They recorded ballads of bad men and folk heroes, like Stack-O-Lee and John Henry, songs full of restlessness and rambling and lost love, worried minds and wry humor, trains, with their black smokestacks and bells that shine like gold, highways and dirt roads and blood-red rivers, rain and floods and sun that would shine in your back door someday.

Every area of the country, it turned out, had a different style, and the recordings began carrying these styles out, like notes in bottles, for others to hear in other places. Texas delivered the haunting gospel singer Blind Willie Johnson and Texas Alexander, whose singing sounded like field hollers. Urbane Memphis had jug bands and jaunty medicine show singers like Frank Stokes and Furry Lewis. There was Atlanta, with its twelve-string guitar tradition including Barbecue Bob and the great Blind Willie McTell, whose high, plaintive voice is one of the most identifiable in the blues; there was slick Lonnie Johnson from St. Louis; Blind Blake from Florida, who could make his guitar sound like a whole band; the great fingerpickers from the Piedmont area in the Carolinas; barrelhouse pianists who played in lumber camps in Mississippi and Alabama and created the beginnings of boogie-woogie. And, perhaps the most intense of all, there were the singers from the plantations and small towns of the Mississippi Delta, like Charley Patton, Tommy Johnson, Son House, and Skip James, whose dark, driven sound seared the soul for keeps once you had heard it.

White singers knew about this stuff, too, and many rural white performers began recording blues. The most famous, and the greatest, of these was Jimmie Rodgers, whose "blue yodels" became a sensation. From the beginning, blues was an integral part of country music, and early performers such as Dock Boggs, Frank Hutchison, and the Carter Family recorded convincing blues performances, as did some of the pioneering Cajun performers, like the great accordionist Amédé Ardoin. Decades later, both the father of bluegrass music, Bill Monroe, and the great country singer-songwriter Hank Williams claimed to have taken early "lessons" with local bluesmen while coming of age.

And, of course, jazz bands played the blues. King Oliver and Louis Armstrong both accompanied the classic blues singers on recordings and translated the blues into instrumental jazz terms. Duke Ellington, Fletcher Henderson, Don Redman, and a number of others were learning to orchestrate idiomatic blues for large jazz orchestras; as writer Albert Murray has pointed out, their instrumental and expressive techniques, the grammar of their style, evolved in large measure from the palette of the blues. The jazz critic Whitney Balliett once wrote that "Jazz would be an empty house without the blues," and during this period there might not even have been a house in the first place without the blues. The centrality of blues to American music wasn't lost on George Gershwin, either, who deliberately incorporated blues elements into both his popular songs and his more ambitious compositions such as "Rhapsody in Blue."

This late-1920s period was a Golden Age of American music, and it lasted until the Depression knocked out record sales for just about everyone.

5.

The Great Depression hit poor blacks especially hard. Record sales were down all over, but the blues's main audience was at the low end of the economic ladder, and they rarely had extra money to spend on records. "Some people say money is talkin'," the Atlanta bluesman Barbecue Bob sang, "but it won't say a word to me." Across the country, people faced bread lines, subsistence conditions, and worse, and naturally enough the blues began to reflect this reality. Franklin D. Roosevelt's New Deal programs began to provide some relief, and they themselves became a topic for blues in songs like "WPA Blues" and "Welfare Store Blues."

As the 1930s went by more Southern black people moved to Northern cities, especially Chicago, where the opportunities for work were somewhat better. Swing—the dance music of the time, based on jazz—was the popular music, and it began to leave its imprint on the blues. Rhythms got smoothed out; the irregular vocal lines of Blind Lemon Jefferson and Charley Patton, so close to memories of field hollers and cotton-patch work that many emigrants to the cities may have wanted to forget, got streamlined, and the most popular performers, like Peetie Wheatstraw, Leroy Carr, Tampa Red, Big Bill Broonzy, Big Maceo Merriweather, and John Lee "Sonny Boy" Williamson, provided a solid, jazz-edged rhythm, often with bass, piano, and drum accompaniment.

The influence didn't just go in one direction, of course. Many of the most popular big bands of the time relied heavily on the blues. Count Basie, whose band featured the great blues singer

Jimmy Rushing, brought the sound of the Kansas City blues tradition to a national audience, and Duke Ellington used his compositional genius to ring more changes on the blues form than anyone has before or since. Clarinetist Woody Herman even dubbed his ensemble the "Band That Plays the Blues." A number of the best popular singers, too, showed the influence of the blues, above all the great Billie Holiday, who delivered even the sappiest pop tunes with a strong blues sensibility.

There was still a market for the earlier, rougher kind of blues, although it was shrinking. A late entry turned out to be one of the most extraordinary singers and guitarists who ever lived—Robert Johnson. Influenced by Son House, still absolutely a Mississippi Delta bluesman, Johnson had also clearly heard pop singers like Bing Crosby. Johnson's mid-1930s records were dark and intense and driven, like House's and Patton's, yet his style was just a bit more finished around the edges, and his stunning guitar playing laid the groundwork for the rocking bass of Chicago blues. His recordings would become a major influence on many of the blues revivalists of the 1960s. His murder in 1938 cut short one of the great blues careers.

6.

And then, of course, came World War Two, and everything changed. The war shuffled the entire deck of American society— people from different backgrounds were thrown together in the armed services, and also in the rapidly growing cities where there was an accelerated demand for war workers in factories. Chicago, Detroit, Indianapolis, and many other cities swelled with black and white workers. The scene was stimulating, but there was also a sense of dislocation, which gave an edge to the blues (and to a new form of white country music called honky-tonk), a double edge of bittersweet nostalgia for the familiarity of life back home, wherever home was, mixed with a realization that one could never really go back.

One of those who moved north to Chicago was a young man named McKinley Morganfield, who had been living on a plantation just outside of Clarksdale, Mississippi. Muddy Waters, as he called himself, began making a name at house parties and, later, nightclubs, playing an electric guitar and doing intense versions of down-home tunes like "Rolling and Tumbling" and "Walking Blues." Along with other Southern transplants like Howlin' Wolf, Sunnyland Slim, Little Walter Jacobs, and Rice Miller, he changed the sound of the blues. What came to be known as Chicago blues was in essence Mississippi Delta blues run through an amplifier—the music of Robert Johnson and Son House and Charley Patton, keyed to a new pitch of urban tension and urgency. Over insistent bass lines and accompanied sometimes by drums, piano, and throbbing amplified harmonica, this was destined to become one of the most influential types of blues.

After the war, there was an echo of the confidence of the 1920s as people began spending money more freely. And, as in the 1920s, the recording companies were under pressure from a new media rival—television, this time, rather than radio. Once again, the companies would take a shot on just about anything— once, at least. Audiences were changing, too; black people and white people had been thrown together in new ways, creating new kinds of tensions and opportunities. The younger black audiences in the cities had been listening to the jump blues of Louis Jordan and, later, Amos Milburn, Wynonie Harris, Joe Liggins, and suave Charles Brown, as well as the amplified gospel blues of Sister Rosetta Tharpe. Dozens of independent labels sprung up like wildflowers, with names like Atlantic, Chess, Savoy, King, Swing Time, Imperial, and Specialty, both to cater to these newer tastes, and to see what else would fly.

In their search for new sounds that would sell, the little record labels documented the early work of such important blues, and blues-based, performers as Fats Domino, Big Joe Turner, Lightnin' Hopkins, Professor Longhair, T-Bone Walker, John Lee Hooker, Percy Mayfield, and, perhaps greatest of all, Ray Charles. In 1951 the small Sun label in Memphis released a record by a relatively obscure singer named Jackie Brenston, with an exuberant vocal riding over an aggressive shuffle beat, answered by a sandpaper-rough saxophone, and many consider that disc, "Rocket 88," to be the first real rock and roll record. Records by performers like Ike Turner, Roscoe Gordon, Big Mama Thornton (who scored an immense hit with "Hound Dog"), and the charismatic singer and guitarist B. B. King were selling well to black buyers but were having trouble getting heard beyond what was still a more or less segregated "rhythm and blues" audience.

But then, in 1954, Sun Records founder Sam Phillips recorded young Elvis Presley, and all hell broke loose. Presley's versions of blues-based material—covers of Arthur Crudup's "That's All Right," Junior Parker's "Mystery Train," and, later, "Hound Dog," among many others—were inflected, too, with the feel of country music, and that fusion helped the blues cross over to a national white mass audience. Chuck Berry, Little Richard, Bo Diddley and white singers like Carl Perkins and Jerry Lee Lewis brought the sound and the feeling of the blues into the main vein of American popular music.

While this was going on, technology was opening its own un-expected doors. Through the new medium of the long-playing record (LP)—which could fit much more on a side, at the slow speed of $33^1/3$ revolutions per minute, as opposed to the earlier records' 78—reissues of extremely rare old records began to make the earlier music available to a younger generation, who were often at quite a geographical and cultural remove from the sources. Harry Smith's famous six-record *Anthology of American Folk Music* and Samuel B. Charters's pioneering collection *The Country Blues* turned on these younger listeners, some of whom made it their business to begin learning the old music, note for note—the beginnings of what came to be known as the folk revival.

Young record collectors and fans also began trying to locate the men and women who had made those treasured old recordings, and trips south turned up figures like Skip James, Son House, Mississippi John Hurt, Furry Lewis, Sippie Wallace, and quite a few others. They emerged from the past (along with a number of seminal white rural performers, like Dock Boggs), in many cases playing every bit as well as they had on their recordings thirty years earlier. They were brought north to play in concerts and coffeehouses, and at the enormously important Newport Folk Festival, and they made an indelible impression on everyone who heard them.

7.

At the same time, there was an odd ebb in the blues quotient in pop music. From about 1959 to the assassination of President John F. Kennedy in November 1963, things got . . . comfortable. Although blues was still being recorded and listened to by black audiences, and classic recordings by the likes of Ray Charles, Jimmy Reed, Slim Harpo, and Bobby "Blue" Bland were still being made, on the airwaves it was largely the era of white teen idols like Frankie Avalon, Paul Anka, and Pat Boone; the blues was in a partial eclipse.

But it is one of the odd coincidences of the era that, within three months of JFK's assassination, the blues came back in force, from an unexpected direction: England. The Beatles arrived to an upsurge of hysterical appreciation, singing their Chuck Berry– and Little Richard–inspired rock and roll, and after them came the entire British Invasion. Just when it looked as if maybe the blues were gone, the Rolling Stones, the Kinks, the Yardbirds, and John Mayall reminded white America of what its culture was really all about.

America was ready for it. After the 1950s the complexities that the country faced—the emergence of the civil rights movement, the acceleration of the Vietnam War, the assassinations, the increased consciousness among the young that things were not as they seemed on the surface—began to give everyone a case of the blues. The blues as music found a new resonance with a wide public, which needed a way to prevail and continue to operate in the face of injustice and trouble, a way of affirming humanity without turning a blind eye to the facts of life in America.

One of the most important performers at this time was the protean genius Bob Dylan. From his first recordings, in 1962, Dylan was mixing material from the black and white rural traditions, performing songs such as Bukka White's "Fixin' to Die" and Blind Lemon Jefferson's "See That My Grave Is Kept Clean." After the British Invasion, Dylan began plugging in and delivering a more aggressive, blues-based form of rock and roll on albums like *Bringing It All Back Home* and *Highway 61 Revisited*, on which he brought his own brand of imagist poetry to a series of kaleidoscopic variations on the blues form.

In the mid-1960s a number of young white and black performers and bands, fueled in part by the British Invasion and in part by the reissuing of older performances, began playing blues as a main part of their repertoire. The Blues Project, the Paul Butterfield Blues Band (which had accompanied Dylan in his first electric performance), the Lovin' Spoonful, Janis Joplin, Taj Mahal, the Grateful Dead, Jimi Hendrix, Canned Heat (which took its name from a recording by Delta singer Tommy Johnson), and the Jefferson Airplane (which cribbed part of its name from Blind Lemon) all spun their own variations on traditional blues.

These developments also meant a new lease on life for Muddy Waters, Howlin' Wolf, and others who had been playing the blues all along. To their credit, a number of the blues-influenced rock bands made a point of steering audiences to the sources of their music. The Rolling Stones made it a condition of one of their appearances on the television music show *Shindig!* that Howlin' Wolf appear as well. In the 1960s and 1970s performers like Wolf, Waters, Albert King, and especially the brilliant B. B. King began playing to much larger crowds than they had known before, and different crowds. As the audience for blues began to dwindle somewhat among urban African-Americans, the slack got taken up by young white audiences. The impact of seeing the earlier players live—still powerful and vital—made an impression that many never forgot. Some of the most popular rockers of that time were those most rooted in blues: the Allman Brothers, Led Zeppelin, Johnny Winter, Eric Clapton. Young musicians who heard the older blues musicians live were marked by that experience, and the careers of Bonnie Raitt, Stevie Ray Vaughan, Lucinda Williams, and many others would have been unrecognizable without it.

8.

Today, blues is having another of its periodic resurgences—in the music of the White Stripes (who have recorded songs by Son House, Blind Willie McTell, and others), Jon Spencer, Keb' Mo', Corey Harris, Chris Thomas King, Susan Tedeschi, Cassandra Wilson, David Johansen, and some hip-hop artists, most notably Chuck D. It has made its way back to its ultimate source, as well, influencing the music of such contemporary African performers as Ali Farka Touré. It has proven to be so durable partly because it is not just a way of playing music but a way of living in the world.

The blues is a reminder of the painful facts of life in the midst of good times, but it is also a reminder that hard times can't last. In the world of the blues, nothing lasts forever—except, perhaps, the constant struggle with the blues. Acknowledging that fact, the blues seem to say, is the key to living realistically. The incredible diversity of voices and approaches, the breadth of soul, that has found expression in the blues, is a testament to the durability and usefulness of that worldview.

The blues has always met resistance from those who don't, for one reason or another, want to be reminded that life will always be hard. And there are some, to this day, who prefer not to hear its message. But what would American music sound like without the blues? What would Louis Armstrong sound like? Or Chuck Berry? Or Bill Monroe and his bluegrass, or Elvis Presley, or Hank Williams? Or Cajun music? Or George Gershwin, or Duke Ellington, or Bob Dylan? Not just jazz but all American music would be an empty house without the blues. It would be a town without a river, a ship without a sail, a train without an engine. And by that measure alone, if no other, the blues will never die. It is perennial, like the showers of rain—and the sun that will surely follow.

In 1989 I flew from New York to Memphis to do a short travel piece. While I was there I rented a car and made a side trip down to Clarksdale, Mississippi, near where Muddy Waters had worked on a plantation and made his first recordings, in 1941 and 1942, for the Library of Congress. I visited the Delta Blues Museum, which at the time was located on the second floor of the public library. It was a quiet, still room on a hot afternoon; little dust motes floated in the sun that came through the partly closed blinds. A few cases with some 78s, a few artifacts, not a lot, but it evoked a period and a feeling, and I loved it. (It has subsequently moved to new quarters and expanded greatly.)

On my way out, the librarian, a very gracious middle-aged white lady who had shown me the way to the second-floor museum, asked if I wanted to go and see "Muddy's house." The cabin where Muddy Waters had lived was apparently still there, just a few miles outside of Clarksdale, in what was now a town called Stovall. She drew me a little map, and, thrilled, I set out to find Muddy's cabin. After not more than five minutes I was outside of town, surrounded by endless fields stretching off under a grey sky; another five minutes or so and I easily found the cabin, set just off the road on a slight rise, surrounded by more fields. Its brick-red paint was almost all gone; the doors were gone, the windows were gone, and the roof was gone. There it was.

I got out of the car, and with no one to stop me I climbed up onto the doorjamb and stepped inside a large room, open to the sky above. I walked around on the bare planks, looked out the window across the fields, walked back across the floor, pulled a loose nail out of a wall for a lucky piece. I wish I could say that I heard the echoes of long-ago music, or that an entire world was summoned up for me, but mainly what I heard was time rushing by.

Eight years later, I returned to Clarksdale to do this interview with Muddy Waters's cousin, the Reverend Willie Morganfield. While there, I drove out again to see Muddy's cabin, but it was gone—purchased and moved, apparently, by a well-known and well-heeled blues maven. It has since been returned to Clarksdale, and it now sits in a room in the restored train depot that houses the new Delta Blues Museum.

SACRED AND PROFANE IN CLARKSDALE

Saturday afternoon at the Western Sizzlin restaurant in Clarksdale, Mississippi. Outside, just beyond the parking lot, runs Highway 61, which in Clarksdale is the strip with the fast-food places, the chain motels, the turning lanes, the mini-malls—the oasis in the desert for those passing through the Delta south toward Greenville or north toward Memphis. Inside, Reverend Willie Morganfield, trim at seventy years of age in a beige windbreaker and brown touring cap, walks past the end of the salad bar and affectionately greets a couple of waitresses, flirting politely and generating good-natured laughter.

On Sunday mornings, when Reverend Morganfield emerges from his wood-paneled basement office at the Bell Grove Baptist Church and ascends in glory to the pulpit, he gives the impression of great size, like a barrel wrapped in a bright blue double-breasted suit. Here, though, as he makes his way to the restaurant's back room, he looks compact, spry, something like a fight trainer—quick on his feet, able to notice small increments of advantage and disadvantage in a developing situation. To an outsider, his eyes present a pleasant, guarded, searching expression, as if he were waiting to be tipped the first part of a password. He is Muddy Waters's cousin.

As he settles down at a table in the Sizzlin's back room, he lights up a Virginia Slims menthol. "I don't like the members of the congregation to see me smoking that much," he explains. "It's okay around a certain small group of them, but . . ."

The reverend is one of the best-known preachers in the Mississippi Delta. He is also a prolific recording artist with several sermons committed to record as well as a string of gospel songs (many written by him) stretching back nearly forty years. A preacher in the Mississippi Delta has a peculiar problem, to this day, because he has to coexist with a secular tradition—the blues—as profound as any sacred tradition. The blues offers an implicit, comprehensive, existential philosophy that operates outside the framework of Christian belief, yet which is haunted by it just the same; they are the Delta's spiritual poles—one sacred and the other profane—and I am here to ask Muddy Waters's cousin his thoughts about them.

As a preacher, Reverend Morganfield's technique runs toward the "Behold, I set before you a multitude of details" variety, as opposed to the intensely anecdotal, narrative, even poetic style favored by preachers like Reverends C. L. Franklin and Jasper Williams Jr. Reverend Morganfield tends to lecture his congregation on performing church duties, or on the need to contribute more money to the church. In one of his recorded sermons he estimates what an average church member might spend on cigarettes, soda pop, chewing gum, and other nonessentials in a given year, and contrasts that with what he or she might give to the church.

If his preaching tends toward admonishment on the subject of communal duty, his singing is a totally different story. Any preacher is something of a divided soul, split between the administration of public and social duties (for which the church is a center), and the essentially private business of revelation and personal relation to God. Reverend Morganfield may be an extreme example of this inner division; when he sings, his spirit becomes airborne with his voice, his high, burnished tenor broadens on long syllables into a wide vibrato, and something tender and vulnerable shows through at the heart of his sound. The modest bureaucrat of the church disappears, and his voice becomes a flag in the wind of his own faith.

Reverend Morganfield was a singer before he was a preacher. He got started singing early, leaving Clarksdale after World War Two to sing with various groups until the army drafted him, in 1950. After his discharge he continued singing, but despite some success he always had trouble making a living from it. He spent years away from Clarksdale, in Cleveland, Memphis, and elsewhere, performing, writing, and recording gospel songs for Jewel Records, out of Shreveport, yet also working construction jobs to make ends meet, before he started to preach in 1971. He came back to Clarksdale in 1975 and became pastor of Bell Grove Baptist Church, a solid brick structure that accommodates a hundred or so members every Sunday morning on Garfield Street, a narrow residential road across Highway 61 from downtown.

He is careful and politic in answering questions; he sits listening, squinting a little, smoking, then, as if feeling his way along, he begins talking.

"Well . . . any kind of music is power. You can go all the way back to Africa—those people couldn't count up to four, but they had a crude way of playing music that would get attention. Music is designed for certain different things. Biblically, music was designed to praise God. In later years, man developed a liking for music to the extent where he wanted to do it for his own benefit.

"Blues and gospel are not the same. Gospel is more . . . flexible. Like a blues singer would sing a song if his wife is gone, or a girlfriend: 'My baby gone and she won't be back no more.' That derives from the feeling of the things that happened between he and she. The average person would sing that the same way every time; very seldom do you hear a pop or blues song in a different spirit at different times.

"Now, when it comes to gospel, today you sing, 'Precious Lord, take my hand,' because you in such a downward mood until you don't know what's happening, and you say, 'Take my hand and lead me on. I can't make it unless you take my hand.' But then maybe I'll sing it, and I'm singing it because he's already blessed me, and I want him to continue . . .'"

He looks at me now with that searching expression, as if he is trying to read whether this is what I am looking for. As he pauses, another waitress comes over and says, "They didn't tell me you were here." He gets up, kisses her, gives her a little squeeze around the midsection, introduces me ("He's doing an article on me."). I say hello, but I'm thinking about what he has said. It seems to me that he is making an effort to be diplomatic; when the waitress leaves I ask him straight out if he thinks of the blues as sinful.

"Well"—there's the searching expression in his eyes again, trying to see why I'm asking—"it's the things that's done from the blues. I would think it was sinful if it's not pertaining to right and righteousness. I'll have to see it that way because of my position. I don't fight that person that does it, because I feel like he's doing what's beneficial to him, or best for him. But you'd have to look at it as being something that's being contrary to the will of God. Because if you're drawing people from the church . . ." He pauses, puts out his cigarette, thinking.

"I had a guy to tell me once," he says, exhaling, "about a certain artist; he said, 'He could be just as good a Christian as anybody.' I said, 'No, he couldn't, because, first thing about it, he's drawing folk away from God.' So he said, 'Well, he could be singing during the week and go to church on Sunday . . .' I said, 'Well, if you had a wife, would you like for her to stay with another man for three nights, and then come back and stay with you?'

"Now, I sang rock and roll," he goes on. "I haven't always been goody-goody. And I'm not goody-goody yet. I've gone to Muddy Waters's concerts . . . I've even sung on his concerts. I was staying with him up in his home on Forty-third Street in Chicago. A man offered me a lot of money to sing rock and roll. I turned it down. I had been recording gospel for a while, but I wasn't making any money. So this guy offered me this money, and Muddy told me, 'He wouldn't have to ask me but once.' But I turned it down."

"Why?"

"I just couldn't do it, because it wasn't me. I couldn't sing something that I'm not a part of. It just wouldn't work. My daddy was a preacher, and he had written me a song—'I Can't Afford to Let My Savior Down.' He wrote it for me, and I recorded it. And that night, when I was trying to make up my mind to sing the rock and roll, that song stayed with me all night. And the next morning, I said, 'I'm not gonna do it.'

"You see, you got enough folk doin' whatever's to be done for you not to ever get involved. There's enough folk playing football for you not to ever have to play it. There's enough folk getting drunk, so you don't have to. If you do, you just want to. Is that right? And they doin' it because they want to do it. And that's what I'm saying about the singing—I don't have to sing rock and roll, 'cause there's a lot of folk out there doing it, so it really don't have to be me. I can stay in my field and let that other person stay in his field. You don't have to endorse it. You don't have to condone it. Just let 'em go on and do it. Now if you can change them over to stop them from doing it, good. But if you can't, they still going to do it.

"What you have to look at . . . The store across the street sells clothes. You have to wear clothes. And over here they sell food. You have to eat. So it's a difference in whatever come up. That person survive off of selling clothes, this person survive off of selling food. But by the same token, the company he buys food from, they survive off of selling it to the restaurants. Everybody have a different thing that they are doing, and all of them work together, because you wear clothes and you eat food. So you can't fight the person that's selling clothes just 'cause you selling food. Does it make sense?"

"It makes sense to me," I say, "as a practical philosophy for how you conduct yourself, but finally, there is some kind of tallying up. Food is not necessarily in opposition to clothes. You do have to have both. But," and here I struggle for a good counterexample, "if one person has a store and they're selling fur coats, and someone comes up and says it is morally wrong to kill animals for their skins . . ." It's not a good example, but it is the best I can do.

"Well, we won't get into the wrongness," he says, "because if that's the case, it's a whole lot of things that's wrong. It'll be bad for you to buy a steak for a dollar and a half and sell it to me for nine dollars. . . . Is that right? So what we need to do is get to the median.

"You got to remember this. I said previously that blues and gospel are not the same. Music was designed to praise God, and man have made it to praise man, and that's what makes the difference. If it's praising God, good. If it's praising man, good for the man. I'm not . . . fighting because someone likes music. Anybody that have good sense like music."

"But," I go on, wanting to force him into an actual answer, "I would still think that a person who believed in Jesus as the savior would have to find blues sinful. Because you're not asking God for help, in the blues. That's not correct?"

"You're right."

"Football is one kind of thing—it just takes time away. But it seems like blues is spiritually opposed . . ."

" . . . to the gospel."

"Right."

"Well," he says, "now here's what you got to watch. There are two sides to everything. If you have hate, the opposite word is love, or vice versa. Right? So both of 'em can't be the same. You can't be wet and dry all at the same time." He laughs. "If you pushing, you not pulling. There has to be two sides. So you have to determine within yourself what side is more profitable to you. Say, if I sing the blues I'll make a lot of money. But are you thinking about the money, or are you thinking about the hereafter? That's what's important.

"Now, Muddy Waters was a good fellow, when it comes to being nice to his family . . . He was nice to us, you know—I stayed with him, I went to his home. Many times. He'd come to our home, call my mother and tell her what he want to eat, she'd fix it for him, you know. But Muddy never accepted Christ. That's going to be the difference. His daddy was ninety years old when he died, and *he* never accepted Christ. But my daddy was his daddy's brother. My daddy preached for one church for forty-two years. They fellowshipped—they got together, you know. But it's a difference in what the ultimate end is."

"What is the ultimate end?" I ask.

"Being with Christ. Now, you have to do this by faith. Some people say, well, I don't know what's going to be at the end. I don't either, but I'll tell you what, I don't want to take no chances. I'd rather be with Him, then go and not have Him. Because the Scripture said, 'Hell is a bottomless pit.' You know what bottomless mean?" He regards me across a plume of exhaled smoke. "Ain't no bottom."

"The Lord said, 'Behold I set before you good and evil. You choose. Your choice is your choice. If you want to accept good, okay; if you want to accept evil, it's okay. But now you have to pay the penalty for whichever one you accept.'"

"Did you talk to Muddy about religion at all?"

"Mmm-hmm," he says, "He went to church with me. Yep." He is silent for a moment. "Geneva, now, she went to church pretty good. His wife. She died before he did. But you see, it's a difference in going to church and being churchy. There's a lot of people in the church, but nothing in the people. You know, you can have a purse full of money, but a person full of nothing. But, now, if you don't go to church, you can't be churchy. Because He said, 'Forsake not the assembling of yourselves together.' See, you need to be together. And then He said, 'I'll meet you in my house,' and

His house is the church house. So that mean, if He don't meet you there, then you might not be meetin' Him.

"And I don't mean that you can't feel Him, or have an urge, at home, right here—but, say for instance if you got a job, you got to go to the job to get paid. So that's the way it is about church. You fellowship, and you learn about folks . . . you learn their desires, their shortcomings, and you learn how to accept that person as he or she is. You can't do it if you don't be around them."

"What role does music play in church?"

"Well," he says, "singing is to preaching what gravy is to steak. Gravy is not steak, but it makes the steak taste better. Singing is not preaching, but you can sing and soften the heart of an individual, and while the heart is softened you can inject the gospel in. There are a lot of things that, you know, you tell your children, and the way you tell them, it makes a difference how they react. You can say to your son [*harshly*], 'Go out there, boy, and mow that lawn.' He knows he's supposed to be obedient, he'll go out there and mow the lawn, but he'll break the mower. You wish you hadn't told him. But if you say, 'Son, would you like to mow the lawn for your daddy?' That's a different spirit. He says, 'Yeah, I'll do it.' He'll go out there, and if the mower looks like it's fixin' to break, he'll stop and fix it. Because of the way you told him.

"So the sound does make a difference. You can sing a song one way"—he starts singing the gospel standard "Precious Lord" in a strong voice—"and another person sings it this way"—he sings the same words as if he's falling asleep.

"It makes a difference in the feeling of the person that's playing it," he continues. "That person that plays it or sings it, that feeling is within them, and that can be injected into the people by it. People know the difference when you puttin' on and when you not. A lot of people are not really sincere. See, the devil tell you to take 'Amazing Grace' and pick up the tempo and you get more recognition. But you taken the spirit out of it. Music is designed, as I said, to praise God. If you play music just because you love music, I don't see anything wrong with it. But if you play it to try to get a certain point over for your benefit . . . that's selfishness.

"Now, I listen to blues, like I do any other. I don't turn my radio off just 'cause it come out . . ."

"If you hear blues on the radio," I ask, "do you enjoy it?"

"Not necessarily," he says. "What I do is I listen to any record for the point that's tryin' to be made on it. If I don't get the point, then I don't get anything out of it. You know, I listen to country and western—I like music, period—and I heard this guy sing, 'Who stole the train off the railroad track? / Whoever stole it sure better put it back.' I don't know what he meant by that [*laughs*]— you understand what I'm saying?—but it sounds good. So this is the way it is with music—sometimes the music give you more enlightenment than the words."

"Can the lyrics of a song have one message and the music have another?"

"Uh-huh," he says. "Yep. But, see, your lyrics is what really makes your song, where I'm concerned. It's not the music; it's the lyrics. What does it mean? What are you trying to convey? What are you trying to make folks see? Even if you sing rock and roll you ought to have a meaning behind it, or else you're really not going to get it over like it should be.

"Like, one guy put out, 'This is a man's world . . .' Well, the Bible say he a liar. The Twenty-fourth Psalm said that the earth is the Lord's. And the fullness thereof. The world is His and they that dwell therein. So that means this is not a man's world, it's God's world. Now, man has a certain amount of control, like a steward. You understand what I'm saying? But it doesn't belong to him. And if he doesn't use it in the right way, then when he go to give an account to the owner, then it's gonna be some flaws. Now, the Scripture said, in the twelfth chapter of Luke, verse forty-six, -seven, and -eight, 'He that knoweth to do of his father, and don't do it, will be beaten with many stripes'—you know to do right, and won't do it?—'but he that knoweth not, he'll be whipped with a few.'

"So what I'm saying is, if you know what's right, and do what's right, then you get a reward. Now, your reward don't necessarily have to be here . . ." He lights another cigarette.

"I talked with Muddy about it a lot of times," he goes on. "I said, 'Man, that stuff you singing ain't no good.' "

"You would say that to him?"

"Uh-huh. Muddy said, 'Look out there and see what I'm riding in.' His car. 'If it ain't no good, I wouldn't be riding in that.' "

"What do you think about someone like Ray Charles?" I ask him. "Someone who sings secular words to gospel tunes?"

"If you're not going to do it as a blues . . . If you read the Song of Solomon, you don't find nothing but romance there. He says that her breath is sweet as peaches, or something on that order. He said, 'Love is strong as death, but jealousy cruel as the grave. . . . Many waters can't quench it, floods can't drown it.' So this is really romance, you know what I'm saying? He said, 'I have virgins unnumbered,' you know, and it lets you know that he have a mind of romance, but he was talking about God. So this is what's important—that you know what you're saying, and what are you saying it about? You don't take the thing that Solomon said and try to make your girlfriend accept it.

"The question is, where do you want to spend eternity? There are certain criteria that's involved in either one of them. The Scripture said you don't want to be weighed in the balance and found wanting. So this is what I'm asking, in regards to what you like or dislike, where do you want to spend eternity? Now, you can't spend it in both places. Now, what you want to do? Do you want to live here and go to hell, if you want to use that, or live here and die and go where Jesus is? Now, wherever He is, I don't know, but He said, 'Where I am, there you may be also.' Now, if we don't believe it, then we live any way we want to. But I believe it. I believe there's a hell and a heaven. And I don't want to go to hell. I catch enough hell here." He laughs and puts out his cigarette.

It is getting late in the afternoon; outside the windows, long shadows cut across the parking lot. I ask him about a couple of recent revivals he has conducted. He warms at the memory, says they went well. "In Aliceville I sold five hundred dollars' worth of tapes. In Nashville I sold seven hundred—two hundred before I started singing!"

We walk toward the front of the restaurant; he has two of his cassette tapes for one of the cashiers. The owner comes over to say hello, a sleepy-eyed, pink-faced man in a white shirt. Reverend Morganfield introduces us, and the owner says, "Come around later and I'll give you the real story about him," and everyone laughs appreciatively.

Outside in the glare of the low, late sun, as he gets out the keys for his midnight-blue Lincoln Town Car, he says, pensively, "I really started making more on the singing when I started preaching. The singing . . . I suffered with it, suffered with it, suffered with it, and then I suffered with it. But eventually it paid off. I don't know how it happened. But you know, God will put things on your mind. And if you don't do what He want done, you suffer for it. But if you go ahead and do it, He open up avenues for you. So that's what happened to me—when I went on and started preaching, I had no problem. Everything began to fall in place." He opens the big car door.

"And it's okay if I come to service tomorrow morning?" I ask, double-checking.

He looks me in the eye and smiles faintly. "I'm looking for you," he says, and gets in behind the wheel.

From the Oxford American's *Second
Annual Music Issue, Summer 1998*

The following is the first piece I wrote for the Oxford American. *The magazine's editor, Marc Smirnoff, had been in touch with me after the publication of my story collection* Blues And Trouble, *inviting me to contribute something to an upcoming* OA *issue focusing on crime. I appreciated the invitation, but I was working on a novel and I had no special ideas about crime at the time, so I declined.*

Some months later he got in touch again. They were planning their first music issue, and he wanted me in it. I wasn't in the mood, and I hit him with an idea that I doubted he would accept. If they would send me to Nashville to find the bluegrass legend Jimmy Martin, I'd do a piece for him. Unlike Bill Monroe or Ralph Stanley, Martin was more or less unknown outside the tightly knit world of bluegrass musicians and fans. To my surprise, Smirnoff said to go ahead and do it.

My reasons for wanting to write about Martin are explained in the piece. When "True Adventures with the King of Bluegrass" came out in the first OA *music issue, it became a minor phenomenon in the country music world; musicians faxed it back and forth all over the country, and for years whenever I was around country musicians, somebody would ask me for more details on that night at the Opry. Jimmy was an amazing performer and a very difficult man, and I was very grateful to be able to catch him in action.*

Following "True Adventures" is a short piece I wrote for the OA *after Jimmy's death in 2005. He really was the last of a breed.*

TRUE ADVENTURES WITH THE KING OF BLUEGRASS

I.

It's pitch-dark and cold and I'm sitting in my car at the top of a driveway on a small hill outside Nashville, trying to decide what to do. In an hour and a half, the Grand Ole Opry starts, and I'm supposed to attend with the King of Bluegrass himself—or, rather, the King-In-Exile, the sixty-nine-year-old Black Sheep of the Great Dysfunctional Family of Country Music—Jimmy Martin, veteran of Bill Monroe's early-1950s Blue Grass Boys and one-time Decca recording star in his own right. Inside the nearby house, which is totally dark, Jimmy Martin is submerged in some advanced state of inebriation, waiting for me. Outside my car, two of Martin's hunting dogs are howling their heads off in the cold, black night air in a frenzy of bloodlust.

I've hit the horn a few times, but no lights have gone on, no doors have opened. The Dodge van and the Ford pickup are there, with the coon-hunting bumper stickers ("When the tailgate drops, the bullshit stops"), as is the midnight-blue 1985 Lincoln stretch limousine in which we took his garbage to the town incinerator yesterday, so I know he didn't run out on me. Finally, I tentatively open my door to see if I can make it to the house, but one of the dogs comes peeling around the front bumper and I close it again, fast. I decide to pull out and call him from the gas station on the corner of Old Hickory Boulevard.

It's kind of beautiful out here, actually. Hermitage is an eastern suburb of Nashville, about fifteen minutes out Interstate 40 from downtown. Rolling hills, shopping centers, subdivisions, plus the usual swelling of motels and fast-food joints around the highway interchange, like an infection around a puncture wound. The main attraction is President Andrew Jackson's house, the Hermitage, where historically minded Nashville tourists can go for a couple hours' respite from the Eternal Twang.

I have always wanted to meet Jimmy Martin. I'd heard that he was a difficult person, but I don't know if anything could have prepared me for the past two days. But you may not even know who Jimmy Martin is, so first things first . . .

One night in 1949, a completely unknown twenty-two-year-old singer-guitarist from Sneedville, Tennessee, walked up to Bill Monroe backstage at the Grand Ole Opry and asked if he could sing him a song. Monroe agreed, and before an hour had passed he invited the young man on the road with his band, the Blue Grass Boys. At that time, Monroe and his mandolin had already pioneered the sound that would become known as bluegrass, a form of country music reaching back to earlier mountain styles and adding an emphasis on instrumental precision and virtuosity. Monroe's two most famous sidemen of the 1940s, the guitarist-singer Lester Flatt and the banjoist Earl Scruggs, were as important in many ways to the music's development as Monroe; when they left the Blue Grass Boys in 1948, they were stars in their own right.

Martin's arrival brought another element into the group; his high, strong voice, stronger than Lester Flatt's, gave a new edge to the vocal blend, and his aggressive guitar added a stronger push to the rhythm as well. His early-1950s recordings with Monroe, including "Uncle Pen," "River of Death," and "The Little Girl and the Dreadful Snake," are classics. After five years with Monroe, Martin went on his own, first teaming up with the very young Osborne Brothers and then forming his own group. The 1957–61 incarnation of the Sunny Mountain Boys, as he called them, with the mandolinist Paul Williams and the banjo prodigy J. D. Crowe, is widely regarded as one of the greatest bands in bluegrass history.

Martin had a string of hits in the late 1950s and early '60s, including "Ocean of Diamonds," "Sophronie," the truck-driving anthem "Widow Maker," "You Don't Know My Mind," and his signature tune, "Sunny Side of the Mountain." Martin's vocals—high, plaintive, and lonesome—wrung every bit of meaning and feeling out of the lyrics. Like many country performers, he was capable of astonishing sentimentality, musical crocodile tears, like his duet with his young daughter on "Daddy, Will Santa Claus Ever Have to Die?" But at his best, his phrasing, the impact of the urgency behind his long, held notes, could be staggering.

Although his early recordings are considered bluegrass classics, to my ears he seemed to take more chances and gain in expressiveness as he got older. In 1973 he received a gold record, along with Roy Acuff, Doc Watson, Merle Travis, and Maybelle Carter, for his contribution to the Nitty Gritty Dirt Band's first *Will the Circle Be Unbroken* album; his performances are arguably the best thing about that record.

Despite all this, Martin has remained a kind of shadowy figure, with much less of a public profile than some of his bluegrass peers, like Ralph Stanley or the Osborne Brothers. He is seen in Rachel Liebling's excellent 1991 bluegrass documentary film *High Lonesome*, but the glimpses are only tantalizing. In some ways Martin doesn't fit into the categories that have evolved in the country music world. He is too raw for the commercial and slick Nashville establishment, and in a way too unapologetically country in the old sense—mixing sentiment and showmanship with George Jones– and Hank Williams–style barroom heartbreak—for the folk-revival types to whom bluegrass was, and is, essentially folk music. On top of that, the King of Bluegrass, as he called himself, had a reputation as a heavy drinker and a volatile personality. As I asked around, I began to realize that Nashville insiders traded Martin stories back and forth the way 1960s Washington insiders used to tell Lyndon Johnson stories.

Still, his obscurity was hard for me to fathom. When I got into bluegrass, after twenty-five years of listening to jazz, Martin seemed, and still seems, to be the greatest. On heartbreak songs he could tell it like it is, with no posing, only pure truth . . .

Tomorrow's just another day to worry.
To wake up, my dear, and I wonder why
Must a sea of heartache slowly drown me?
Why can't I steal away somewhere and die?

He sang to the hilt, as if the full weight of a human life hung on every line. His phrasing was alive with expressive turns, his voice breaking at times, or falling off a note he had held just long enough. His nasal, reedy tones reached back all the way to country music's deepest Scotch-Irish roots; at its highest and lonesomest, his voice conveyed the near-madness and absolutism of bagpipes in full cry. The only comparison in my experience was to the keening sound of certain jazz players, the altoist Jackie McLean or, especially, the tenor giant John Coltrane. Why, I always wondered, wasn't he everybody's favorite?

I did some digging and got his phone number and in early October of last year called to try and set up an interview. From the first he was guarded, suspicious, and it was clear that he was in no rush to have me visit. His voice was unmistakable from his records—high, nasal, and deep country—and he spoke loud and in italics much of the time. After some confusion over my name ("*Tom T. Hall?*"), he gave a series of grunted, grudging responses to my initial comments about why I was calling. When I told him he was my favorite bluegrass singer he shifted gears a little, thanking me and saying, "I can't *tell* you how many thousands of people have told me that over the years. When did you want to come up and see me?" I suggested a date in November, and he began hedging, saying that he would be spending a lot of time out of town coon hunting. We agreed that I'd call him in a week or two to see how his plans were shaping up.

A week and a half later I called him again to try and zero in on a date. It was immediately obvious not only that he didn't remember our previous conversation ("Tom T. *WHAT?*"), but that he was drunk. I started explaining that I wanted to write a piece on him, but he cut me off in mid-sentence.

"*Whut* . . ." he began, dramatically. "Is *in* this . . ." Another dramatic pause. "For *Jimmy Martin?*" His speech was heavy and overdeliberate, rather than slurred.

Before I could answer, he broke in and said, "Pub*lic*ity?"

"Well, yeah . . ." I began.

"I mean," he said, "what kind . . . of *money* . . . is in it?"

"Well," I began, again, realizing that he probably hadn't had a lot of magazine articles done on him lately, "magazines don't really do that. They don't pay the subjects of—" And here he broke in again—

"*You're* . . ." he said, "telling *me* . . . what *magazines* do?"

Uh-oh, I thought.

"I've had *all kinds* of write-ups," he went on, cranking up, his voice suddenly seething with a weirdly intimate rage. "I'm the *KING OF BLUEGRASS*, and *you're* . . . telling *me* . . . what *magazines* do?"

I wasn't sure what I was supposed to say to this, so I kept quiet.

"I'm just saying," he went on, picking up a little speed now, as if there were a response expected of me that he could see I was

going to be too dim to get, so he was going to have to lob me
the serve one more time, "is there gonna be a *few dollars* in it for
Jimmy Martin to buy himself a *fifth* of *whiskey*?"

This, I began to sense, was some kind of test. Feeling my way,
I said, "I tell you what . . . If you want to do the interview . . . I'll
bring you the fifth of whiskey *myself*."

"*ALL*-right," he hollered, sounding hugely pleased. "*COME 'n'*
see me. When you wanna come up?"

I suggested a date in mid-November, and he said it would be
fine. Then he said, "Listen . . . I gotta go. I got a black girl here
tryin' to talk to me. You know what . . . every white girl I ever
went with, she got a *home* offa me. Now I'm gonna see about a
black one and tell the others to *kiss my ass*. How does *that* sound
to you?"

I said it made sense, and he said, "Good. Call me closer to the
time," then he hung up and I sat at my desk, shaking my head.
After that call I had a pang of misgiving about the whole idea, as
if I might be getting myself into something I'd prefer to stay out
of, but I was too curious to give up. Boy, I thought. Whatever you
do, don't forget that whiskey.

Over the next month we talked two more times. The first
time, he sounded sober and friendly, even asking me one or two
questions about myself. He had a happy memory of New Orleans,
where I live ("I played down there when Johnny Horton had his
hit on 'Battle of New Orleans.' We played 'Ocean of Diamonds'
and 'Sophronie' and tore his ass to pieces"), and we were able
to set a date of November 20, a Wednesday, for me to come up,
but there was only one hitch. What I had to do, he said, was
call the weather report for Richmond, Indiana, that week and see
what the temperature was going to be. If it was going to be in the
thirties up there, it would be too cold to go coon hunting and I
could come see him in Nashville. But if it was going to be in the
forties or fifties, then I might as well stay home because he'd be
in Indiana, hunting. I had no intention of calling the weather

report in Indiana; I decided to just call Martin again a few days beforehand.

On November 17, the Sunday before I was to go up, I called him to confirm, and he was the old Jimmy again; he grumbled, chafed ("Now, that's *how* many days you're taking up?"), but I finally got him to agree that I would drive up on Wednesday, we would visit on Thursday, and then we could take it from there. Thursday, right? Yep. Okay. See you then. Hang up.

That's it. I was going.

The drive from New Orleans took ten hours. As soon as I arrived at the Holiday Inn in Hermitage that Wednesday night, I called Martin.

"Oh, hell," he said, gloomily. "I was fixing to spend tomorrow rabbit hunting. But I guess I'll spend it with you . . ." He sounded like a teenager forced to bring his kid brother along on a date. We agreed that I'd come over at ten in the morning; he gave me directions to his house, and that was it.

Thursday dawned grey and raw; yellow leaves blew around the motel parking lot. I had breakfast and ran through some of the things I wanted to ask Martin, but I was already realizing that the questions I wanted to ask him weren't really the point of this trip. Whatever I was looking for I probably wouldn't find by asking him a bunch of questions. But it was a place to start, at least.

His house, it turned out, was closer than I realized, and five minutes before ten a.m. I pulled up to the big iron gates he had described, at the foot of a long blacktop driveway leading up to a large, ochre-colored ranch house on several hilly acres of land. At the top of the driveway I could see a figure moving. I made my way up the driveway and parked in some mud off to the right, the only paved spots being taken up by a couple of vans and a long, midnight-blue stretch limousine, the rear license plate of which read KING JM. Across the lip of the limo's trunk, yellow and or-

ange letters spelled out the title of his best-known hit, SUNNY SIDE
OF THE MOUNTAIN. The moving figure was, of course, Martin,
attended by two dogs that bayed lustily at my approach. Martin
didn't stop what he was doing or register my arrival in any way;
by the time I opened the door of my car he had disappeared into
the limo, and as I got out his taillights squeezed bright and the
limo started to back up.

I grabbed my stuff and approached the limo, the tinted driver's-
side window rolled down halfway, and there was Jimmy Martin
looking up at me, unsmiling, suspicion in his red and slightly wa-
tery eyes, his head as big as a large ham and very jowly, with long
grey sideburns and thin grey hair combed straight back and left a
little bit long by the collar of his black nylon windbreaker.

"Leave your bags in your car," he said. "I gotta do an errand
here; you can come with me."

By the time I climbed into his passenger seat, Martin was trying to maneuver the limo into a five-point U-turn so that he could
get it out of his driveway. He worked the gear shift, which was on
the steering column, with dogged concentration and without saying a word. The hood was as big as a queen-sized bed. On the first
leg of the turn the limo stalled, and Martin cursed and restarted
it with effort. The car stalled twice more before he got it through
the turn; at one point he spun the wheels and they splattered mud
all over my car, which was about twenty feet behind the limo. Finally, the turn was completed and we coasted down the driveway
with the engine gurgling uncertainly, and out onto the road.

Once we were under way I tried a few conversation openers,
but it was like trying to play tennis in the sand. It took three
long minutes, driving at about fifteen miles an hour, to get to our
destination just off the main road; the back of a one-story brick
building where somebody was busy throwing wood and other
garbage into an incinerator.

"Wait here," Martin said, getting out and slamming the door.
For the first time I turned and looked in the back area of the limo,

which was upholstered in blue velvet, but not very well cared for, littered with scraps of paper and junk. In the middle of the back seat were two giant bags of garbage and a broken crutch. Martin opened the back door, grabbed the garbage, and closed it again. I watched him bring it over to the guy; they stood around talking, inaudibly to me, for about five minutes while I sat in the front seat.

When they were finished Martin got back in without any explanation, and we headed back to the house, with the limo stalling only once more.

The dogs were really whooping it up when we arrived, and Martin hollered at them as we got out and they skulked away quietly. At the end of the driveway stood a big STOP sign, with stick-on letters added, reading BAD DOG WILL BITE TAIL. I grabbed my bags out of my car and followed Martin inside.

We walked under a carport and through a storm door into an unheated den, where the floor was piled with boxes of cassettes, CDs, an upright bass, sound equipment, and other stuff. I followed him up a few steps, through a door and past a daybed, where a collection of mesh caps of all sorts was displayed, then through another door into a vestibule with a bathroom and a bedroom off of it, which led directly into the kitchen. It was obviously a bachelor's house: clothes were set out to dry on a chair by the heater, and at the Formica kitchen table space would have had to be cleared amid papers, mail-order catalogs, letters, and empty cassette cases to make room for a second person to eat. I unpacked my cassette recorder and notebook while Martin wordlessly looked through some mail, but before we got started I was going to give him the whiskey I had promised him.

I had put some thought into the choice, actually. I had initially bought him a bottle of Knob Creek, a very good Kentucky bourbon. But after I bought it I wondered if there wouldn't be some state loyalty involved in Martin's whiskey preference. He had begun life in Tennessee, after all, and had spent the past twenty-

five years living there. Tennessee was the home of the Grand Ole
Opry, etc., etc., and for all I knew some kind of horrible blood
rivalry might exist between Tennessee and Kentucky. So I went
back to the liquor store and picked up a bottle of Gentleman Jack
as well, to cover the Tennessee base.

Now I reminded him of the conversation, made a little speech
about my rationale for the choice, during which he looked blankly
at the bottles, and then I handed the bottles to him, feeling proud
of myself.

"I drink Seagram's 7," he said. Then he walked across the
kitchen, stashed the bottles in a cabinet, and that was that.

The interview started slowly. We discussed a few things per-
functorily for a while (Do you have a favorite country singer?
"George Jones." Why? " 'Cause he's the best."). He also said he
liked Hank Williams, Roy Acuff, Ernest Tubb, Bill Monroe, Lester Flatt and Earl Scruggs, and Marty Stuart. His favorite guitarists were Chet Atkins and Doc Watson. Not Merle Travis? I
asked. "Well, yeah, I would have to say Merle Travis. Put Merle
Travis in there . . ."

Before long, though, he steered the conversation to what turned
out to be his main preoccupation: the fact that he has never been
invited to join the Grand Ole Opry. His exclusion clearly causes
him pain; he has various theories about why he has been passed
by, but he has not given up hope of being asked. He produced letters from a number of people in and out of the music business in
which they sang his praises and expressed wonder that he wasn't
on it. It is obviously the great frustration of his life. To grasp why,
one has to realize that to someone of Martin's generation, who
grew up listening to it on the radio, the Opry *was* country music.
All the greatest stars were on it; it was the pinnacle of exposure
and prestige. Being on the Opry was tantamount to being in a
family; being asked to join was the final seal of approval on a
performer, an entrance into a pantheon that included all of one's
heroes—Hank Williams, Roy Acuff, Bill Monroe, Ernest Tubb,

and on and on. Martin has been lobbying for his inclusion for years, and we talked about the question for a good while before I could lead him on to other things.

Once we got past the topic he relaxed a little and actually started to be fun company. He has a good sense of humor, which balances out his tendency to talk about how rough he's had it. He really started to warm up when he talked about hunting. A perfect day, he said, is one on which he can "get my beagle dogs and take 'em out and run 'em and just enjoy their voices." It turns out that he has named most of his hunting dogs after other country singers. "My beagle dogs," he said, "are named George Jones, Earl Scruggs, Little Tater Dickens, and Marty Stuart. My coon dogs are Tom T. Hall, Turbo, Cas Walker, Cas Walker Jr. . . ."

"Turbo?" I said.

"He's named after that motor in them hot rods; we say his voice sounds like Number Five just went by." Martin then did an eerily realistic dog bark—guttural at first, then quickly louder and tapering off, like a loud car passing really fast. "I go out huntin' sometimes with Marty Stuart [referring now to the man, not his canine namesake]. Earl Scruggs just called the other day; he just had a quadruple bypass operation. Little Jimmy Dickens goes hunting rabbits with me. Ain't nothin' no better than a rabbit fried in a skillet, good and brown, and make gravy in the skillet, then make you some biscuits, then you can just tell Kroger's what to do with their steaks." At this he laughed a beautiful, infectious laugh.

"Country music," he said, "what makes it is you're singing by the way you've had to live. And if you had a hard life to live, then you sing a hard life song. Then you turn around and sing about how good you wish it *could* have been. When I sing, whether it's recording or at a show, or just sittin' down here with you, I give it all I got from the heart. And if it'd be something sad in there, I've *hit* that sad road. 'Cause I used to be barefooted, no shoes on my feet, had no dad when I was four years old, nobody to give me

a dollar to go to a show. Had to walk five miles to town to see a
show. We'd get one pair of shoes when it frosted, and time it got
warmin' up your toes was walkin' out of 'em. You wore 'em day
and night and everywhere you went.

"In writin' songs," he went on, "you gotta have something good
to write *about*. You can't just sit down and say I'm just absolutely
gonna write a song out of nowhere—and that's just about the way
the song sounds. It has to *hit* you."

Referring to a recent song he had written, he said, "*That* song
started and I'm sittin' on the damn *commode*—all reared back
and I start in to write that thing. And I've heard a lot of people
say that's where it *started*, on the commode. Well, I'll tell you,
the best place to read the newspaper, get you a glass and sit on
the goddamn commode and read and read and read and enjoy it
better'n anything in the world." Again he laughed and laughed at
this. He was so out front with everything, and I decided I really
liked him, even if he was hard to deal with.

I asked him if he had a favorite time in his life. He thought
for a second and said, "I was glad that Bill Monroe hired me, but
sometimes that was rough there. Traveling six in a car, with the
bass tied on top, used to sleep on each other's shoulders, that was
the pillow, worked seven days a week, seven nights . . . I guess
for enjoyment, when I had Paul Williams and J. D. Crowe with
me, on the Louisiana Hayride, and in Wheeling, West Virginia.
We could really sing it, really pick it; we had it down just right.
J. D. Crowe was fourteen years old. I learned him how to sing
baritone and how to tone his voice in with mine. Paul, too. We
slept in the same house and could rehearse and get it down like
we wanted to.

"Seems like that's when I liked to sing, and . . . We'd ride
along in the cars and sing our songs and enjoy it, get it to soun-
din' good. In those days everybody liked to sing, and liked to
hear that harmony, liked to get it better so they could make more
money. Playin' in them little bars for five dollars a night and tips.

And sayin', 'Oh, God, please help me get good enough to get out of here.' And *mean* that. Now the boys meet me at the festivals backstage, we show up—"Are you in tune?" "Yeah, let me see if we are"—go on, do the show, and go off . . . It just ain't as good as it was then. And I hate to say this, but it never *will* be, because it's run different. Most of the bands don't even travel in the same car and come to the shows together. They come with their girl-friends, or their wives, or whatsoever, so it's a girlfriend deal, it's not a professional deal. And it shouldn't be like that; business should be *business*. If you're gonna make a living at it.

"They're payin' big money, though," he said, with a tinge of bitterness audible now. "But there's little rehearsin'. *No* rehearsin', to tell you the truth. My band don't know what it is to rehearse. If they get out there the night before I do, or stay a night after, they might jam out there and play everything in the world, but there's no rehearsin'. Nothin' *serious*. You can't go into a job just laughin' and having fun and expect to show what you're doing. If you're driving a bulldozer you're liable to run over somethin'. You got to have your mind down to the *business*. And I've been told this many times: 'You just take your music too serious.' I don't see how you could be too serious about somethin' that's gonna feed your family and make you a living the rest of your life. I don't see as you could *get* too serious about that." At my expression of surprise, Martin said, "The man who said that couldn't *pick*. A man that don't wanta get serious about somethin', he don't wanta get *good*. Am I right?" He was, of course, right, but the pressure behind the way he said it spoke of some buried frustration, a sense of injustice, of not being sufficiently recognized for his own abili-ties while standards were falling apart all around him . . .

As I was thinking this, he looked at me and said, "But the big-gest thing I have been asked by the public is, 'Why ain't you on the Grand Ole Opry? Why can't we hear you on the Grand Ole Opry?' I just laugh back and I say, 'Well, I guess I just ain't good enough.'"

He showed me a photo of a plaque commemorating his induction into the International Bluegrass Music Association Hall of
Honor, which he was very proud of. Then we started to wind
down. We had gotten along well, after all, and I liked him. He
was opinionated as hell, cranky and overbearing, but he was honest and had a great sense of gusto for life, and real passion about
his music. He was himself, nothing else, and that alone is hard
to come by. Still, I felt we had only scratched the surface, and I
wanted to see him in some other context if possible, get a feeling
for how he related to other people. He said he enjoyed our conversation, and we talked about getting together again later in the
weekend, since I was staying in Nashville until Sunday.

At one point I mentioned that I was going to try and get to see
the Grand Ole Opry, and he cautioned me to get my ticket quick
if I didn't have one already. Then he suggested that we might go
together.

"Really?" I said.

Sure, he said, they all knew him backstage, and we could just
go inside that way.

I didn't want to scare him off by seeming too excited about
the idea, but it was perfect. He asked me to check and see who
was going to be on the Opry, which runs on Friday and Saturday
nights, and we agreed to talk about it the next day.

On my way out, walking through the den, Martin gave me
two of his cassettes out of a couple of big cardboard boxes, and
sold me two more at ten dollars apiece. Then he pointed out a selection of mesh caps in various colors, emblazoned with a "Jimmy
Martin—King Of Bluegrass" logo. I chose one in burgundy with
gold lettering, which I thought was a bargain at five dollars. Now
I had the rest of the day to look around Nashville.

Roughly speaking, Nashville today is at least two towns. First, and
best, is downtown, where you can find the old Ryman Auditorium

(home of the Grand Ole Opry until its move to suburban Opryland in 1974), the original Ernest Tubb Record Shop (where they used to have the post-Opry broadcasts on Saturday nights after the crowds left the Ryman), Tootsie's Orchid Lounge, and other landmarks. Downtown is the province of the ghosts who make country music something worth thinking about seriously—Hank Williams, Roy Acuff, Lefty Frizzell, and on and on. It attracts the hipper tourists, and musicians with a sense of tradition, as well as quite a few aging, struggling characters in denim, Western shirts, and cowboy boots.

Farther west, along Broadway, lies Music Row, the heart and soul, if you can call it a soul, of New Nashville, where you find the big music publishers, record companies, ASCAP headquarters, the Country Music Hall of Fame, and gift shops owned by Barbara Mandrell, George Jones, and other luminaries. Music Row can be a little rough on you if you think country music is still about deep, soulful expression from the hills and honky-tonks. The Country Music Hall of Fame, for example, is a lot of fun for anybody with an interest in country music, full of great artifacts and video installations. But most of the Hall of Fame's visitors waltz past the rare Hank Williams photos and Uncle Dave Macon videos vacant-eyed and clueless, in order to gape at the Reba McIntyre and Garth Brooks exhibits. Well, there's nothing wrong with that, but it is a clue to the sensibility of the New Nashville's bread-and-butter constituency.

Music Row contains no shadowy cubbyholes full of interesting stuff, the way old downtown does. The senior citizens who get off the tour buses in matching warm-up suits don't want shadowy and interesting; they want bright and aggressively heartwarming. They graze happily among the T-shirts and souvenir spoon rests and coffee mugs at Barbara Mandrell's store, where a Christmas-sale sign reads, SPECIAL: NATIVITIES 25% OFF, which just about says it all, and at the George Jones Gift Shop, where rows and rows of glass display shelves under bright fluorescent lights are crammed with frilly dolls, little ceramic figurines, souvenir spoons, salt and pepper shakers, coffee mugs reading "I'm not grouchy—I'm constipated . . ."

All of which, I thought, helps explain why Jimmy Martin might be anathema to New Nashville. Imagine the souvenir-spoon crowd listening to him sing "Steal Away Somewhere and Die." Not likely. Yet all the garishness and bad taste is no aberration; it's part of the fiber of the world that country music serves. You can't really separate one from the other, any more than you can just forget about Martin performances like "I'd Rather Have America" and "Daddy, Will Santa Claus Ever Have to Die?"

That night I had dinner with a friend, a well-known songwriter and performer who has lived in Nashville for almost thirty years and was part of the so-called New Breed of younger figures who shook up the town in the late 1960s. My friend is actually something of a connoisseur of Jimmy Martin stories, and he added a few to my stockpile, including one about a trip, involving Martin and a couple other musicians, to see Clint Eastwood's movie *Unforgiven*. At one point in the movie a small country shack came on the screen, and Martin supposedly stood up at his seat and hollered, "That shack there is just like the one Jimmy Martin grew up in, back in Sneedville, Tennessee, that y'all been asking me about, folks." Everybody in the theater turned around wondering what the hell was going on, while Martin's companions sank low into their seats.

After we laughed about this, my friend went on, "But, at the same time, I'll never forget once we were having this benefit concert for a local band who had had an accident on the road and needed money. The whole bluegrass community had rallied to their support and held a benefit concert, which Jimmy hadn't been invited to appear on. Late in the evening, though, he showed up backstage anyway, real quiet, with a big jar, like a Mason jar, full of coins and bills. He had had a show earlier that night and he had collected all that money from his audience himself, and he wanted to contribute it. It wasn't a showy thing at all; he just gave it and left quietly.

"Another time," my friend went on, "the son of some dear mutual friends of Jimmy's and mine had died under extremely tragic circumstances, and one of the visitors during the worst of this episode was Jimmy. He walked in and he had obviously been crying beforehand. He had some little plaster statue he had bought for them, maybe it was a Madonna, and as soon as he got in, he just let it all out, crying and saying how sorry he was that it had happened and how much he loved them . . ." My friend stopped talking for a moment, and I realized he was trying to keep from crying himself. "He only stayed for about five minutes," he went on. "But of all the visits during those days, that's the one that was maybe the most moving."

He kind of shook his head. I could relate; even in the short time I had spent with Martin I could see those disproportions—the deep loneliness and the huge ego, the self-assertion and the sensitivity and the defensiveness. When I mentioned the possibility that I might go to the Opry with Martin, my friend looked at me and raised his eyebrows. "If there's any chance of doing that," he said, "don't miss it. Something interesting will happen."

"I know," I said. "That's what I'm afraid of."

2.

That was last night. Earlier today Martin and I talked on the phone and he said he wanted to go; he told me to get dressed up ("not like what you come to see me in yesterday") and meet him at his house at six o'clock. My first stab at doing that, ten minutes ago, was unsuccessful, and I had to call him from the gas station to get him to let me in. From the sound of his voice he's in no shape to go anywhere, but he insists he wants to go.

Now, as I pull up to his house again, I finally see him, in my headlights, struggling to open the screen door, and I turn my lights and motor off. He's yelling at the dogs, and they quiet down. I get out of the car, but he has already disappeared back into the house. I follow, groping my way through his den in the dark.

The only light on in the house appears to be the overhead one in the kitchen. As I enter the room Martin is sitting down in his chair at the kitchen table. He's wearing his blue jumpsuit, and his eyes are unfocused.

"I'm higher than a Georgia . . . kite," he says. "I know what they'll say . . . 'Jimmy Martin's been drinkin' again . . .' But I don't owe them anything." He looks up at me. "Do I?"

I can see his eyes pull into focus. "Where's your Jimmy Martin cap?" he says, squinting at me.

"I left it back at the hotel," I say. His eyes narrow into slits. "I can borrow one of yours," I offer, "if you want me to wear one."

"You got one of your own, didn't you?"

"You said on the phone you wanted me to get a little dressed up, so—"

"So it's fuck Jimmy Martin."

Silence.

"Listen," he says, steadying himself with his forearm on the table. "If I give you the keys to the limo . . . will you drive? Can you drive the limo?"

The *limo*?

"Jimmy," I say, "why don't we just take my car—"

"*NO*," he says, his voice rising. "We're takin' the *limo*, with 'Sunny Side of the Mountain' along the back and everything. They'll recognize it. They *know* me. Can you drive it?"

"Why don't we—"

"*We're takin' the limo*," he says. "We can drive right inside. Whoever says hello says hello." He stands up, unsteadily. "Me and you are goin' to the Opry," he says. "Did you get you a drink?" he says.

"No," I say.

"Well, go and git you one. Right there."

"Where, Jimmy?"

"*In the cabinet*," he says. I find the cabinet he's indicating, and inside it the bottle of Knob Creek I gave him yesterday, with about an inch and a half of bourbon left in it.

"Me and you are goin' to the Opry," he says, shuffling past me and leaving the room. "Don't drink too much."

I'm standing here and I don't know what to do. I'm almost overwhelmed by a feeling of not wanting to be here. The single overhead light, this chaos, the malevolent magnetic field he generates. I want to get out. But at the same time, it's *Jimmy Martin* . . .

Now I hear a grunting sound coming from a small room off the kitchen. I say, "Are you okay, Jimmy?"

"Come see what I'm doin'."

I walk back to the garage end of the kitchen and look in the doorway to where he is, and it's his bedroom, small, barely enough room for the double bed on which Martin is sitting, utterly transformed. His hair is neat and he is wearing black slacks, a fire-engine-red shirt buttoned at the neck, and white leather boots with little multicolored jewels sewn on.

"Wait a minute, now," he says. He gets a black Western jacket out of the closet and puts it on, then a clip-on tie, white leather with little tassels at the bottom. "All right, hold on," he says, and from a chair in the corner he grabs a white straw cowboy hat with feathers arranged as a hat band.

"How do I look?" he says, now, presenting himself to me. "Huh?"

"You look great," I tell him. I'm not lying. Getting dressed up for these guys is a form of warfare, total plumage warfare, and Martin hasn't been a pro for forty-eight years for nothing.

It is not quite 6:30 by the time we leave the house. The night outside is cold, cloudless, and moonless. Just outside the carport, the limo is a long, sleek, indistinct presence in the darkness. Opening the driver's door is a small project in itself; the seat is cold through my slacks, and when I pull the door shut it closes like the lid of a tomb. Martin is next to me in the passenger seat.

I turn the ignition and the limo grumbles to life while I fish around for the lights. The rear window, way back there, is about the size and shape of a business envelope, so I lower my window to look out behind. I slide her into reverse, a hard shift, and ease off the brake.

"Cut her back and to the right as hard as you kin," Martin says. "Cut her."

I'm cutting her and hoping I'm not going to hit the tree that I know is back there. When I get what I think is far enough back I shift into drive and it stalls out immediately.

"Oh boy," Martin says. "Go ahead and start her up again."

I start her, pull her into gear, and move forward until the front bumper is almost against the Dodge van's rear bumper, where it stalls again. My own car is sitting halfway under the carport, boxed in now by the limo, and I look at it nostalgically in the headlights. I try to start the limo again; Martin is saying, "Cut the lights! Cut the lights!"

I cut the lights and try again quickly, but it won't even turn over.

"We done it now," Martin says.

I try to get it going another time or two, but the limo is dead. "Son of a bitch," Martin says, opening the passenger door. "Crack the hood."

Martin disappears into the house. I get out and open the gigantic hood; I can hear the dogs moving back and forth somewhere in the darkness. My car is completely blocked in by the dead limousine.

Now Martin reappears; he's carrying something about the size of a shoebox, and trailing a long, heavy-duty orange extension cord. He hands me the plug from the box and the end of the extension cord.

"Plug this in there," he says.

The end of the extension cord seems like it's been melted, and the plug tines won't fit into it easily. I'm struggling with the fit, and I feel it start to slide in when I'm blinded by a bright shower of sparks in my face. I drop the cord and the plug on the ground and stand there trying to get my sight back.

"Which one of these is red?" I hear him asking me. I blink my eyes a few times; he's holding out the charger clamps. I squint, but it's hard to see them; it's too dark . . .

"Can't you tell which one of these is red?" he says.

I look at him for a second. I breathe slowly through my nose. "Why don't you turn on a light?" I say.

He heads off someplace again, and I try the plug again and get it in this time. Martin comes back and gets the clamps attached, and I go and turn the ignition and it zooms to life. While it is charging, Martin tells me to get the jumper cables out of his Ford pickup and throw them in the back of the limo. He disconnects the clamps and puts the charger away and we get back into the limo, and I maneuver it through its turn, and we head out, slowly, down the driveway and out onto the road. I'm trying to breathe nice and slowly.

"Me and you are goin' to the Grand Ole Opry," he says now. "And your name is *what*?"

"Tom Piazza," I say.

"Tom," he repeats, as if going over a set of difficult instructions. "And you're doin' a article."

"Right."

"Okay."

We pull onto I-40 West, heading toward Nashville. We need to get to Briley Parkway and go north to Opryland. Outside the car, the Tennessee hills pass in the dark like huge, slumbering animals. I'm holding the limo steady right around fifty, and most cars are passing me, but that's okay. I'm in no hurry. This is an island of tranquility here. God only knows what's going to happen when we get to the Opry. I know Martin has feuds with various members of the Opry; he's not crazy about the Osborne Brothers, and I've heard that he especially has a problem with Ricky Skaggs, one of the younger generation of bluegrass stars. Evidently Skaggs was a guest on Martin's latest CD and wouldn't sing the tenor part that Martin wanted him to sing because it was too high. Martin feels that Skaggs's refusal was a form of attempted sabotage, motivated by professional jealousy, although Skaggs, of course, is the one with the spot on the Opry.

Now Briley Parkway comes up, with the sign for Opryland, and this is the last definite turn I know; from here on I have to rely on Martin. I take the exit and follow the curve along to the right.

"Do I look all right?" he asks.

I tell him he looks great.

"When we go down here I want you to be close to me now, and everything," he says.

"I'll be right next to you the whole time," I say.

"Tell 'em who you are."

"Okay."

"You a magazine man—Tom, right?"

"Right."

Now, off to the left, Opryland appears, a city of lights in the darkness. Big tour buses pass us as we make our way along in the right lane; the traffic is much denser now. We go under a bridge, exit, and curl up and back around over Briley Parkway, and there, ahead of us, are the gates to Opryland. I'm happy to be somewhere near civilization. I follow the line of traffic through the entrance. "When's the last time you came to the Opry?" I ask, breathing a little easier now that we've found the place.

"I can come down here anytime I *want* to," he says.

"Yeah," I say, "but when's the last time you did?"

"I'd say it's been about six months," he says. "But they'll know me well enough. They'll know me. Just walk in there with me. Your name's what?"

We're being funneled into Opryland, with giant tour buses looming outside the windows like ocean liners over a rowboat. "Boy, ain't that got it?" he says. Out the front windshield, spread all out before us, is a huge jungle of tiny white Christmas lights among the trees of Opryland. "Ain't this Opryland? Huh?"

After a few wrong turns we find a service road that takes us alongside Opryland to a place where the chain-link fence opens and a guard, bundled up and holding a clipboard, stands in the middle of the street under bright lights.

"Pull over here," Jimmy says. "Lower your window. Roll your *glass* down, now. Roll your glass on down. You need to talk to this guy right here. *Hold* it . . ."

We pull up to the guy and I say hi and he says, "Hi, y'all," and bends down to look in my window, at which point Jimmy yells out *"HEY"* in a happy greeting, and the guy says, "Hey, Mr. Martin!" cheerfully, and Jimmy, looking across me out my window, hollers back, *"Mister Martin? Mister?* Just say *Jimmy* . . . I'm goin' rabbit huntin' tomorrow . . ."

A woman comes over, another guard, also bundled up and carrying a clipboard; she approaches, hollers, "Hi, Jimmy. You got you a driver now?" and Jimmy says, "Who is *this? Candy?*" "Yes," she answers, coquettishly, and Martin says, "Candy . . . I *love* you," "I love you too," she answers. Jimmy says, "Can we just pull in over here some place?" and the guy says, "Just pull in the dock, over on the other side of the van," and Candy says, "Over on the other side of that van, there by the canopy in that second dock," and Jimmy says, "Just where I can get out of everybody's way," and they both smile and say, sure, go ahead, and as we start pulling away, Martin hollers, *"LOVE* you . . . *MERRY CHRISTMAS* . . ." As we pull away I breathe deeply in relief; they knew him, they were happy to see him, he was on good terms with them, and I begin to think that the evening might smooth out after all. A tall, rangy-looking guy in denim with a cowboy hat and carrying a guitar case is walking in front of the limo, toward the entrance in front of us, and I slow down a little. "I don't want to run over this guy with the guitar, here," I say.

"*Fuck* 'im," Martin says.

I get the limo situated right next to a loading bay; before we get out Martin finds the bottle of Knob Creek, which he has been looking for, and we both take swigs, then get out and head for the stage door.

Swarms of people mill around inside the brightly lit reception area, under the gaze of a security officer and a tough-looking middle-aged lady at the security desk; people are greeting each other, coming and going, musicians walking in with instrument cases, and the first impression is of a high school on the night of a big basketball game. The lady at the desk knows Jimmy and waves us in, and before ten seconds have gone by, he is saying, "Hey! Willie!" to a short guy with short, salt-and-pepper hair and a well-trimmed moustache. His name is Willie Ackerman, a drummer who played on a number of Jimmy's recordings in the 1960s. "I put the bass drum in bluegrass music," he says. "Good to meet you," I say. We mill along together for a few moments in the crowd and he and Martin exchange some small talk.

I am at the Grand Ole Opry, backstage. It feels, indeed, like a big night at the high school, down to the putty-colored metal lockers that line the hall, the dressing rooms off the hall, with people crowding in and spilling out into the general stream— laughter, snatches of jokes and gossip overheard as you pass along—the halls even have the same dimensions of a high school hall, crowded with people, men and women, men with very dyed-looking hair and rhinestone-studded suits and guitars around their shoulders; at one point I recognize Charlie Louvin, of the Louvin Brothers. I follow Jimmy, who is alternately oblivious and glad-handing people as if he's running for senator. He attracts a fair amount of attention, even here, where flamboyance is part of the recipe.

Eventually we come to the dark, cave-like stage entrance, with heavy curtains going way up into the dark rigging above. The curtains at the front of the stage are closed, and I can hear the audience filing in out front. People in this area come and go with a more focused sense of purpose than out in the noisy halls; by the entrance to the area stand a guitarist and another young man and woman, harmonizing a bit. We walk into the bright, comfortable green room, just to the left of the stage entrance, and someone, a big man with stooped shoulders, comes over to Jimmy.

"Jimmy, how you doin' there?" he says, putting his arm around Martin and shaking his hand. "How's the old Hall of Fame member?"

"Well," Jimmy says, "I'm a Hall of Fame member, and the big booker ain't booked me *shit*."

Glancing at me a little embarrassedly, the other guy says, "Well, you never know; tomorrow's a brand-new day." We stand for a minute listening to the little group singing their song. "They're singing some bluegrass right over there," the man says. Martin grunts. This must be difficult for him being here, I think, like crashing a party. He seems to go in and out of his drunkenness; sometimes he's lucid, other times he has trouble putting a sentence together.

Now another man comes up and asks him, "Are you on the Opry tonight?"

Martin says, "No. They won't let me on it."

"Well, when are you going to get the hell on it?"

"Hey, Charlie," Martin says, grinning, "I can get out there and sing it and put it over!"

"I know it. I've seen you do it. Get out there and sing one."

Martin seems pleased by the encounter. He gets the two guys seated; he's going to tell them a joke. Two women are walking around a shopping mall, carrying heavy baskets full of all the stuff they bought. They get tired at one point and they sit down. After they've been sitting fifteen, twenty minutes, one of them says, "I tell you, I got to get up here; my rear end done plumb went to sleep on me." The other one says, "I thought it did; I thought I heard it *snore* three or four times."

Great laughter at the joke. "Now you beat *that*, goddamn it," Martin says, triumphantly. We walk away, toward the stage area.

This is going okay, I think. He's seen some old friends, his ego's getting stroked, people seem to like having him around. Who knows? I think. Maybe they will invite him to join after all.

We approach the small group that had been singing, and Jimmy stops. He says, "You're going to play on the Grand Ole Opry?"

"Yes, sir," the young man with the guitar says. He puts his hand out and says, "How are you doing, Mr. Martin?"

"What are you going to sing on it?" Jimmy asks.

"I'm playing with Ricky Skaggs," he says.

"Yeah?" Jimmy says.

"Yeah," the young man says. "Gonna play a little bluegrass tonight."

"A little bluegrass," Jimmy says.

"Yeah."

"Well," Jimmy begins, "he's about the *sorriest* fuckin' bluegrass you could ever hope to be on *with*, I'll tell you."

All three look at him, still smiling, but a little stunned; the woman says, "Ohhhh," as if he must be trying to make a good-humored joke that he has just taken a little too far, and the young man with the guitar, smiling more broadly, says, "Well, bless your heart . . ."

"Well," Martin says, even louder now, "I'm just telling you, he's about the sorriest bluegrass, and *tell him I said it*."

"I'll do it," the young man says, smiling even more broadly, as Martin lumbers off.

I start off after Martin, who abruptly stops, turns around, and adds, "*Hey*, bring him over here and let *me* tell him that."

"He's back there," the young man yells after us.

Now we're making our way along through the dark backstage area, and I'm thinking maybe I should just lead Martin out of here before something really bad happens. He's heading for another well-lit area, where some instruments—fiddles, banjos—are tuning up, sawing away, warming up. "Didn't I tell him?" Jimmy says to me, proudly. "Let's see if we can see anybody back here."

Now we enter a brightly lit, garage-like area, with musicians milling around, and a number of older men who look like a certain type you still see behind the scenes at prizefights—slit-eyed, white-shoed, pencil moustaches, sitting in chairs, watching everything. "Hello, Jimmy," someone says, a middle-aged man walking toward us, with a banjo, wearing a plaid sports shirt. "Good to see you, man," the man says, with genuine warmth. They shake hands. They make some small talk, mostly Jimmy talking about his hunting plans. The banjoist seems to know all about the hunting and the dogs. Then Jimmy tells him the joke about the two women. The banjoist laughs and laughs. "I don't want you to *steal* this on me, now," Jimmy says. Everything seems to be cool again.

Then Jimmy says, "Let's me, you, and Brewster do a tune." The banjoist calls the guitarist and singer Paul Brewster over. Across the room I see a big guy walk by, with a kind of combination crew cut and bouffant hairstyle, carrying a mandolin; it's Ricky Skaggs.

From my left side I suddenly hear Martin's voice, loud, hollering, "Is that the *BIGGEST ASSHOLE* in Nashville?"

Immediately the banjoist launches into a loud, unaccompanied solo, Earl Scruggs–style, an old Bill Monroe–Lester Flatt tune from the late 1940s called "Will You Be Loving Another Man?" and it is beautiful, ringing, pure and uncut, and, his attention distracted like a bull's by a red cape, Martin begins singing the refrain, the banjoist and the guitarist joining in with the harmony, then Martin sings the first verse over just the banjo, his voice piercing and brilliant, then the refrain again, with the harmony, and the banjo comes in for a solo, so spangling and stinging and precise, the melody appearing out of a shower of rhythmic sequins and winking lights and now Martin comes in for another chorus, with the banjo underneath him telegraphing a constant commentary, goading and dancing around Martin's melody, and it's as if they have all levitated about six inches off the floor, pure exhilaration, and by far the best music I have heard during my time in Nashville.

When it's over there is that lag of a few seconds that it always takes for reality to be sucked back into the vacuum where great music has been, and as reality returns, along with it strides Ricky Skaggs.

"Hey, Jimmy," he says, pleasantly, walking over to our little group, strumming his mandolin, perhaps a little bit nervously. "How you doin'?"

"Okay," Martin says, making it sound, somehow, like a challenge. "How *you* doin'?"

"Okay." Strum, strum.

"Think you can still sing tenor to me?" Oh no, I think.

Skaggs laughs, strums a little more. "I don't know. If you don't get it too high for me."

"Ricky, it's left up to you," Martin says. "It's not left up to me. If you want to make a ass out of yourself and don't want to sing tenor with me, don't do it. *He* can sing tenor with me . . ." He indicates Paul Brewster, who had been taking the high part in the song they had just sung.

"He sure can," Skaggs says, strumming, already regretting that he has come over. "He sings a good tenor to me."

"But *you* can't sing tenor to me," Martin persists. "You did with Ralph Stanley, didn't you?"

"I was sixteen then," Skaggs answers.

"He lost his balls, huh?" Martin says, to the few of us gathered around. "He lost his balls; he can't sing tenor with Jimmy no more."

Strum, strum.

"I can sing lead with any sumbitch who's ever sung . . ." Martin says.

"You sure can," Skaggs says.

"Huh?"

"You sure can," Skaggs says, no longer looking at Martin.

Not to be placated, Martin goes on, "You let me down."

"I couldn't sing it that high, Jimmy."

"You didn't *hurt* me," Martin says, "about making money. I made it."

"That's right, you sure did," Skaggs says. Then, wearing a Mona Lisa smile and nodding politely, he says, "Good to see you guys," and steps away.

Skaggs and his band rehearse a few numbers now, and Martin stands watching them, and they sound good, especially the banjoist and the lead guitar player, who is astounding. Jimmy stands listening, more or less unimpressed. At one point a short man in a white cowboy hat and blue cowboy suit comes over and it turns out to be Little Jimmy Dickens, one of the legends of the Opry, and the two of them stand there with an arm around each other's shoulders, watching Skaggs's band rehearse, and I'm glad Jimmy's found a port in the storm.

Now I kind of pull back and listen; I just want to enjoy being here a little bit. If Martin can survive being that much of a pain in the ass to someone, then he can probably weather just about anything. A while goes by, and then quicker movements begin to thread through the crowd, among the laughter and the picking, and someone calls out, "Five minutes till segment," and it's getting time for the Opry to start.

We move to the backstage area, the wings; the backup musicians are taking their places, and the backup singers are gathering around the mikes, the curtain is still closed, and the band hits a fast breakdown song, and before I know it the audience is visible, and cheering, and Porter Wagoner is leading things off, a gleaming white silhouette in front of the yawning cavern of the audience, a glowing nimbus around him and his bejeweled suit.

The first act on the bill is Little Jimmy Dickens himself, who hits the stage like a bomb going off, gyrating and singing "Take an Old Cold 'Tater and Wait," which has been his Opry signature tune since the 1950s; his guitar is almost as big as he is, and he shakes so much that he looks as if he's wrestling an alligator. After Dickens leaves the stage, to huge applause, Wagoner talks to the audience a little, then introduces Skeeter Davis, who sings her old hit "The End of the World." During each tune, the upcoming performers gather behind the curtain just off to the side of the stage to watch the act preceding them.

Everybody does one song apiece, eighty-year-old Bill Carlisle comes out and does an act combining singing and high-jumping, and it's a good variety show, but as I stand and watch I can't help thinking that it's almost as if Jimmy Martin would be too strong a flavor to introduce into this stew, like uncorking corn liquor at a polite wine tasting. The performers appear one by one, as if they are making cameo appearances in a movie about the Opry, and I can't see Martin fitting into it. Anyway, in his frustration he does everything he can to make sure he won't get on. He lashes out almost as if he's trying to give himself some sense that he's the one in control, that he's the one on the offensive, and not just sitting there helplessly. Whatever his reasons, he is doing exactly what he needs to do to keep himself off the Opry.

During Jimmy C. Newman's number, it occurs to me that Martin has been very quiet. He was talking to someone for a while, but now he is standing at the theater rope that demarks the small area of the wings where the performers are about to go on, and he has been standing there silently for quite a while. I look at him, and his gaze is fixed straight ahead, and I'm thinking something doesn't look right, maybe it is just the difficulty of watching the party going on around him, but I say, "Hey, Jimmy—everything okay?"

No answer; he keeps staring straight ahead.

"Jimmy—is everything all right?"

Now he turns his head just a little in my direction and squints as if to say, Hold on a minute, I'm thinking about something.

Then, nodding in the direction of a small group of people standing just offstage behind the curtain, he says, "Go over there and tell Bill Anderson to come over here. I'm going to knock his ass right off him."

"What are you talking about?" I say.

"Will you just go over there and tell him to come here and we can go outside—"

"I'm not going to do that," I say. "Hold on a second—hey," I say, trying to get his attention. "What happened?" This is not cool; Anderson is one of the Opry's biggest stars and has been since the mid-1960s. What this is about I have no idea.

"He talked to me in a way I don't like to be talked to, and I'm going to knock his ass off. I'll go over there *myself* . . ." And he moves as if to climb over the theater cord, and I grab his arm and say, "Hold on, man, what are you doing? You don't want to do this. *Hey* . . . Jimmy . . ." People are starting to notice now.

"I *will*," he says. "I'll knock him down right *here*—"

"Hold on, man," I say, under my breath. "You don't want to do this. Don't"—here I have an inspiration—"don't *lower* yourself into that. The hell with Bill Anderson," I say, laying it on thick. "What does it matter what he says? Come on," I say, "let's get out of here, okay? I've seen enough . . . I'm bushed . . . Let's get out of here and have a drink . . ."

It's too late, though; as I'm saying this, Bill Anderson walks past us with a couple of other men, not looking at us, heading toward the greenroom, and Martin lunges toward them. I step in front of him to hold him back, and as I do this I can tell that it is some kind of charade, because he doesn't struggle. As soon as the group passes Martin hollers out to the people who have been watching, "He walked right *by* me . . . If he hadn't a-been holdin' me *back* I woulda knocked his *ass* off," and meanwhile someone out onstage is singing about yet another Lonely Heartbreak, and it occurs to me that it will be a miracle if they ever even let Jimmy Martin set foot backstage again at the Opry after this, much less perform. Calling someone an asshole is one thing, but moving on someone in front of witnesses is another. I've got to get him out of here, and I say to him now, "Come on, let's get the hell out of here, screw Bill Anderson anyway," and he kind of nods.

But before I can pull him away he stands for a long moment looking out toward the stage, and the singer and the audience. Impatient to get him out before something worse happens, I, who have come to the Opry very late in the game, say, "Come on, Jimmy, let's go." Then Jimmy Martin, who might well be taking his last look at the biggest dream of his life, turns around and walks out.

I spent Saturday tooling around the city, buying CDs and souvenirs and just looking around, with the previous night looming in my mind like a weird nightmare. I called Martin in the afternoon; he had a hunting buddy over visiting him and he sounded rested and happy.

On Sunday morning I called again to say good-bye, and he volunteered to come down and meet me for breakfast at the Hardee's by the Holiday Inn. While I waited for him I tried to think if there was anything I wanted to ask him that I hadn't already asked him, but there wasn't.

He arrived late—car trouble, of course—in the limo, and we had breakfast. Martin ordered fried chicken. We talked for a few minutes about different things, but what was most on Martin's mind was a set of videotapes of stars of the Grand Ole Opry he saw advertised on television and which he thought I should get. "All of 'em is on there," he said, "Rod Brasfield, Minnie Pearl, Roy Acuff, Uncle Dave Macon," and on and on, and he talked about each one lovingly, especially Brasfield, a comedian whom Martin called "the best thing ever to hit Nashville." Martin wasn't making a nominating speech for himself this morning; he was just thinking about the people who made him want to do what he has been doing for almost fifty years, with an enthusiasm that reached back to the little shoeless kid's awe and love for those voices coming out of the radio. "Get 'em," he said, "if you wanna see the real thing—the *real* thing," he said, with lots of meaning in the emphasis.

Eventually it's time for me to go, and we head out into the bright morning. Before I go, though, he wants to tell me a joke. "There was this guy, said he could go around and talk to statues in town, and they'd talk back to him. So one day he walked up to this one, and, God, it was a big 'un, and he says, 'Old man statue, this is so-and-so.' The statue said, 'Yeah, glad to meet you.' So he says, 'Listen, what would be the first thing you would do if you could come alive for an hour?' And the statue answered him back, said, 'Shoot me *ten million pigeons* . . .'"

I don't know if he means this to be a little parable of our couple of days together—I doubt it—but it occurs to me that it works as such, and I laugh along with him.

Then Martin, in his blue jumpsuit, black nylon windbreaker, and dirty white mesh cap, gets into his limo, which starts up with a gurgling roar, and I watch and wave as he backs her out, wheels her around, and rides off into the distance up Old Hickory Boulevard in a midnight-blue blaze of country grandeur, the goddamn *KING OF BLUEGRASS* himself.

From the Oxford American's *First
Annual Music Issue, 1997*

JIMMY MARTIN, RIP

He was one of a kind. He insisted on his own way, as a singer, guitarist, bandleader and as a man in the world, and he respected others who insisted on their own way. Especially he loved and respected the musicians whom he felt had carved out an unmistakable place of value for themselves in the world of country music and bluegrass—Bill Monroe, Lester Flatt, Earl Scruggs, Hank Williams, George Jones, Roy Acuff, and most of the other members of the earlier generation of Grand Ole Opry stars. Implicitly and explicitly, he numbered himself among them, and he was right to do so. He reserved expressed admiration for a relatively small handful of younger performers—Marty Stuart, Tom T. Hall, a few others.

Jimmy Martin, the self-crowned "King of Bluegrass," who died of bladder cancer on May 14, 2005, at the age of seventy-seven, was larger than life, and he will turn out to be larger than death, too. He was incapable of the kinds of dissembling, duplicity, politenesses, and homogenization that make for a smooth career in today's Gentleman's Business of country music, where every outlaw has his own hairdresser. He did everything to the hilt, whether it was telling a joke, hunting, eating, feeling sorry for himself, or playing music. Above all, playing music. He had a kind of contempt for half-measures and timid souls, and his first project would be to try and find out how steady you were on your feet.

He took things seriously, including fooling around and cutting up. He didn't like ass-kissers, politicians, wishy-washy types. He wasn't above trying to ingratiate himself with people who might be able to do him some good; he just wasn't very good at it. He wanted to be remembered as one of the greats; he was inordinately proud of his induction into the International Bluegrass Music Association Hall of Honor, and it was the frustration of his life that he was never invited to be a member of the Grand Ole Opry. It was the Opry's loss. When it seemed that the world wasn't going to rush in to build him a monument, he did it himself; several years before his death he designed and erected his own tombstone in a Nashville cemetery, taller than he was standing, a stone's throw from Roy Acuff's somewhat more modest plot. He had himself photographed in front of it, and he put the photo on the front of one of his CDs.

The documentary film *King of Bluegrass* is worth seeing, but you could easily come away from it thinking that Jimmy Martin was a more or less normal person, just with the color turned up a little high. He wasn't. He was, to quote his friend Marty Stuart, "part preacher, part prophet, and a card-carrying madman who is completely filled with the musical holy ghost." That spirit erupts like a genie from every recording he made. He found a way to discipline his turbulent and sometimes anarchic soul through music, and his musical reputation is going to continue to grow. Jimmy Martin will be remembered long after many of his contemporaries. In an age dominated by spinmasters and bean counters, Jimmy Martin was the unvarnished Real Thing. Wave good-bye, and holler.

From the Oxford American, *2005*

Carl Perkins was one of the nicest people I've ever met. He came to New Orleans in 1996 to film a promotional video for his about-to-be-published autobiography and its companion CD. He was warm and genuine, utterly without star pretensions of any sort, and a living product of the fleeting era after World War Two when country honky-tonk music, bluegrass, and Memphis blues got real friendly and produced rock and roll. Included here are two pieces on him: a profile that appeared in the Sunday New York Times, *and a remembrance that appeared in the* Oxford American *after Perkins's death in 1998.*

The Gillian Welch essay was another of my Oxford American *columns, and is more or less self-explanatory.*

THE LOST MAN OF
ROCK AND ROLL

It is just after twelve noon, an October Saturday in New Orleans. Carl Perkins, composer of the song "Blue Suede Shoes" and the original rockabilly singer and guitarist, waits outside a small guitar store in an ordinarily quiet uptown neighborhood for filming to resume on a promotional video for his new CD. He flew down this morning from his home in Jackson, Tennessee, where he has lived for the past forty-five years. He takes all the flurry of activity in stride, joking with crew members and photographers, harmonizing on country songs with onlookers, and telling stories.

At sixty-four, Perkins is slim and handsome, with sculpted cheekbones, a prominent chin, easy smile, and a curly, steel-grey toupee which is the topic of frequent jokes by its owner. He wears blue jeans, a tight, ribbed crewneck shirt, thick aviator glasses, and, yes, blue suede shoes.

"Back in the days when that song was popular," he says, in a thick Tennessee country accent, lighting a cigarette as cameramen and technical crew members swirl around him, "somebody would always come up with a camera and want a picture of themselves stepping on the shoes. I used to carry a wire brush in my back pocket so I could reach down and brush 'em back to life. They sold the brush with the shoes."

From the street, someone passing on a bicycle stops and yells, "Hey! Carl Perkins! How's it goin'?"

Grinning widely, gesturing around at all the activity, Perkins says, "Well, country as I am, I don't really know. It seems like it's rocking right along."

Things are, indeed, rocking right along for Carl Perkins right now, although he seems admirably unimpressed by that fact. Mr. Perkins is, in a sense, the Lost Man of early rock and roll. He was there in Memphis at the Creation, the Big Bang of rock, a contemporary of Elvis Presley and Jerry Lee Lewis when country music, Southern gospel, and blues fused into a new hybrid. His 1956 song "Blue Suede Shoes" became as much of a rock-and-roll anthem as "Great Balls of Fire" or "Roll Over Beethoven."

Yet as the rockets of Jerry Lee and Elvis and Little Richard and Chuck Berry and Buddy Holly shot off into the great American night of legend, Mr. Perkins spent decades touring the middle and the bottom of his profession, battling alcoholism for long, honky-tonk years and searching for an ever-elusive follow-up to his big hit.

Now, with a just-published autobiography, entitled *Go, Cat, Go!*—the title comes from the famous refrain of his most famous composition—and a new CD of the same title—including Perkins duets with everyone from his old Sun Records labelmate Johnny Cash to Beatles George Harrison, Paul McCartney, and Ringo Starr, to Tom Petty, John Fogerty, Paul Simon, and Willie Nelson—Carl Perkins seems poised on the brink of a long-overdue rediscovery.

Mr. Perkins was the archetypal rockabilly. He spent his early years in a Lake County, Tennessee, shack without electricity or indoor plumbing; he acquired his first guitar from an older black neighbor who traded it to the boy for a couple of dollars and a one-legged chicken named Peg.

He emerged from that background into a post–World War Two milieu in which country people were gravitating to large towns and small cities. "It was a time in America when the war was over," he says, during a break in the weekend's filming. "People were happy. And it was a time when black and white were fusing musically. See, there was a little circle in West Tennessee, where we combined the blues influence coming up from Mississippi, and the bluegrass from out of Kentucky, but I don't think none of us even ever quite knew what it was. It didn't have a name; we called it feel-good music. A few guys got brave enough to get out and start playing it in the honky-tonks."

Perkins formed a band with his two brothers that became extremely active in the area around Jackson, playing a mixture of country and rhythm and blues material for dancing. The honky-tonks were rough places where the atmosphere was suffused with the highly charged possibilities of both physical love and violence, and the demands they placed on musicians were straightforward and unequivocal: stimulate dancing and drinking. The honky-tonks may seem, in retrospect, an unlikely setting for the complex, introspective, often sentimental man one meets today, yet they were the crucible that shaped both the band's sound and Perkins's emerging songwriting talents.

Spurred by a chance meeting with Elvis Presley, who had just made his first recordings for Sam Phillips's Sun Records, Perkins and his band headed for Memphis, hoping to audition for Phillips. He persisted despite initial rebuffs, eventually got Phillips to listen, and in October 1954, three months after Elvis's debut, Perkins cut his first record. The two tunes, both Perkins originals, were a beautiful, Hank Williams–ish country ballad called "Turn Around" and the jumping "Movie Magg," a quintessential rockabilly song about the exhilaration and dangers of courtship.

The recordings gained the band important local exposure, and Perkins often found himself on the same concert bill with Presley.

Even today, Perkins is awestruck by Presley. "He was the first boy I heard on record playing the songs the way I always done. I think Elvis was the complete entertainer. I believe when Elvis was born, God said, here is a messenger, and I'm gonna make him the best-lookin' guy, and I'm gonna give him every piece of rhythm he needs to move that good-lookin' body on that stage. I was fightin' a battle workin' with him, knowing I looked like Mr. Ed, that mule, and here was a guy that could go out and clear his throat and have ten thousand people scream."

In December 1955, Perkins struck gold with his third record for Phillips, a brand-new song he'd written entitled "Blue Suede Shoes." It became Sun Records's first million-seller and landed Perkins an important break, a national TV appearance on *The Perry Como Show*. The appearance could have done for Perkins's career what the Dorsey Brothers' television show was doing for Presley's, but it was not to be; in March 1956, en route to New York for their Como appearance, Perkins and his band collided with a truck on a desolate stretch of road in Delaware. Perkins went into a coma, and his brother Jay suffered a broken neck. Perkins's physical recovery took months; the professional wounds, however, never wholly healed.

After his recovery, Perkins's career languished. Overshadowed at Sun first by Presley and then by the younger Jerry Lee Lewis, who made his first recordings as a sideman on a Perkins record, Perkins left Sun for recording-industry giant Columbia, which didn't quite know what to do with him. Although his Columbia recordings are excellent, they did nothing commercially, and as the 1960s got under sail, Perkins's career was stalled in the doldrums.

It is a puzzle. The recordings he had made, and continued to make after the accident, are among the classics of rock and roll. Unlike Presley, Jerry Lee Lewis, or Little Richard, Perkins wrote his own hits. Songs like "Matchbox," "Everybody's Trying to Be My Baby," and "Honey Don't," all three of which were recorded by the Beatles on early albums, as well as "Boppin' the Blues," "Put Your Cat Clothes On," and many others, fused blues, country, and gospel music over a slapping, pulsating bass, with Perkins's tough, sinewy guitar and vocals seemingly straining at an invisible leash. At their best, Perkins's lyrics reveal a wit and an eye for detail that could give even Chuck Berry a run for his money.

Still, despite these strengths, Perkins never quite managed the transition from the honky-tonks to the national arena that his famous contemporaries achieved. When the music played in the honky-tonks stepped onto a national stage, it began to change its meaning from mere lubrication on the gears of flirtation and animus into a dramatization, by the star, of those possibilities in his own personality. Performers like Presley and Lewis made this a kind of shared joke or secret between themselves and the audience; an instinct for self-dramatization became part of the necessary equipment for rock-and-roll stardom. Perkins, an electrifying performer at his best, somehow lacked that instinct, which might have allowed him to fully occupy the enlarged stage to which he now had access. In his heart, he was still playing the honky-tonks.

He spent the early 1960s searching for a niche, alternating between country music and harder-edged rock and roll and spending long months touring, battling a deepening alcoholism. Along the way he suffered a series of personal disasters, including the death of his brother Jay and the near loss of two fingers in a freak accident. He was cheered by a 1964 meeting with the Beatles, who had idolized him from his Sun Records, but it was a bleak, wandering time for him, personally and professionally.

In 1966, he accepted an offer to tour with his old friend Johnny Cash, an arrangement that lasted for nearly ten years and provided him with a solid economic base. He continued recording on his own for several labels, and gradually, with the help and understanding of his wife, Valda, began to get a handle on his drinking.

When he left Cash in 1975, Perkins was a middle-aged man who had begun, the hard way, to come to a measure of wisdom and stability. In the late 1970s he began touring with a band that included two of his sons, Stan and Greg, who are a source of constant pride to him. "I didn't try to pull 'em into the music," he says. "But when Stan was little he would take two pencils and beat on his mama's coffee table, and I said, 'Oh Lord, that boy's gonna be a drummer.' I don't like to hear anybody bragging on their kids, but I played with a lot of people in my life, and when those two boys look at the back of this old man's head and start playing, it hits a groove and it just works."

A longstanding dispute with Sam Phillips over the royalties to "Blue Suede Shoes" also got ironed out, adding further financial security to his life. He opened a restaurant in Jackson, called Suede's, and in 1981 founded the Carl Perkins Center for the Prevention of Child Abuse, for which he organizes an annual telethon. Then, during a 1991 recording session, he began experiencing difficulty singing. The consequent visit to his doctor turned up the worst card he had yet been dealt: he was diagnosed with cancer of the throat.

Two years later, after a long course of radiation therapy, which Perkins ranks just behind prayer and his wife's love as a curative, he was pronounced cancer-free. "It was a miracle," he declares, unironically and convincingly. In the ensuing three years he has resumed touring with his sons for about half of each year, spending the rest of the time at home, writing songs, and visiting with family and friends.

Perkins today is a warm, relaxed man who would just as soon play guitar and sing during an interview as talk, although he is prodigiously gifted as a storyteller, raconteur, and informal living-room preacher. His emotions are close to the surface and he breaks into tears easily when remembering a kindness done him, or when talking about his family. He seems to be constantly surprised by the fact that he has survived, and that he seems to have outrun his demons.

"I'm not a society man," he says. "I don't go to the country clubs, I don't go to Nashville and hang out. I never fit in with that. My friends at home work at the service station. I like to go fishing, I like an old cotton field, and I like to spend time with Valda. I never get tired of her."

Perkins has more friends than just his fishing buddies, however, and most of them, it seems, appear with him on *Go, Cat, Go!*, his new CD. The record runs a gamut from country-flavored duets with Willie Nelson and Johnny Cash, to two excellent collaborations with Paul Simon, to a remake of his 1968 rocker "Restless" with Tom Petty. One of the best tracks on the disc is a version of a new song, called "Quarter Horse," on which Perkins's unaccompanied voice and guitar weave magic on a sentimental tune about childhood dreams.

Somehow, over the years, Perkins has learned to live with a set of conditions that may have exempted him from the pantheon of martyrs to the Fast Lane but apparently gave him something better in exchange. "I never envied Elvis his mansion and all that. All these boys—Elvis, Jerry Lee, Roy Orbison—they all lost their wives, their families . . . I never was in envy of them when they hung their platinum records on the walls. People say, 'What happened to you, Carl? All of them went on to superstardom. Where'd you go?' I say, 'I went home.'"

From the New York Times, *Fall 1996*

ELEGY FOR CARL PERKINS

arl Perkins died this past January, and most of the obituaries have already been written. All mentioned his paternal role in the history of rockabilly music, his authorship of its anthem, "Blue Suede Shoes," and the fact that his career never quite followed the same upward trajectory as the careers of Elvis, Jerry Lee, and the rest.

Almost all of the obituaries also acknowledged that Perkins had managed to escape, or at least outrun, many of the ravaging effects of what is usually called success in America. By the time he died—of a series of strokes, at age sixty-six—he had beaten alcoholism, throat cancer, and the odds against a public figure growing up and having a meaningful life in this culture.

The following is offered as an addendum to the official eulogies. I spent some time with Perkins in the fall of 1996, when he was visiting New Orleans to film a video. We visited for a while on a bright Sunday morning in a private French Quarter home with a lovely living room, overstuffed pastel sofas, curtains; outside French doors the sun shone in a lush courtyard, a far cry from the rough Tennessee farmland Perkins had grown up sharecropping. When I arrived, Perkins's blue Stratocaster was out, the amplifier on; he and his hosts had been relaxing singing gospel songs. It was clear immediately that he was primarily a country boy; he liked to sit around and tell stories, and sing. He was a man whose first band was made up of his brothers, and whose last was largely made up of his sons. He kept repeating how much he liked New Orleans. The previous night he had played with a local band at the Mermaid Lounge, and he had been greeted by a cadre of rockabilly freaks dressed in retro style. He got a kick out of the way they used period slang when they talked to him; there was one blond girl he couldn't get over, who kept telling him how "cool" he was. His manner was unfailingly generous and self-effacing.

Conversation was interspersed with Perkins's guitar playing, which was crackling, relaxed, and exuberant; he played a quasi–Merle Travis version of "The World Is Waiting for the Sunrise," sang the new tune "Quarter Horse" from his recent CD, and sang a few gospel numbers as well. Then at one point something remarkable happened: Perkins wrote a song on the spot.

Among the first generation of rock and rollers, only Chuck Berry and Buddy Holly stand with Perkins as songwriters. Little Richard wasn't a songwriter, nor was Jerry Lee Lewis, nor Elvis. Perkins's lyrics at their best are wry, sharp, and funny; songs like "Dixie Fried," "Pointed Toed Shoes" ("Everything's all-reet cause I got 'em on my feet"), "Put Your Cat Clothes On," "Movie Magg," and a number of others are rock-and-roll classics.

At one point, Perkins was fooling around with a little whip-lash lick in the key of G that he played on the high strings with his index and middle fingers, set against a driving rhythm on the low strings that he played with his thumb. After he played it once through a jumping blues chorus, I asked what it was and he laughed and said, "I don't know what that's called . . . I just been foolin' with that little old lick, hopin' a song'll jump out that I can use it on." He played it again, and said, "It's just kickin' the string back a little . . ." Then, out of nowhere, over that little rockabilly riff he started singing:

She was walking down the street
Struttin' down in New Orleans
She was hot and hard to handle
She'd be everything I need
She was cool . . .
They say, "Cool, man; cool, man . . . cold."

(big chuckle from Perkins)

Lord, that gal got to me,
She buried herself down in my soul.

(then a series of rhythmic breaks)

Lord, I got on me a Learjet
And I just headed south
I got to New Orleans and . . . Whoo! . . .

(a moment of free fall in which he searched
for a rhyme and the rest of us hung on for dear life . . .)

. . . There went my mouth!

(. . . and we all cracked up as he went on singing)

I saw her walking down the street. . .
All I ever need, she's for me.

(spoken: "Yes, she is . . .")

Lord, you all know what I mean
I got to get back to New Orleans
'Cause it's cool, man . . .

. . . and after a few more guitar licks the songs broke up in laughter. When it was over I asked if that was something he ever played
before.

"Naw," he said, shaking his head once and lighting a cigarette,
and laughing. "Just popped out."

Over the course of a few hours we talked about all kinds of things. Roy Orbison, Johnny Cash, Elvis (whom he worshipped), Bob Dylan (whom he loved). He spoke frankly about his family, his faith in God, and his struggle with alcoholism ("I *had* to drink. That's where I got the courage to get in front of those drunks in those honky-tonks. If I hadn't been drinking with them I'd-a got scared and run home").

At the end of our visit, I asked a question that had come to me in an odd moment. Maybe because he was so strongly identified with one tune, "Blue Suede Shoes," it had occurred to me that the two and a half minutes he spent recording it on that particular day in 1955 became thousands of hours of other people's lives. I started by assuming that "Blue Suede Shoes" had sold a million copies. (It had sold more.) Say you could play the record twenty-five times in an hour. That means you could play it a hundred times in four hours, and in forty hours you could play it a thousand times. So it would take 40,000 hours (238 weeks, or over four and a half years) for everybody who bought the first million records to play the song only once. And we know that people played it a lot more than that and that it sold more than that. So two and a half minutes of his life had become years and years of other people's lives. Had he ever thought about that?

He looked at me for a long moment. "No," he said, slowly. His face slid into a thoughtful frown. "I . . . I never have. That's awesome. It really is. I . . . I . . . I had never thought of that." He looked past me, suddenly subdued, thinking about it. "I started getting these awards from BMI [a company that licenses music for radio play] when it passed a million plays. I'm past two million airplays for 'Blue Suede Shoes.' They have ways of keeping up with this. That's not counting what you're saying—that the kids who buy it, and the people who listen . . . No, that is . . . It's very weird. I never thought of that. I've wasted a lot of people's time."

As I watched his face I began to realize that he was genuinely disturbed by what I had said.

"They could have . . . built a *city* in the time they spent listening to that tune," he went on. "I don't know how I feel about that. I feel weird. It's an awesome thought. Maybe on my tomb rock they'll carve the words 'I'm sorry for taking up so much of your time . . .'"

This was too much; I hadn't wanted to ruin his sense of what he had done with his life. I explained that I had only wanted to ask him a question I had thought of in other forms, at other times, a mystery close to the heart of any profound human action, a kind of grace, how one moment can expand, like the parable of the loaves and fishes . . . I floundered, trying to articulate what I meant. Perkins listened, seemed to brighten a little, and eventually stopped me.

"I . . . I follow you," he said. "I'm in that same place that you are. You stirred up something I'll think about the rest of my life. Thank you for working that out. I mean, it is an awesome thing, to think, only two and a half minutes of my life, but look what it spread into, you know. I don't know . . . I never really thought of it that way." His eyes focused on me again, and he seemed to return to the room. "And I don't know what I'm going to do with it now that I've got it." And with that he laughed again, and the dark mood broke, and I breathed a little easier.

Later that afternoon he flew back home to Tennessee and never, to my knowledge, visited New Orleans again. I thought many times about our conversation. How many performers would have seen the question I'd asked as anything other than a cause for celebration? Somehow Carl Perkins had managed to stay real enough to think seriously about the value of his life and his actions.

The CD never did engender a Carl Perkins renaissance. I have a feeling that was okay with him. He'd been through it all, and he had achieved something more important than megastardom. I always hoped I'd see him again; he was the kind of person who made you feel that way, as if you had made a friend. And if you expand that feeling through all the people who listened to and enjoyed his music, maybe you have something like immortality.

From the Oxford American, *1998*

TRUST THE SONG

We have entered an era of mass confusion between people's ability to perform public tasks for which they are, presumably, trained, and their personal lives, which in healthier times are considered nobody's business. Former vice president Dan Quayle has even announced that marital fidelity will be "the issue" in the next presidential race. Sure—the heck with foreign policy, education, the economy, public works . . .

"Trust the song, not the singer" is age-old wisdom. I'm glad that the singers and musicians, male and female, whose work I have loved over the years did not have to display certificates of marital fidelity in order to qualify as performers. Likewise the fiction writers. No one asked them to be moral exemplars in their personal lives. It was their work that was important.

Lately the agenda of aesthetic discussion, along with politics, seems to have been lifted from an afternoon talk show. One example from recent memory: Philip Roth's Pulitzer Prize–winning novel *American Pastoral*, which I read and admired. At least three quarters of the people to whom I mentioned the book didn't really care what was between the covers of *American Pastoral*, but wanted to know if I had read Claire Bloom's memoir of her apparently troubled marriage to Roth.

To some people, an artist's work is only an avenue by which to get to the real point, which is the artist her/himself. A kind of sacrificial element comes into play, a desire to consume the body and drink the blood. "Who are you, *really?*" is the question. But most creative people are trying to escape from the cage of "who they are." It is a mistake to think that most artists and creative people are trying to express the self; they are more likely to be trying to escape the day-to-day self, complete it, even find its opposite.

These thoughts are occasioned by the career of the singer and songwriter Gillian Welch since her brilliant 1996 debut CD *Revival*, and perhaps even more so since her second recording, *Hell Among the Yearlings*, was released last year. Both discs consist of original material, strongly inflected by different kinds of traditional music, as well as some rockabilly, folk, and so on. Easily one of the most talented and distinctive singers and songwriters to come down the pike in a long, long while, she and her partner and cowriter, the excellent guitarist and harmony singer David Rawlings, have gained a wide and appreciative following for themselves.

Along with that following, though, like hyenas following a wagon train, has come a chorus of scattered carping voices, issuing from places like the *Los Angeles Times* and *Rolling Stone*, questioning Welch's right to use themes and musical elements from traditional music in her songs. The problem, for them, is that Welch grew up in Los Angeles, to music-business parents. Maybe the writers looked at her picture, thought she was a mountain girl, and then were embarrassed when they realized they'd been fooled. Who knows.

What we can know is that the voices questioning Welch's right to do what she does are putting the emphasis in exactly the wrong place. They are the same type of people who felt betrayed thirty-five years ago when it turned out that Bob Dylan was a Jewish kid from Minnesota instead of Billy the Kid's younger brother. They are operating out of an inquisitional mode that is anathema to anybody who actually derives pleasure from the arts. It is a particularly creepy form of puritanism.

Here's the thing: First of all, Gillian Welch is not playing, or claiming to play, "traditional music," strictly speaking, any more than Bob Dylan was. She knows the repertoire and some of the techniques, but there are all kinds of elements in her music that are hardly orthodox old-time elements, and that are clearly there as part of an intentional effect. As for the often rural, and even rural-gothic—murder, moonshine, failed crops—subject matter of her songs . . . well, what about it? "Caleb Meyer," the song all the reviewers mentioned from *Hell Among the Yearlings*, is about a foiled rape attempt somewhere in the vicinity of "them hollering pines." It's a good song, and I don't believe one needs to have been the victim of a rape attempt or live near the hollering pines to have written it, or to appreciate it. If there's a better devotional song than "By the Mark," from *Revival*, I don't know what it is. It makes no difference to me whether Gillian Welch believes in Jesus or not; the song carries its own weight. Besides, it is about a kind of truth in life that one can recognize as truth whether or not one believes in Jesus in the first place. But both discs are full of terrific songs (and singing)—"Good Til Now" (with its faint echoes of Blind Boy Fuller's "Weeping Willow"), "Acony Bell," "My Morphine," "Winter's Come and Gone," "Barroom Girls," "Only One and Only" . . . To make an issue of who is behind the lyrics and the voice moves the discussion into a completely different arena.

It seems to me that it takes an extreme poverty of imagination to propose, implicitly or explicitly, that people can write only about their personal experience (or, worse, about the experiences peculiar to their ethnic/gender/regional/national group). It takes poverty of imagination, and hostility to the idea of the free human spirit. Any hope one might have left for a society like ours depends on the constant assertion of the possibility of that kind of empathy. Of course, as an artist, the further from your personal experience you try to reach, the more effort, intuition, honesty, humility, and/or luck it takes. The further you reach, the easier it is to do something that just doesn't work, doesn't ring true. But the question is *whether it works*, whether it rings true, *not* whether you have an inherited visa to enter that territory.

A few years ago, while I was attending the Iowa Writers' Workshop, Saul Bellow came to talk to us for a few days. In addition to a reading, he conducted a workshop and a question-and-answer session. During the Q&A one student asked him about "stealing" from other writers—borrowing techniques, structural ideas, entering other cultural milieus. Bellow smiled wanly and said, "You are entitled to steal anything you are strong enough to carry out."

Amen.

From the Oxford American

The following four pieces come at the work of Bob Dylan from four different angles. The first appeared in the commemorative program for the 1997 Kennedy Center Honors, the year when Dylan was honored along with Lauren Bacall, Jessye Norman, Charlton Heston, and Edward Villella. He had just released his stunning, Grammy-winning return-to-form disc Time Out of Mind, *and was at a new, or renewed, creative peak. All the honorees got to invite someone of their choice to write an encomium for inclusion in the program; I was honored to be invited to write this.*

The second piece appeared as booklet notes accompanying the DVD The Other Side of the Mirror: Bob Dylan Live at the Newport Folk Festival, 1963–1965, *which contains extraordinary footage of Dylan remaking himself over the course of three summers. Those were crucial moments not only for his life and career but for the direction of American popular music and culture.*

The very short third Dylan item here accompanied the disc Gotta Serve Somebody: The Gospel Songs of Bob Dylan, *a collection of Dylan's Christian songs performed by African-American gospel performers such as Mavis Staples, Shirley Caesar, the Mighty Clouds of Joy, and Rance Allen.*

The final Dylan piece, "World Gone Wrong Again," was commissioned for, and published in, the collection Studio A: The Bob Dylan Reader, *edited by Benjamin Hedin. It represents my attempt to understand, up to a point, the role that Dylan's revisiting of traditional material on his two solo albums* Good as I Been to

You *and* World Gone Wrong *played in his creative revival of the 1990s. The odd structure and tone of the essay had something to do with the sinister progression of events in the early years of the new millennium, specifically the ongoing disaster of the George W. Bush administration, whose choices seemed to be eroding the already tenuous social contract many Americans felt they shared, and which had always seemed to me to be incarnated in American music, and most specifically in Dylan's. It was published in 2004. The next year, the shit really hit the fan.*

BOB DYLAN, 1997

The central question for an American artist—both as an American and as an artist—is how to remain indivisibly oneself while, in Walt Whitman's phrase, containing multitudes. Few in our time have done both as fully as Bob Dylan.

By now it probably goes without saying that he is the foremost American songwriter of the past thirty-five years. Even a short list of his best-known songs, from "Blowin' in the Wind" through "Mr. Tambourine Man" and the songs from classic albums like *Highway 61 Revisited, Blood on the Tracks, Infidels,* and this year's triumphant *Time Out of Mind,* would take up half this page. In the course of writing and performing them he has changed everyone's expectations of the kinds of complexity and meaning that popular songs could deliver.

But beyond his preeminence as a songwriter and performer, Bob Dylan has remained a quintessentially American artist in the largest sense, a true American original. By combining African-American blues, white country music, rural folk music, imagist poetry, and rock and roll, Dylan created a new musical and literary form, both popular and serious at the same time, which many have emulated but of which Bob Dylan is still not only the prototype but the unchallenged master.

From the beginning, Dylan's work has occupied a special, central ground where forms and genres that had previously been seen as separate or incompatible combined and were transmuted into something both wholly his own and wholly in the American grain. From many sources came one voice—*E pluribus unum*—and in his constant reimagining of these materials he has proved, over and over, that the elements of American culture, in all their contradictory, painful, exhilarating, and sometimes indigestible glory, are infinitely elastic, and infinitely renewable.

For years, reviewers of popular culture have reflexively referred to Bob Dylan as the voice, even the conscience, of a generation. And it is true that the period of the 1960s, in nearly all of its aspects—its political and moral preoccupations, its apocalyptic overtones—was reflected in his recordings of the time as it was in no other single artist's work, regardless of genre. Yet he has remained an abiding presence in American culture, his work growing and changing as he and the culture at large have grown and changed during the past three decades. He and his work represent something perennial in our culture.

"I always thought," he said once, "that one man, the lone balladeer with the guitar, could blow an entire army off the stage if he knew what he was doing." That sense of the power of the lone creative voice can be traced, its pulse felt, through the great river of creative imagery and action that stretches back centuries in the United States: traveling lecturers, tall-tale spinners, itinerant entertainers of all sorts, blues singers, old-time fiddlers. It is there to be heard in the work of Jimmie Rodgers and Blind Lemon Jefferson, Emily Dickinson and Bessie Smith, Walt Whitman and Jack Kerouac, the sense of the individual voice, intensely personal, indivisible, taking on American life, in all its epic contradictions.

In his song "Bob Dylan's 115th Dream," on his 1965 album *Bringing It All Back Home*, the singer spins a long, tall yarn in which he arrives in North America before the arrival of Columbus and has a series of funny, dreamlike encounters, skirmishes, and near-misses with a gallery of bizarre characters. At the end of the song the singer greets Christopher Columbus himself as the explorer arrives on the continent, and Dylan wishes him a deadpan "good luck."

It is a tall tale in a tradition going back to Mark Twain, and well before him, yet it is something more as well. In it we watch a vivid imagination cutting a mythic reality down to size—projecting itself, in fact, right into the middle of that reality. With wry humor, the singer celebrates a discovery of a land that is confusing and out of whack yet full of possibility, and claims, in a more than symbolic sense, the territory for his own.

There is a recognizable stance here, and in all of Dylan's work: a sense that the individual sensibility—aesthetic, political, spiritual—could claim a role at the heart of the nation's ongoing drama, in the middle of its ethnic and regional polyphony, locate what was of value there, and sing a new self, even a new country, out of it. As if the very activity of incorporating, coming to terms with, those multitudes of influence and utterance is itself somehow at the heart of the American ideal.

A large part of Dylan's enduring claim on our imagination and attention is that his example has restated that ambition and that possibility, year after year, to this day. His has been an example not only to songwriters but to fiction writers, playwrights, poets, and filmmakers, constant proof that this culture, in all its contradictions, is still there to be claimed yet again, seen anew, through the agency of the human heart and imagination.

From the commemorative book for the
Kennedy Center Honors ceremony, December 1997

LEAVING THE FARM

After a certain point, most of what you can say about a person only obscures the truth of who he is, like vines covering a house. Rarely can a document strip away the encrustation of legend, lies, projection, and wish fulfillment and make you see the outlines more clearly. This film is one of those documents.

So much has been written about the early days of Bob Dylan, and about his first appearance with an electric band at the 1965 Newport Folk Festival, that it seems futile to add to it. The endless interpretation can make it harder to hear the songs. But in *The Other Side of the Mirror* director Murray Lerner cuts through all of the midrash and shows Dylan himself, in the context of those early-'60s changes, and the film speaks more pointedly than volumes of explanation could.

The Newport Folk Festival, where this film was shot, was started in 1959 by impresario George Wein and promoter Albert Grossman. It was a spinoff of Wein's Newport Jazz Festival, which had been bringing the likes of Thelonious Monk, Duke Ellington, Louis Armstrong, and Miles Davis to the upper-class enclave of Newport, Rhode Island, every summer since 1954.

From the beginning, the project of the Newport Folk Festival was not just cultural but political. In fact, for some of the

most powerful guiding spirits of the Festival—Alan Lomax, Pete
Seeger, Theodore Bikel, members of an older generation that had
come of age with the left-wing politics of the 1930s and 1940s—
there was little or no distinction between the cultural and the
political. Music—song—was for them, at its truest, an expression
of the spirit of common people, and a tool by which those people
might gain greater power and leverage in society. Traditional
ballads and songs preserved a sense of continuity with the past;
topical songs advanced a critique of the present and a vision of
the future. Individual performers, no matter how talented, were
subordinated to the tradition, and to the larger project of social
change.

When Bob Dylan came along, with his youth and his personal intensity and his overwhelming songwriting talent, the folk
establishment must have smelled spring in the air. There had
been important topical songwriters before Dylan—Joe Hill, Pete
Seeger, Aunt Molly Jackson, and, especially, Woody Guthrie,
who was Dylan's most potent early influence. But Dylan had a
genius that lay beyond any of them. To a degree unmatched by
any other songwriter of his or any other generation, Dylan mixed
the lyric and prophetic modes. The songs' political concerns came
through with such power because they were carried by this combination, aided also by Dylan's strong dramatic instincts.

In 1963, when the earliest footage here was shot, Dylan was
still the prized and private discovery of the extended family of
folk music enthusiasts that had begun to mushroom in the 1950s.
Dylan's songs as performed by Peter, Paul and Mary, Joan Baez,
and others, had made him a reputation that preceded him everywhere, but at Newport large numbers of the faithful could
now see those songs literally embodied in the fascinating and
contradictory persona Dylan represented—tough yet vulnerable,
young yet battle-worn, comically self-effacing and uncompromis-
ingly intense. Finally, the Old Guard must have thought, a brilliantly talented and creative and charismatic youngster who could

bring their own message of social justice to a larger audience. Such hopes have driven many a youngster from his or her parents' house in search of a little fresh air.

The Other Side of the Mirror shows us with vivid economy and directness the progression of Bob Dylan first fulfilling those hopes and then rapidly and inevitably freeing himself from them and finding his own voice, a new persona, a way forward into very different psychic and political and artistic territory. The film does this by merely presenting well-chosen and intelligently sequenced footage of Dylan's performances from the Festivals of 1963, '64, and '65, along with just enough contextualizing material to be able to see the effect he was having on those around him. Some of the footage is taken from the informal daytime "workshops" held during the Festival, and some from the more formal night-time concerts.

The earliest glimpse we have of him is from one of those day-time workshops, performing on a stage shared by Doc Watson, Clarence Ashley, and Judy Collins. Joan Baez joins him to sing his antiwar song "With God on Our Side." Baez, already a star, had by then fallen in love both with the artist and with the man, and she had helped expose him to her already wide and devoted audience. This film brilliantly cuts from their afternoon performance to their reprise of the song at an evening concert. It also shows Dylan delivering his Woody Guthrie–esque "Talkin' World War III Blues" and, with burning intensity and commitment, his bitter, nuanced song about the murder of civil rights leader Medgar Evers, titled "Only a Pawn in Their Game." Finally he is surrounded onstage by Baez, Pete Seeger, the Freedom Singers, and Peter, Paul, and Mary for an ensemble performance of "Blowin' in the Wind." The first song that brought Dylan fame and fortune, "Blowin'" was hardly a conventional topical song, although it was adopted almost immediately by the civil rights movement and the nascent peace movement. It was based not on answers but on questions—repeated questions that pointed to larger questions about the nature of life. This performance amounted to a kind of collective acknowledgment of Dylan's emerging centrality, an implicit anointing of him as the Hope Of The Future.

A lot happened between Newport '63 and Newport '64. Two events, in particular, stand out: the assassination of President Kennedy in November 1963, and, three months later, the Beatles' first U.S. visit. The assassination was in some ways the culmination of many of the political themes about which Dylan had been singing. It signaled a split in the American psyche: a shift in power to a younger, more vital generation had been aborted. Kennedy was replaced in office by the dour, older Lyndon Johnson. Then, with the New Year, came the Beatles, an explosion of fun and irony and sex from foreign shores, just the thing to help a traumatized public forget its trauma for a while. If Kennedy's death had foreclosed a newborn sense of possibility in politics to which young people could relate, rock and roll would step in to fill the vacuum. Something in that equation affected everyone in the United States.

By the time the 1964 Newport Folk Festival came around, an obvious shift had taken place in Dylan. In all these 1964 performances Dylan seems to have a different relationship to the audience, a shift perhaps from shared struggle to shared joke. Instead of burning, uncompromising songs of social indictment, he sings ironic love songs and imagistic poetry. A spoken introduction from folk godfather Pete Seeger precedes an afternoon performance of the not-yet-released song "Mr. Tambourine Man," and one can only imagine Seeger's thoughts as he sits, visible on the side of the stage, listening to Dylan singing about dancing beneath the diamond sky with one hand waving free, instead of about God stopping the next war . . . When Dylan sings the obligatory duet with Joan Baez on "With God on Our Side," the comparison with the year before is fascinating. The climax of the song is delivered not with ardent closed eyes but with knowing, open eyes, a smile not quite hidden around the edges.

But the standout performance from 1964 is surely the monumental "Chimes of Freedom," a mystical poem full of flashing, nonlinear imagery, delivered here with the focus, intensity, and exhilaration of an artist who has found his true freedom and his real voice. When Dylan finishes his performance the audience roars its amazement and hunger for more, refusing to listen to emcee Peter Yarrow's pleas for order, sanity, and all-around good citizenship. Although Odetta and Dave Van Ronk, both major folk stars, were still to come, the sheer force of Dylan's artistry and charisma had blown everything else away. And in Yarrow's lonely, haggard, besieged figure, imploring the turned-on audience to be reasonable and accept the ordered, preordained progression of the evening, we can read the writing on the wall for the Folk Establishment. Performers were supposed to be serving a Larger Good, but Dylan's assertion of personal, artistic freedom was more compelling to that audience than any other kind of Larger Good.

Between Newport '64 and Newport '65, U.S. involvement in Vietnam was ratcheted up dramatically, Malcolm X was gunned down in Harlem, the British rock invasion became a flood, marijuana and other recreational drugs spread far and wide, and the 1960s were in full swing. That winter Dylan recorded his great album *Bringing It All Back Home* and, as summer approached, began work on his subsequent masterpiece *Highway 61 Revisited*; both albums had Dylan playing in an electric rock setting. His songs were now all dense, poetic, imagistic—often cryptic, often comic, often frightening, often all of these at once.

In his memoir *Chronicles: Volume 1*, Dylan wrote, "The folk music scene had been like a paradise that I had to leave, like Adam had to leave the garden. It was just too perfect." In 1965, we see him choose deliberately to step outside the gates of Eden. His surprise performance with the Paul Butterfield Blues Band (minus Butterfield himself) turned that 1965 Newport appearance into legend. After an afternoon workshop where he delivered some of his newer songs acoustically, Dylan came out for his evening set wearing a leather blazer and a deadpan expression and fronting Butterfield's great band, with Michael Bloomfield on lead guitar, and roared his way into "Maggie's Farm," a declaration of independence if ever there was one: "I try my best to be just like I am, but everybody wants you to be just like them." He followed it up with "Like a Rolling Stone," which had just been released as a single.

Much has been written about the reaction from the audience, which had been expecting the cuddly Bobby of years past, and about the shock experienced by some members of the folk establishment, who saw rock and roll as the voice of the devil himself— sensuous, egocentric, commercial, scornful of the Greater Good. You can read countless published accounts of what happened, but here, finally, we can hear and sense the reaction without mediation. After his short and abruptly terminated set with the band, Dylan departs the stage, leaving the crowd confused and agitated; after some cajoling, he returns alone with his acoustic guitar and delivers stunning performances of "Mr. Tambourine Man" and "It's All Over Now, Baby Blue," the most appropriate swan song imaginable.

The astonishing journey of transformation to that moment from the afternoon only two years earlier when he wore a work shirt and sang a steely "North Country Blues" on a stage next to Clarence Ashley has obsessed critics and fans for decades. The essence of it is visible here, now, in under ninety minutes, and we have the filmmaker Murray Lerner to thank. Lerner, who has also made documentaries on the 1970 Isle of Wight Festival, Jimi Hendrix, Isaac Stern, and Miles Davis, speaks for himself in an accompanying filmed interview here. He makes the point that his early interest in the modernist poetry of T. S. Eliot and Ezra Pound, and their technique of using, as he puts it, an "unexpected juxtaposition of two different images to create a third idea" was what led him into filmmaking. *The Other Side of the*

Mirror, like its predecessor, the Newport documentary *"FESTI-VAL!"* (released in 1967), works in exactly this manner, with no voiceover or explanatory titles, nothing but a procession of images (and sound). Of course, the same could be said about Dylan's best work as well. The clarification the film delivers also serves to deepen our appreciation of the mystery at its subject's heart.

From The Other Side of the Mirror:
Bob Dylan Live at the Newport Folk Festival, 1963–1965

GOTTA SERVE SOMEBODY

Bob Dylan's songs are nearly always the record of a struggle—between appearance and reality, or between justice and its opposite, or between the demands of the self and some higher truth. Nothing is taken for granted; one is always choosing.

When Bob Dylan let it be known, in 1979, that he had been born again, it seemed to some that he had renounced the complexity and questioning of his earlier work in favor of what they saw as the prepackaged answers of religion. As time has gone by, though, it is clear that Dylan encountered the Gospel the same way he has encountered everything else he has looked into—with the full complexity of a whole human heart and mind.

When there is the possibility of choice, there is always, just behind it, the reality of judgment. The awareness of judgment hovers behind the insistent questions in "Blowin' in the Wind"; it stares out at the listener from between the lines not only of what he once called his "finger-pointing" topical songs, like "Masters of War," but also his more imagistic song-poems of the mid-1960s, such as "Maggie's Farm" and "Like a Rolling Stone," although the targets are a little more ambiguous. In the years just before his conversion, in albums like *Blood on the Tracks* and *Desire*, the finger begins to point, ever more unmistakably, toward the self.

"I think of a hero," Dylan once remarked, "as someone who understands the degree of responsibility that comes with his freedom." When Dylan began performing the Christian material publicly, he presented himself, in a sense, as Exhibit A. The songs were a form of personal testimony, and they were accompanied by spoken testimony as well. Yet before too long Dylan eliminated this directly evangelical component of his performance. Perhaps he felt a trap waiting there, one more head on the hydra of vanity, a disproportionate emphasis on his own persona, while it was the song that was, and is, the important thing. He has never stopped performing the songs.

In any case, for a while, on this recording, we can separate what Dylan is saying in his gospel songs from the drama of his saying it. Here, as in his other work, you find the range of human experience; there is serenity, turbulence, joy, gratitude, the hot iron glow of temptation and guilt and pride; there is damnation and hope, mystery and plain talk, all riding the constant and sometimes torturing undertow of the flesh and the world's concerns. In this way we see, again, how rooted Dylan is in the grain of American music, the Saturday night/Sunday morning tug-of-war that has lent tension and fire to the fact of the gospel in the singing of Ralph Stanley, Little Richard, Charley Patton, Muddy Waters, and Hank Williams, among so many others.

Truth, whatever its specifics may be, is never argued for; it is revealed. And in these songs the truth of the human heart is revealed, striving after that which will heal it, ennoble it, and, finally, save it from itself.

From Gotta Serve Somebody: The Gospel Songs of Bob Dylan

WORLD GONE WRONG AGAIN

I.

"It's so grandiloquent to speak of 'the national character,'" Norman Mailer once remarked, before going on to speak of the national character.

In the centrifuge of the accelerating world, unlike elements once held in solution have separated out. Things go by fast; you have to label them quickly.

America is the incarnation of good; America is the embodiment of evil. Cast your vote; it only takes a second. This is not an essay question; please just mark "yes" or "no."

America . . . Meaning what, again? Cowboys and Indians? New York City? Hollywood? The Civil War? The CIA? Interstate Highways? Main Street? Wal-Mart? John Wayne? John Wayne Gacy? Earl Scruggs? Muhammad Ali? Rosa Parks? Don Rickles? Flaco Jimenez? Edmund Wilson? Redwood forests? Gulf Stream waters? Ellis Island? Los Alamos? America wants to include all possibility, hence it takes up, potentially, all the space there is. It expands. Something so internally contradictory is, of course, a target for every kind of projection. The mind has trouble accepting such intense contradictions within the same entity. Their presence creates a profound anxiety. Learning to accept them is a discipline.

Is it because the culture as a whole contains such extremes of good and bad that there is such a pull to identify with only one vein or corner of the culture?

To identify with the culture itself means identifying with a high level of tension among elements. It means identifying with the tension itself.

I don't know . . . It used to be important to me. Maybe it still is. I'm trying to figure it out.

But the worst elements in the world are either wrapping themselves in the flag or hoping to exorcise their problems by burning it.

2.

People like to make generalizations about artists, but you really can't. Generally speaking. Any time you say something like "artists need freedom," right away you realize that artists also need necessity. If you say they need a tradition, it is also immediately clear that they need to be able to work against a tradition. Or, rather, some do. And some don't.

But it is probably true that most people who are artists as we tend to mean that word have very contradictory needs and impulses, and that their work is among other things a way of mediating between opposite forces in their own nature. Melville's poem about art says, "Humility—yet pride and scorn / Instinct and study; love and hate / Audacity—reverence. These must mate . . ." in order to "wrestle with the angel." It is an impulse toward wholeness and balance.

Certainly most significant artists implicitly or explicitly pose questions about the relation between the individual and society. Everyone, of course, leads a dual citizenship as an individual and as a member of a larger group, just as we all live both in the present moment and in a continuum with some past and future. In the United States, these relations are unusually complex, because the society is based not on a fixed grid of social organization against which intelligible individual dramas play out, but on an ideal of fluidity in which identity is nothing if not elastic and individuals can re-create themselves, or try to, by moving down the road, making a fresh start. That's the mythology, at least.

"Significant artists," "American artists" . . . the terms are vaguely embarrassing. Even the word "artist." It is too big a concept. You need to make distinctions among the types. But how useful are the distinctions? Michelangelo, Ravi Shankar, Sarah Vaughan, Akira Kurosawa, Chuck Berry, Beethoven, Sviatoslav Richter, Charley Patton, Emily Dickinson, Romare Bearden, Dock Boggs, Laurence Olivier, William Faulkner, the Notre Dame stone masons, Bessie Smith, an Asmat shield carver, Dante . . .

Today the distinctions between types of artists seem to be less important than they once were. To some people, of course, it is still vitally important to maintain the distinction between, say, "fine art" and "folk art." Others like to state loudly that there is no difference. But there's a difference. Any time you can make a terminological distinction there's a difference. But how important is it, and to whom? And—if you are interested in this kind of question—why?

It's easy to be dismissive of the kind of anxiety that fuels a strident emphasis on the setting of boundaries for terms. But the disintegration of a culture, or of an individual personality, often begins when it is no longer possible to pose intelligible questions about boundaries. If there are no locatable boundaries, then there is no locatable center, either. There is a paradox here for any culture or individual that seeks to continue growing. As a paradox, it is inherently insoluble. You have to embrace the paradox itself, perhaps, to keep from being smashed to pieces. Like a gyroscope that has to keep spinning in order to stay upright. A lot of times the struggle results in a religious conversion of some type.

3.

Good as I Been to You and *World Gone Wrong*, Bob Dylan's two early-1990s solo recordings, recorded just after he'd hit his fifties and more than a decade after he got Saved, sit like a two-headed sphinx in the middle of Dylan's recorded work. People never talk about them all that much. Two records in a row of Dylan, all by himself, performing only traditional (or at least old) songs from the repertoires of Blind Willie McTell, Frank Hutchison, the Mississippi Sheiks, not one Dylan original among them. Nothing but Dylan; everything but Dylan.

For at least the three years preceding 1992's *Good as I Been to You*, the best parts of a Dylan concert were likely to be his performances of other people's songs, especially traditional songs like "Girl on the Greenbriar Shore," "Roving Gambler," "Barbara Allen," "Golden Vanity," songs he'd known from the beginning, back when people didn't mind stepping on him. It was almost as if he was tired of being himself. Whoever that was. Onstage he often seemed lost in the wilderness. The songs, however, had clearly lasted, and were demonstrably true. They had lasted not just outside him, in the culture, but inside him. They could provide a sense of magnetic north, bearings, orientation.

From the beginning, Dylan pieced together a persona, both social and creative, from found elements. That bag of found elements seemed to give him a meaning, or a rationale, a spiritual or psychic exoskeleton, a set of forms in which he could invest his roiling polymorphous energies. But any exoskeleton can become a cage, too. The thing that supports you from outside also constrains the free exercise of the polymorphous imagination. Being labeled—a marketing device for some, a security blanket for anxious listeners—is the ultimate trap. Eventually the id, or whatever you want to call it, will want to bust up the fixed form by which the world has come to know it. "That's not me," the Jokerman inside howls. "Never assume you know who I am." A series of masks or guises, because the inner thing is unknowable itself. Its name is unsayable.

On the evidence, Dylan has been both strongly attracted to absolute claims and yet also extremely wary of them. He apparently operates under an extremely high level of tension. The absolute claim of independence ("Don't follow leaders!"); the absolute need to serve somebody ("Property of Jesus!"). The need to choose moral sides ("It may be the devil or it may be the Lord"); the resistance to shouting "Which side are you on?" The containing of those urgent and apparently incompatible claims within one framework is a very American thing.

4.

Nobody knows what really goes on for an artist. It's presumptuous to think you can, any more than you can know what really goes on inside somebody else's marriage. Unlike elements are engaged in a constantly evolving dialogue.

"I don't know who I am most of the time," Dylan told David Gates in a 1997 *Newsweek* interview. "It doesn't even matter to me. . . . I find the religiosity and the philosophy in the music. I don't find it anywhere else. . . . I believe the songs." In the interview he was speaking specifically about gospel songs, but it is no stretch to imagine that it also applies to the whole body of folk- and blues-based music that informed his work. The songs gave him a text to go on, a Holy Book containing not an orthodoxy but a kind of anti-orthodoxy in which the most disparate elements were all given space at the table. In the mid-1990s he started appearing onstage dressed like the reincarnation of Hank Williams. It may not be too much to say that his intense reconnection to the traditional material at that point amounted to a kind of secular conversion, a renewal and realigning of what was of value, what was necessary, and what was possible.

Parallel things had happened previously in his career, of course. After arriving in New York City in 1961 as the hobo angel boy from everywhere, performing traditional material and then infusing it with more and more of his own inner light and darkness, the wheels stopped in 1966; he went back to the basics with the material that came to be called the Basement Tapes and came out with *John Wesley Harding*. The process began again, and then toward the end of the 1970s the wheels stopped again and he came out with *Slow Train Coming*. One could say that the subsequent *Infidels*, and its outtakes, bears the same relation to *Slow Train* as *Highway 61 Revisited* bore to *The Times They Are A-Changin'*—the calculus of doubt and conflict and irony and corrosive anger and livid imagery supplanting the algebra of faith and direct statement. As if Dante had started the *Divine Comedy* in the *Paradiso*, or at least the *Purgatorio*, and ended in the *Inferno*.

Whether there is a causal relation or not, Dylan's live performances began pulling together sharply in the year or so after *World Gone Wrong* came out in 1993, and he also began work on the material that would comprise two of the best records he ever made, *Time Out of Mind* and *Love and Theft*.

Dylan cited his sources for the *World Gone Wrong* songs in the disc's booklet; the sources for the *Good as I Been to You* songs have been discussed in print with varying degrees of accuracy. In *Behind the Shades Revisited*, Clinton Heylin quotes Ian Andersen, the editor of something called *Folk Roots*, as writing that there is "no shadow of a doubt" that "the rich old has-been" (that would be Dylan) copied his arrangement of "Frankie and Albert" from Mississippi John Hurt's 1928 recording. Really? You listen to it and tell me. Dylan's vocal approach has a lot more in common with Charley Patton's version of "Frankie and Albert" than with Mississippi John's. In fact, what is striking about the performances on *Good As I Been* is the extent to which Dylan turns each song to his own expressive purposes. Heylin, with his trademark penchant for broad, definitive, dubious, and eerily hostile statement, claims that, of Dylan's performances on *Good As I Been*, only "Tomorrow Night" "had the stamp of originality." I wonder if he knows Blind Boy Fuller's original version of "Step It Up and Go," or Tom Rush's recording of "Diamond Joe," the most likely source for that tune (not to be confused with the song of the same name that Dylan performs in *Masked and Anonymous*, which comes from the Georgia Crackers, probably by way of the New Lost City Ramblers . . .). In fact, "Tomorrow Night" may be one of the least original arrangements on the disc.

In any case, on both discs Dylan pulls songs from sources as different as English and Irish balladry, the blues, and nineteenth-century parlor songs, and from performers across the range of the folk tradition—as Harry Smith did in compiling his *Anthology of American Folk Music* for Folkways Records—and claims all of the territory as his own.

5.

Of course, if you say "American artist," right away a tension is set up. The dual citizenship. Dylan has been one if anyone has. Not by wrapping himself in the term "American," but by being very aware of the culture and place and time in which he has found himself, and trying to make sense of it. Or give an imaginative shape to it. What was "Bob Dylan's 115th Dream" about? Or "Masters of War"? Or "Clean-Cut Kid," or "Hurricane," or "John Wesley Harding," or, for that matter, "Foot of Pride"? There is the abiding realization that the fate of the individual and that of the culture as a whole are intertwined. The individual in fact recapitulates his or her sense of the culture within himself.

Possession, demonic or otherwise, implies that one part of an organism has taken control of the whole, putting things out of balance and destroying as much of the organism as possible before someone either exorcises the demon or destroys the host organism from without.

America has always been extremely vulnerable to fears of possession, and it has gone through famous periods of panic over it. The Salem witch trials, populist rhetoric about special interest groups, anticommunist fever, Eisenhower's warnings against the military-industrial complex . . . sometimes the concerns are justified. But the most opportunistic elements in the society usually look for a way to exploit the concern in order to gain greater power. Which in turn fuels greater concern . . . This tendency toward entropy seems built into the logic of our society, and it is a paradox from which we may not recover.

In the 1970s Dylan could conceive of going out on the road with the Rolling Thunder Revue and reclaiming the spirit of America—freedom, possibility, creativity, inclusiveness— from the clutches of the folks who brought us the Vietnam involvement and Watergate. Today we have bigger problems. The spirit itself, the sense of entitlement, is questionable. In the aftermath of 9/11, the oil companies scrambling to enrich themselves, the media full of sentimentality, the rush to jettison constitutionally guaranteed liberties, shopping as a patriotic duty . . . Is that really what it was all about all the time? Does it really all amount to a big Coke commercial? Who says the greediest and most rapacious bastards in a society get to define what it means? Can a culture get so defiled that its own citizens don't recognize it?

Everybody pieces together their own America in the brain, whether they want to or not. Dylan's career still suggests a way of operating within such painful confusion. In making a harmony of such apparent discord, it reminds us that freedom is a curse and a blessing at exactly the same moment. But that's how you know it's alive.

From Studio A: The Bob Dylan Reader,
Benjamin Hedin, editor (2004)

Two

Before I moved to New Orleans, in 1994, I spent three years in Iowa City, two of them at the Iowa Writers' Workshop. In my final term there I studied with Margot Livesey, the wonderful fiction writer and teacher. In our first workshop, Margot said to us, in her deceptively hesitant-sounding cadence, "For this term, I would like to suggest that if you are used to writing quickly, write slowly. And if you are accustomed to writing slowly, write quickly."

I was a slow writer. I had written my first good short story five years earlier, and had subsequently produced six more. One of them had taken me two years to get right. It wasn't an encouraging pace. Nonfiction was different—reviews and journalism could arrive on a deadline. But fiction seemed to demand endless revision. The ghost of Flaubert, padding around Croisset in his dressing gown and his Egyptian slippers, laboring for the *mot juste*, loomed large for me, as it probably does for most writers. Ditto Proust in the cork-lined room, James Joyce going blind rewriting, and so on and on. And, of course, long labor could produce masterpieces. Sometimes it produced Madame Bovary. But then sometimes it produced Bouvard et Pécuchet.

When Hurricane Katrina hit, in August 2005, a lot of new and unfamiliar information—logistical, emotional, and spiritual—was abruptly forced on me, as it was on everyone else, and I needed, badly, to make some kind of provisional sense of it all in the only way I had, which was by writing. What did I know? What was necessary? What was not necessary? What role had community played in my life? What would be lost if it disappeared? Where do you go when you are put out of your house? How do you feel when friends lose everything they own? What about when they kill themselves? Why is your hand shaking? What is the meaning of this?

I wrote one book, Why New Orleans Matters, *very quickly, in the five weeks immediately following the storm, mostly in a spare office in a Missouri cotton gin. Since it was the first book to come out of New Orleans after Katrina, it got a lot of attention, and I did a lot of traveling and speaking, gave a lot of interviews, all of that. The book was a response to the idea, which was being advanced in some quarters, that New Orleans should not be rebuilt. I developed what amounted to a stump speech on behalf of the city. I'd go out on the road for a week or two, talk to community groups or college students, then come back to New Orleans, to some fresh vista of grief and loss.*

At dinner one evening, maybe four months after the disaster, when I still had trouble getting through a conversation without breaking into sobs, I was seated at a nice New York City restaurant next to a well-intentioned person who asked me what it was like to live in New Orleans post-Katrina. The city was still in ruins; bodies were still being found in soaked, moldy houses; people I knew had gone through unspeakable things; I was living out of a suitcase. Although I recognized the gesture toward empathy, in true posttraumatic stress fashion I was irrationally furious with this person for not realizing how stupid the question was. I mean, how are you supposed to answer a question like that?

I turned to him and said, quietly, "You want to know what it's like?"

He nodded.

"AAAAGGGHHHHHHH!" *I yelled, right in his ear, slamming the table with the flat of my hand and jangling the silverware and plates.*

The entire restaurant went quiet. My companion looked at me agape, truly frightened.

"The way you're feeling right now?" I said. "That's what it's like."

Most of the pieces in the second half of this book come out of that feeling. They were written quickly, for the most part, during a time when I was also writing my novel City of Refuge. Most were written in response to invitations after the publication of Why New Orleans Matters. Writing that book had been like diving out of a plane or walking across hot coals: You had to do it before you realized that you couldn't do it. The same goes for most of the following work.

New Orleans, 2006. You had lived through Katrina, you had stayed in town and were rebuilding. You had gone through the shock, the sadness and grief, the fear, and then, to a degree, the unreasonable bubble of elation at having survived, at each encounter with a friend who had also survived and was still there. You huddled together for warmth, you made the necessary plans, you filled out the forms, you helped the people whom you could help, if you could help, and others helped you. Gradually the smoke began to clear, and you began to be able to imagine some kind of provisional way forward.

That got you through the spring.

Then summer hit, and that little mirage of optimism evaporated and the grim truth settled in, of just how big the challenges were, and how deep and wide the damage was—not just physical but spiritual—and the mood in the city turned darker again. Across the nation, the sugar rush of interest and empathy was starting to ebb, replaced by the predictable crash of boredom with New Orleans and even, at times, a kind of nasty backlash. Anyone who has been through the death of a loved one knows the drill—effusions of support, people bringing food to the house, tender and sincere expressions of comradeship and love. But two months later nobody wants to hear about your grief. Who can blame them?

That summer of 2006 was the hard one to get through. In the middle of it, I wrote this piece for Eric Banks, at Bookforum.

CHARLIE CHAN IN NEW ORLEANS!

I.

Summer is never one of the buoyant seasons in New Orleans. The heat is oceanic. It's not just a fact among other facts—it becomes the one glaring, inescapable Ground Of All Facts. This summer the heat seems worse than usual, but maybe that's because it brought its pals along with it: depression, dread, loneliness, breakdown of services. The fact that the rest of the world may soon have to get used to this kind of heat is no consolation.

Air-conditioning helps, of course. Except that last November, three months after the roof blew off the house during Hurricane Katrina, my landlord hired the Moe, Larry, and Curly Repair Company ("Look out with that ladder, you nitwit!") to fix the collapsed ceilings, and they sheetrocked over the main air vent in my apartment.

I wouldn't mention it if it weren't a Representative Anecdote. Even ordinarily competent people here are increasingly unable to function. They drive erratically, forget obvious words and familiar names, have eye problems and skin rashes. They don't recognize old friends, or they act as if they know you when they don't. Everybody here, and from here, is crazy. The evacuees who are stuck in Houston, or Atlanta, or Salt Lake City or Baltimore or Phoenix, living with cousins, are crazy, and so are the people who returned to houses full of obscenely proliferating mold of various colors, like camouflage all over their walls and furniture and treasured photographs and books.

Some people came back to houses that were no more than a pile of sticks and rags under a collapsed roof, and some came back to houses that were more or less intact, and they are crazy too. The streets are full of potholes with no one to fix them, and there is one working hospital, which has a three-year wait for the emergency room. You can't get insurance if you are trying to buy a house, the traffic lights don't work at most major intersections, and the city had to bring in the National Guard to patrol the streets of ruined neighborhoods whose houses have been cleaned out of their meager contents by looters both amateur and professional. It's like the Vienna of *The Third Man*.

The weird thing is that you can still have a great time visiting. Many of the best restaurants are up and running and doing overload business—Bayona and Brigtsen's and Upperline and Lilette and Mosca's and Clancy's and more. Liuzza's in Mid-City, which sat in six feet of water for weeks after the storm, finally opened in May, serving beer in frosted mugs and stuffed artichokes. That was the menu at first, but it was enough, for a while at least. The French Quarter is more or less okay, as is the picturesque heart of the Garden District, and the university area uptown. You can eat and drink and walk around and have fun. Come on down.

But living here is a different story. And now that it is summer and the Tulane and Loyola and Xavier students have left town, and many of the residents who stuck it out through the spring to let their kids finish the school year have put their houses on the market and left town, and you run into your friends here and there and talk about how nobody from outside will ever understand what this was like and then you find out that some of those friends are leaving too, and you start asking yourself, What am I doing here? How can I stay in this?

But how can I leave?

And so on. Something on the order of $12 billion in aid is about to be pumped into the city to jump-start businesses and services, rebuild hospitals, clear land, build new housing. What is left of the city may be in for the biggest boom since the Marshall Plan. Or it may be about to collapse completely. Living with pairs of incompatible yet equally plausible scenarios is another part of why everyone is crazy.

We are entering a new Phase of Grief, I think, calculus compared to Kübler-Ross's algebra, one that affects everyone differently at different times, like Red Kryptonite. I have made a provisional decision to shore up what is left of my own sanity with a mountain of books and CDs and DVDs; somewhere in there I will find the key, the right attitude, or the right stance, an exoskeleton, a persona, someone who will show me How to Be, because frankly I have run out of ideas.

2.

That is why when I heard about the "Buy Two DVDs and Get One Free" sale at the Barnes and Noble in Metairie, the big suburban white-flight enclave just across the Jefferson Parish line, I almost wept with gratitude. Happiness, escape, paradise. I could spend hours browsing with a purpose, comparing prices, putting together possible groupings of DVDs to get the Best Value, mixing and matching. I had a few boxed sets in mind that I wanted to steer for—the new John Wayne/John Ford box set with the special edition of *The Searchers* along with *They Were Expendable* and *She*

Wore a Yellow Ribbon, the brand-new four-disc Super Collector's Edition of Taylor Hackford's great 1987 documentary on Chuck Berry, *Hail! Hail! Rock 'n' Roll*. Maybe I would use my freebie to pick up the two-year-old box set of late Marx Brothers films, including *A Night at the Opera* and *A Day at the Races*, worth having despite the inclusion of dogs like *Room Service* and *The Big Store*.

I went, I grazed, I was happy, like the Eloi in *The Time Machine*. The simple, beautiful, idiotic Eloi were fascinated by shiny, spinning discs that contained important information from the past, just like me. But to them the information was meaningless, inscrutable. Up and down the blessedly air-conditioned aisles I browsed. I found the Ford/Wayne, Berry, and Marx Brothers sets and put them in my shopping basket.

In an ordinary season that might have been enough—mission accomplished—but it wasn't now. I had, after all, known and thought about these in advance. I wanted more adventure, more Thrill Of Discovery. I could easily work my way through these three sets in a week. By then the sale would be over, and what would I do? Around the three sets a certain amount of dread began to seep; the protection they provided felt slightly unsound, as if it could give way. I needed high levees, deep pilings, more to watch than I could possibly get through any time soon.

So I kept going. I passed on Universal's new W. C. Fields collection even though it contained his masterpiece *It's A Gift*; it repeated *The Bank Dick*, which I owned in the Criterion Collection version (now out of print). I examined the new Legacy Collection editions of *The Mummy* and *The Creature from the Black Lagoon*—padded out with dog sequels like *The Mummy's Ghost* and *Revenge of the Creature* . . . I would have bought single-disc versions of all the classic monster movies but I knew I would never watch *The Mummy's Ghost*. I had all the stuff in the new Bogart box except the new two-disc collectors' edition of *The Treasure of the Sierra Madre*, and who needed all these "making of" documentaries and audio commentaries by the assistant director? I was aware of my own desperation; I was raking through the ashes. And then I came to the Action and Adventure section and I found what I was looking for, even though I hadn't realized I was looking for it.

The Indiana Jones movies have always been a guilty pleasure for me. I'm not proud of it, but it is a fact. Pure action, fantasy, spectacle. Escape into the desert or the mountains, hard-charging horse races, sweltering archaeological excavations staffed by Nazi sadists, that wild ride through the cave tunnels in the Temple of Doom . . . Indiana Jones was ready for anything. I'd go ride on his coattails for a while. The set contained all three movies in widescreen editions, along with a "making of" disc that, for once, could answer some interesting questions, like how they did that tunnel chase. This was exactly the kind of thing that the Buy Two, Get One Free Sale was designed for. The set had been out for a while, but I had passed on it because the pleasure was sufficiently guilty. Now I could get it for free, as a dividend. But I needed to find two more box sets that I wanted, so that I could get Indy for free. Obviously the reasoning was feverish, but at least it was a substitute for all the chaos outside B&N's air-conditioned perimeter.

I found what I needed on the next aisle, under Mystery and Suspense, a solution amazing in its simplicity. Ying to Indy's yang. The missing jewel in the crown, two boxes, ten DVDs' worth.

3.

A darkened office, a man's head and shoulders seen from behind, silhouetted against the light from a lamp shining in his face. Across from him sits a man wearing a white suit with a vest and a white fedora on his head and almost plausibly Asian features, peering into the face of the man he is interrogating, really putting the screws to him.

Shadows always surround Charlie Chan. If they are not immediately present in a given scene, he will be heading for them shortly.
He always carries a flashlight. He also carries a gun, but I'm not sure
I've ever seen him fire it. He can crawl through any underground
passageway, including sewers, without getting dirty. If an old house
has a sliding panel leading to a secret hallway, he'll find it. Everybody
important knows who he is, and if they are okay they light up when
he appears and they defer to him. If they are not okay they fear him.
Troublemakers and creeps make an issue of his "foreignness," and
then he wields his politeness like a sword.

An example, from *Charlie Chan in Paris*. Chan, played by
Warner Oland, has just arrived at a young friend's apartment on
his first night in the city, when the doorbell rings and some revel-
ers in evening clothes enter, including one effete drunken boor
who raises his eyebrows, bows to Charlie, and says, "Oh! Me velly
happy know you. Maybe you likey havey little dlinky?"

Charlie Chan smiles faintly and says, in his most courtly manner, "Very happy to make acquaintance of *charming gentleman*."

The boor squirms and Charlie lets him twist in the wind in
front of his friends for just a moment and then, to show that there
are no hard feelings, does his own parody of pidgin Chinese. As
everyone laughs gaily at the discharge of tension, Charlie watches
the boor closely—with reason, as it turns out. Chan is a virtuoso
of the mask.

Most people would probably tell you that Warner Oland was
a better Charlie Chan than Sidney Toler. Whether he was or not,
these two boxes give you plenty basis on which to decide. The
2004 *Chanthology* has six of the Tolers, from 1944 and 1945; the
just-issued *Warner Oland Is Charlie Chan, Volume 1* contains four
of the Olands, filmed a decade earlier—*Charlie Chan in London*,
Paris, *Egypt*, and *Shanghai*, along with *Eran Trece*, a Spanish-
language version of the early, and lost, *Charlie Chan Carries On*.

Simone Weil remarked that we must prefer real hell to an imaginary heaven, but I'm not sure I agree. Right now imaginary anything

sounds good to me, for a few hours at least. These black-and-white *tableaux vivants* are my idea of a good idea, the perfect escape. The Indiana Jones movies, while almost a definition of escapism, have felt jarring to me this time around. The ancient landscapes full of ruins and insects, the fiefdoms of violence in burnt-out purlieus, the occasional outposts of decadent urbanity, the treasures of the past mercilessly exploited by thugs from halfway around the world, everyone sweating constantly under scorching sun and torrential rain—it all reminds me a little too much of New Orleans, post-Katrina.

Charlie Chan's world, on the other hand, is Wholly Other. It is cool, urban, interior; electric lights push back ever-encroaching darkness. The enemies are less visible and tangible than they are in the Indiana Jones movies. They are shadowy, subtle; they let things happen and then do nothing, make coolly furtive phone calls in paneled offices . . . Charlie's antennae for these characters is sharply tuned and almost unerring. The encounter with duplicity, lies, or subterfuge makes him grow calmer and smarter. I find myself imagining him interrogating Michael Brown of FEMA, or President Bush, immediately after Hurricane Katrina, their faces in the bright light, sweating as Charlie circles in for the arrest and conviction.

"Honorable president, why troops and other aid not in place for rapid deployment after terrible storm?"

"Hey, Charlie—heh, heh—nobody could have foreseen the levees breaking."

"Correction—levee break foreseen and described in detail in computer exercise year before. You withdraw funds for further study. One more question—how long could honorable family of president live without nourishment in Superdome?"

"Hey—we got the troops in there as soon as we could."

"Correction—got into Iraq war as soon as could. Baghdad six thousand, two hundred ten miles from White House. New Orleans nine hundred fifty-seven miles from White House. Under circumstances, five days not soon."

Or maybe it would have been better to just leave Bush alone in the attic of a flooded home for a few days and see if that would wake him up. Let him carve his way out with one of his Texas Bowie knives. Or maybe let Indiana Jones take the whip to him . . .

This is known as intrusive imagery, and I have been having a lot of it lately. It does no good at all. As Charlie Chan himself says in *Charlie Chan in London*—"Thoughts are like noble animal; unchecked, they run away, causing painful smashup."

4.

Even with the air-conditioning running full-blast, it is eighty-five degrees in the house. Mary's law practice is currently located on a card table in my living room. We are both on overload, but I show it more than she does. New concepts—about mold remediation, about plumbing and rewiring, about insurance—have entered my life, like uninvited guests at a party that has gotten way out of hand. For a week she has been trying to explain to me what an "umbrella policy" is, but I can't really grasp it. Whatever it is, we seem to need one.

I have started making up my own Charlie Chan–like aphorisms and proverbs. For an hour or so after watching one of the movies, I respond to almost everything Mary says with a gnomic proverb, and I have given up trying to make them make sense. It is a nervous tic, and it is making her crazy, but I am having trouble stopping. Earlier today she asked me, in passing, if I had called the roofer, as I had promised to. We've been spending a lot of time calling the roofer.

"List of tasks like five-course meal," I said. "Can't eat all at once."

"Stop it!" she almost screamed.

Chan was the creation of a writer named Earl Derr Biggers, who based the character on a real Honolulu police detective and former cowboy named Chang Apana, who died in 1933. Although there were three screen incarnations of Charlie Chan before Warner Oland, beginning with George Kuwa in the 1925 silent serial version of *The House Without a Key*, Oland really established the character for the moviegoing audience with his portrayal in 1931's now-lost *Charlie Chan Carries On*. Oland, who emigrated from Sweden as a child in 1892, had played Al Jolson's father in *The Jazz Singer*, as well as the Asian villain Fu Manchu several times before landing in the role of Chan. He was apparently also something of an intellectual badass, who translated Strindberg's plays into English, according to Chan scholar Howard Berlin, and Ibsen's *Peer Gynt*, according to the somewhat more reliable Chan scholar Ken Hanke. Except I thought Ibsen wrote in Norwegian. Whatever.

In any case, Oland went on to play the detective in fifteen more Chan movies, from *The Black Camel*, also filmed in 1931, in which he costars with Bela Lugosi, to *Charlie Chan in Monte Carlo*, in 1937. They are real movies, by and large; well costumed and photographed, well directed. The four films in *Charlie Chan, Volume 1* were made, like the rest of Oland's Chan films, for Twentieth Century Fox in 1934 and 1935 and follow Chan to four "exotic" locales—London, Paris, Egypt, and Shanghai. Oland's manners are unfailingly excellent, and his character appealing, with the sense of great intellectual, and probably physical, resources kept under exquisite control. He is charming and polished.

Toler was picked by Fox to succeed Oland after Oland's death in 1938, and stepped into what would have been Oland's role in *Charlie Chan in Honolulu*, going on to make ten more for Fox before the studio dropped the series. After some searching, Toler moved to the low-budget house Monogram for another eleven. The *Chanthology* box contains the first six of the eleven he made for Monogram. After Toler's death, the all-but-forgotten Roland Winters stepped in for six more, and that was it, unless you count the 1950s TV series starring J. Carrol Naish, which I haven't seen since I was a kid.

There is no question that Toler is slightly stiffer and less expressive than Oland. Also the scripts and, in most cases, the direction are not as good—characters are more stock, and the interactions between Chan and his various assistants more formulaic, dropped in like set pieces. On the other hand, Toler has a hard-boiled edge that can be just the thing on certain days. And his Charlie Chan has a saltier sense of humor than Oland's. At one point in *Meeting at Midnight*, Toler's Chan excuses himself briefly from a tense meeting with the police inspector, and when he returns, claiming to be psychic, he begins telling the inspector what size shoe the man wears, mentions that the inspector is in fact a size eleven but insists on wearing size nine and a half, and claims that the inspector changed barbers the week before, along with a few other things in the tradition of Sherlock Holmes's lists of deductions. Naturally, the inspector is nonplussed and asks Charlie how he can know these things, and Charlie Chan says, "Oh—merely telephoned your wife in next room."

Toler was variously assisted and hampered in his efforts by his son Tommy, played by Benson Fong (there were other sons, played by other actors, but Fong was Number One during the Monogram years), and his chauffeur and aide-de-camp Birmingham Brown, played by the great black comedian Mantan Moreland. They are constantly bumbling around and getting lost, and Moreland gets scared every time he hears a suspicious noise or the lights go out. The infamous Stepin Fetchit appeared in one title in the Oland series, *Charlie Chan in Egypt*, but Moreland was a regular feature of the Toler Monograms. *The Scarlet Clue* even includes one of his vaudeville routines with fellow comedian Ben Carter, in which they answer each other's unfinished sentences, in grand jive manner:

Moreland: "I haven't seen you since . . ."

Carter: "Longer than that."

Moreland: "I moved over to . . ."

Carter: "How can you live in that neighborhood? Where I'm living I only pay . . ."

Moreland: "It ain't *that* cheap, is it?"

And so on. I could watch that stuff all day. It is worth asking why such a great detective has such hapless assistants, and the only thing I can figure is that Mantan was there to discharge any anxiety white audiences might have felt about being outclassed by an Asian. They could still at least feel superior to the easily scared Moreland. The joke is that Moreland was inserted into the series by Monogram in an attempt (successful) to draw black audiences, who loved him, to the films. Interestingly, Warner Oland's Chan was unfailingly gracious to Fetchit's lame-brained character in *Charlie Chan in Egypt*, whereas Toler is almost always a little snotty or at least condescending to Moreland.

In any case, the Chan films always run on a carrier frequency of racial and ethnic tension. Of course, so do the Indiana Jones films. But despite the high adventure and comic-book thrills, the vision of humanity in the latter has started grating almost intolerably. The superficiality of perception about the Other is just too hard to take these days—an astoundingly capable white guy, both impossibly erudite and impossibly physically dominating, kicking ass throughout a world full of menacing foreign stereotypes—the will of the West, under constant siege. It is all too much like the mentality behind our foreign policy, and it isn't funny anymore, if it ever was. I'll admit it—I used to laugh at Karen Allen, being kidnapped in that basket, yelling, "*You can't do this to me; I'm an American.*"

Yes, of course. "*I'm an American.*" That's what the people waiting for food and medical help at the Superdome and the Convention Center were saying. They waited five days for any semblance of help or order to begin trickling in. The people stranded on interstate overpasses for days said it too, as did the people whose parents died in hospitals and nursing homes because there was no evacuation plan in place. The administration can build cities in the desert halfway across the world but it let New Orleans drown. *"I'm an American"* . . . the words are starting to burn coming out.

Calm down . . . deep breath. I need to be more like Charlie Chan. Charlie Chan always takes the high road. He is not the compromised, ambiguous private eye of film noir, certainly not a ladies' man—mainstream American movies weren't ready for an Asian ladies' man yet—and he is partly defined by his marriage and his many children. Charlie Chan stands for the Right Order Of Things. He is disinterested, except in the truth. He has intelligence, self-control, courage; he facilitates marriages getting back together, lovers being reunited, people's names being cleared. He is gracious to the weak, unafraid of the powerful, and he always offers a moment of truth, when he sums things up for everyone, points the finger at the One To Blame, calls a spade a spade. Charlie Chan listens. He listens hard, and he uses his head.

I need to call the roofer. I need to check on the umbrella policy. My friends have left town and I need to call the air-conditioning guy, and I need to vacuum the floor. But I can barely get off the couch. *Calling Inspector Chan* . . . *Calling Inspector Chan* . . . Just give me a minute, here, and let me get myself together.

From Bookforum, *September/October 2006*

"Charlie Chan in New Orleans!" was my second piece for Bookforum. *The following article was the first. In November 2005, during a swing I made through New York City, Eric Banks had invited me to think about writing something for the magazine, and I immediately suggested a review of the just-issued box set of the complete and unexpurgated recordings that Jelly Roll Morton made for Alan Lomax at the Library of Congress in 1940.*

Morton was one of the great characters of New Orleans, and his recorded memoirs are a grand picaresque of the southern and western United States in the period after Reconstruction, with a focus on New Orleans around the time jazz was created. Morton summoned an entire lost world out of memory; having just written Why New Orleans Matters, *I could relate. The Morton Library of Congress box provided an eerie sense of comfort during a time when New Orleans was in a coma, fighting for its life.*

BLUES STREAK

Long before the levees were breached in Hurricane Katrina, New Orleans seemed to many outsiders like the lost continent of Atlantis. Its most characteristic celebrations have always had a funerary cast—from jazz funerals to the literal "farewell to the flesh" of the *carnevale* traditions that gave rise to Mardi Gras. The city's sense of the present is inextricable from its palpable past (not for nothing is its most famous musical landmark called Preservation Hall). Largely for this reason, some say that the city isn't really even part of the United States, alien as it is to the American ethos of clean-slatism and endless self-reinvention. But the flip side of the chameleonic New World desire to start fresh has always been a deep vein of guilt and nostalgia, and from that standpoint New Orleans is wholly in the American grain. The fact of mortality casts a persistent light on all activity there and gives the city's culture its deep chiaroscuro, its spiritual keel—even, or especially, in the midst of the greatest revelry.

As far back as the 1930s, when the pioneering works of jazz scholarship and criticism were being written, New Orleans already seemed like a long-ago place. Works like Frederic Ramsey and Charles Edward Smith's *Jazzmen* and Rudi Blesh's *Shining Trumpets* presented a romanticized vision of the city in the wake of Reconstruction, with all its shifting roles, racial and ethnic ambiguities, and ruptured social and political axioms. Those tensions, and the ongoing effort to resolve or at least contain them, formed the atmospheric conditions that made jazz possible. Legendary characters and locales clung to the names of equally legendary streets like crystals to a string—Rampart Street and Perdido Street and Basin Street, Economy Hall and Storyville, the Great and Unrecorded Progenitors like Buddy Bolden and Papa Jack Laine and Buddy Petit, spoken of by men a half generation younger with the sound usually reserved for the gods themselves . . .

Jelly Roll Morton, jazz's first composer, one of its best early pianists, and its most potent storyteller, was a product of this time. Born sometime around 1885, he grew up in New Orleans and cut a broad swath through its red-light district, not just as a pianist but as a pool hustler, card sharp, and pimp. Early on he began to travel, and he functioned as a sort of Johnny Appleseed of jazz, making his way through the Gulf Coast, the Mississippi Delta, California, St. Louis, Memphis, and other locales before settling down for a while in Chicago. There, in 1926, he began a series of recordings under the name Jelly Roll Morton and his Red Hot Peppers, in which his compositional and orchestrational skills came to their greatest flowering; the Peppers recordings are, along with those of King Oliver's Creole Jazz Band, the high-water mark of New Orleans jazz on record.

In 1928 Morton moved to New York City, where big-band swing was already germinating in the ensembles of Fletcher Henderson, Duke Ellington, and others, and Morton's brand of finely tooled small-band orchestration was marked for the remainder table. Morton himself, however, was slow to recognize this, and when he did he was unable to find the key that would allow him to adapt. His persona, formed in the hothouse environment of Storyville, had worked all right in Chicago, which was still full of recent Southern émigrés, but it was less suited to New York's world-wise cosmopolite tempo. That his importance was not universally acknowledged offended his sense of justice, and he let it be known, but nobody wanted to hear it. Morton struggled against the tide for two years, but in 1930, as far as the record-buying public was concerned, he disappeared off the face of the earth. Although a few of his compositions, most notably "King Porter Stomp" and "Wolverine Blues," became swing-era big band staples, between October 1930 and May 1938 Morton participated in exactly one recording session—as a sideman.

During that time Morton bounced around from place to place with the road narrowing in front of him, before finally finding a perch in the rocks in Washington, D.C., where he worked as maître d', bartender, and entertainer in a tiny nightclub and waited for fate to knock once again. And in May 1938 it did, in the person of Alan Lomax, son of the seminal American folklorist John A. Lomax and himself already a significant collector of folk materials for the Library of Congress. The enterprising young man, tipped off to Morton's presence at the nitery, invited the antique figure from Years Gone By to record some songs at the Library's Coolidge Auditorium, hoping to turn up a new ballad or two, or perhaps some blues verses that hadn't been documented.

Lomax was by his own admission wary of jazz, which he felt at the time was killing the folk music that he loved and to which he was ideologically committed. But he quickly realized that Morton was more than just another down-on-his-luck pianist, and over the course of the next three weeks or so, with a follow-up session in December, he recorded nine hours of Morton's reminiscences of the early days of New Orleans jazz, his travels through Mississippi, Memphis, Mobile, St. Louis, and Los Angeles; the cutthroats and hustlers and musical and funeral traditions of the Crescent City; as well as Morton's demonstrations not just of his own compositions but those of Scott Joplin, John Philip Sousa, and many others.

After decades in which they appeared, disappeared, and reappeared in various forms, these recordings have finally been issued complete by Rounder Records as *Jelly Roll Morton: The Complete Library of Congress Recordings by Alan Lomax*. It would be difficult to overstate not just how important they are, but how interesting, how enjoyable. From the first words, Morton takes us away, away, to a far-off land and time, playing the song "Alabama Bound" softly, under his recitative:

> When I was down on the Gulf Coast, in nineteen-four, I missed going to the St. Louis Exposition to get in a piano contest, which was won by Albert Wilson of New Orleans. I was very much disgusted because I thought I should have gone. . . . I was down in Biloxi, Mississippi, during that time; I used to often frequent the Flat Top, which was nothing but an old honky-tonk, where nothin' but the blues was played. There was fellows around played the blues, like Rocky Johnny, Skinny Head Pete, old Florida Sam, and Tricky Sam and that bunch.

And immediately we have the entire thing in a nutshell— restless traveling, deep South locale, long-ago times, music as a medium of social competition and status, the constant relation between place and expression that is at the center of any understanding of American life. Morton reappeared just as the world was beginning to circle the drain toward World War Two and America was only a few years away from the Faustian realization that it could in fact dominate the globe. Over those soft background chords, Morton speaks and sings a world back into existence, and, along with it, his own place in that world, summoning the pre–World War One America that had given him his chance to create himself in his own image. He restates the tension between Old World and New, the primacy of multiethnicity, superstition, and magic, and attention to the handmade as opposed to the mass-produced. His phrasing, a mixture of high diction and low slang, alternately awkward and deft, enthusiastic and self-conscious, is itself a music that is rare to hear.

Morton also had a natural tendency to codify. In these recordings he outlines his principia of jazz music, the delicate balance among the voices of the ensemble, the importance of dynamics and attention to correct tempos, the crucial role played by the rhythmic displacement he called the Spanish Tinge, the central compositional role of riffs and breaks. He took the tacit operating assumptions of jazz and made them into conscious animating principles. Morton had an essentially dramatic imagination, for which the instruments of the jazz band functioned as the dramatis personae of an ongoing musical narrative. This understanding of jazz was also the subtext of many New Orleans loyalists' antagonism to the well-oiled machine of 1930s big-band swing.

The Morton recordings were first commercially issued in 1947 on the Circle label, in a small edition intended for specialists and collectors, and with boxy, horrible sound that may have contributed to their allure for some of the more Atlantis-minded fans. Lomax also published a book in 1950, titled *Mister Jelly Roll*, stitched together from Morton's winding narrative. In the 1950s the recordings were issued again, this time on the Riverside label, one of the premier jazz labels of the decade, a version that got much wider circulation. They were also subsequently issued on the Australian collector's label Swaggie and in fragmentary form in many other places. In 1993, Rounder put out a four-disc series of the music and not the talking, and included for the first time some of the formerly suppressed, X-rated songs that Morton performed for Lomax only after repeated urging. But the omission of the spoken material was a major missed opportunity, for it is the interaction between the storytelling and the music that gives this material its enduring claim on our attention and that places it near the center of the map of American vernacular historiography.

These sessions, in fact, marked the birth of the oral-history idea, the starting place for everything from Studs Terkel's Homeric compendia of American proletariana to Legs McNeil's *Please Kill Me*, the premise being that the sound, the actual spoken language, of participants in American life, whether on the macro or the micro scale, can give us more of a sense of the texture of lived life than a macerated and processed, disembodied, "objective" history. Of course the idea of personal history was not new, and the popularity of such vernacular and personal memoirs as those of Ulysses S. Grant, Frederick Douglass, and Henry Adams had long since established the value of an intensely subjective witness to larger historical patterns in American culture. But with these sessions the idea got lashed to the technology of sound recording for keeps.

Lomax had a rationale behind all of his work—namely, the advancement of the vernacular culture of the masses, as opposed to the high culture that represented the social structures of the elite. This was a strong motivator for him; it gave his work its moral and ethical topspin, as well as contributing to some of his blind spots and his occasionally idiosyncratic sense of proportion. John A. Lomax, in his 1940 Library of Congress interview with Atlanta bluesman Blind Willie McTell, kept prodding McTell to sing some "complainin' songs." "Don't you know any songs like 'Ain't It Hard to Be a Nigger, Nigger' . . . ?" To some extent, you can hear his son trying to pull some of the same strings in the Morton interviews. In places you can hear Morton's annoyance with Lomax's attempts to steer him, although they are all between the lines.

At one point, for example, Morton is decrying the idea that jazz is frantic and loud. "Somehow," he says, "it got into the dictionary that jazz was considered a lot of blatant noise and discordant tones, and as something that would be even harmful to the ears. . . . Jazz music is based on strictly music. You have the finest ideas, from the greatest operas, symphonies, and overtures, in jazz music. There's nothing finer than jazz music because it comes from everything of the finest class music."

Here Lomax clears his throat in what sounds to me like discomfort at what he takes to be the class anxiety in Morton's rundown, and asks for an example of the kind of discordant jazz Morton is talking about.

"Well," Morton replies, "it's so noisy it's impossible for me to prove to you, because I only have one instrument to show to you. But I guess the world is familiar with it. Even Germany don't want it, but she don't know why. . . . You can't make crescendos or diminuendos when one is playing triple forte. You've got to be able to come down in order to go up. If a glass of water is full, you can't fill it any more. But if you have a half a glass, you have an opportunity to put more water in it, and jazz music is based on the same principle. . . . I will play a little number now of the slower type, to give you an idea of the slower type of jazz music. You can apply it to any type tune. It depends upon your ability for transformation." As he plays his example, he remarks, "I've seen this blundered up so many times it has given me the heart failure."

The values implicit in Morton's nostalgia have everything to do with the sense of possibility implicit and explicit in the ideal of a multicultural society, a multicultural *culture*—the grand oxymoron that actually seemed to come to life, for a while, in certain cities, and in the work of certain of our greatest artists. In fact the actualizing of that principle may be one gauge, maybe the strongest, for the worth and magnitude of a body of work—the degree to which an artist can sustain a dynamic set of tensions among disparate social, class, regional, and ethnic elements—whether that of Herman Melville or Duke Ellington or Bob Dylan. In any case, Morton was a true auteur, and he always rooted his organizing vision in the principles he found in the life of the community that gave birth to jazz. My guess is that this is the secret of Lomax's fascination with him—that Morton's ego as an individual was harnessed in service to what was ultimately a communal ideal.

The Rounder Records box is the first time all of this material has been available in one package. It also includes a full CD of interviews that Lomax conducted with a handful of Morton's contemporaries, including clarinetist Alphonse Picou and banjo and guitar player Johnny St. Cyr, who recorded with Morton's Red Hot Peppers as well as Louis Armstrong's Hot Five. In addition, there is an excellent booklet containing reproductions of photos, newspaper stories, and old advertisements, along with solid annotation by John Szwed and a copy of the newly reissued paperback of Lomax's *Mister Jelly Roll.*

The set arrives, too, at a moment in which the fate of New Orleans is once again at the center of the national narrative, and Morton's love and nostalgia for his birthplace will give anyone with ears a clue to why New Orleanians love New Orleans. Describing the high jinks during a celebratory parade at the dawn of the twentieth century, Morton goes on and on, until words fail him and he says, "It was really a swell time. . . . We had plenty fun, a kind of a fun I don't think I've ever seen any other place. Of course there may be nicer fun, but that particular kind . . . there was never that kind of fun anyplace I think on the face of the globe but New Orleans."

In true New Orleans fashion, these profoundly important, historically resonant recordings proffer a kind of serious fun—both intellectual and aesthetic, set against the precipice of time and mortality and history—that you won't find any other place.

From Bookforum, *February/March 2006*

This was the last piece I wrote for the Oxford American; *it appeared in their 2006 Music Issue. For the first few years of the Music Issue, starting in 1997, the contents had been driven by the writers' ideas about which musicians interested them; the CD that accompanied each issue was the reflection of that traffic jam of idiosyncrasy. But little by little the magazine's content became dictated by the music the editors wanted to see on the CD; a list of musicians would be drawn up, and then writers got to take their choice. The Music Issue may have been just as much fun to read after that change, but it wasn't as much fun to write for, and I went on to other things.*

In 2006, though, the year after Katrina, the lead-off tune was pianist Joe Liggins's earthshaking 1950 track "Going Back to New Orleans," and when editor Marc Smirnoff called to see if I would write a piece about Liggins, I couldn't say no. Here's the result.

GOING BACK TO NEW ORLEANS

I always assumed that Joe Liggins was from New Orleans. His 1950 recording "Going Back to New Orleans" is one of the all-time best musical tributes to the Crescent City, full of insider references to its French and Spanish heritage, its food and special locales.

The tune itself was written by the little-remembered drummer Ellis Walsh, who also cowrote the Louis Jordan classic "Saturday Night Fish Fry" (likewise full of New Orleans references); Liggins's arrangement really summons a New Orleans feeling, making the most of the tune's slightly ominous minor-key cast, and containing an interlude in which a wailing tenor and soprano sax (or clarinet—it's hard to tell) strive to outdo one another. And it appeared on Specialty Records, which, although based out of Los Angeles, had recorded some of the seminal New Orleans R&B sessions by Guitar Slim, Lloyd Price, Big Boy Myles, Roy Montrell, and others, not to mention Little Richard's best early sides.

And, too, there was a big direct line between N.O. and L.A. stretching back to the early days of jazz. The Original Creole Orchestra, with the legendary cornetist Freddie Keppard, had toured California as early as 1911. Jelly Roll Morton spent a couple of years based there before World War One, and trombonist Kid

Ory did the same just afterward, making a couple of the earliest recordings of New Orleans jazz there in 1922. In the 1950s and 1960s it was a famous magnet for Crescent City players, including Mac Rebennack (a.k.a. Dr. John), Earl Palmer, Plas Johnson, Chuck Badie, and too many others to list.

But Liggins, it turned out, wasn't from New Orleans. He was from Guthrie, Oklahoma, born in 1915, and a member of the great forgotten generation of jump blues performers that included his brother Jimmy, Amos Milburn, Roy Milton, Charles Brown, Ivory Joe Hunter, Hadda Brooks, and Camille Howard. They came along in the post–World War Two bubble, after the jazz-centered big band era but before rock and roll blew off the roof. Many of them were not Southerners but came, like Liggins, from the Southwest, particularly Texas and Oklahoma.

Joe Liggins was himself a product of the big band era, and he was trained in that arena. His tastes seemed to run to bands like those of Buddy Johnson and Lucky Millinder and the Savoy Sultans, blues-and-ballad-based dance music, without a lot of the kind of personality that might distract the audience from the business at hand—a dance partner, a drink, whatever. He moved to San Diego in 1932, then Los Angeles in 1939, and began working with local dance bands on the West Coast.

After World War Two, many bands started to scale back in size; by 1950 even Count Basie was working with a septet rather than a full big band. Liggins really hit his groove in this context, crafting smooth, tightly scripted, functional jukebox small-band dance music for black audiences. The war had greatly accelerated the migration of African-Americans from rural areas to big cities like Chicago, Detroit, and Los Angeles. The war work in factories on the West Coast was a big magnet, and the war itself gave a sense of optimism to the African-American community at large, a sense that the country would pull together against the common enemy and that afterward a lot of the outdated discrimination might begin to fall away as we all recognized ourselves as Americans first. The disillusionment was coming, but it hadn't hit yet. Above all, people seemed to want normalcy and common ground.

This black urban audience was served by countless little independent record labels that sprang up after the war to provide music that the major labels weren't really on top of, mostly for the burgconing jukebox market. Some of those labels became as famous as Atlantic and Chess; others stayed as obscure as Bel-Tone and Sittin' In With. Los Angeles was a center for many of them. These small labels recorded a lot of groundbreaking material—Ray Charles's gospel-blues fusion (Swing Time and, later, Atlantic), Charlie Parker and Dizzy Gillespie's bebop (Guild, Musicraft, Dial, Savoy), Muddy Waters's electric blues (Aristocrat and, later, Chess); they were in a position to take chances on things that hadn't yet proved their commercial viability.

But most of what they recorded was workmanlike and predictable, formulaic dance-and-romance music that could be pumped out to service the needs of smaller, often local audiences with easily defined tastes, and make a small profit repeatedly rather than capture a large market. The point of many of those recordings was never to challenge or expand conventions but rather to find a certain angle and work it, to be, at best, a personality within an intelligible ecosystem, the record-industry equivalent of B-movies or potato chips. The audience didn't necessarily want surprises, unless they were easy to assimilate.

Liggins recorded his first big hit, "The Honeydripper," in 1945 for one of these labels, Los Angeles's Exclusive Records, run by New Orleans–born transplant Leon René, an entrepreneur and composer of songs as varied as "When It's Sleepy Time Down South," "When the Swallows Come Back to Capistrano," and "Rockin' Robin." "The Honeydripper" was in many ways an archetypal jump blues record, with its insistent shuffle beat, heavy on the tenor saxophone, and with a chorus of band members singing the jive lyrics in good-natured unison ("He's a killer . . . a solid old cat . . ."). It sold hundreds of thousands of copies and was reportedly heavily bootlegged by the Mob for their jukeboxes.

Liggins's music could be upbeat, or romantic, or suavely bluesy, but it never contained much irony. And it was very, very simple, even at its slickest. The formula made for some of the biggest R&B hits of the late 1940s, including not just "The Honeydripper," but "Pink Champagne" ("that stole my love from me") with its easy bounce and belly-rub tempo, and "Rag Mop," which harked back to older "game" records such as "I'se A-Muggin'" by Stuff Smith and His Onyx Club Boys, and pointed also to later ones like Shirley Ellis's "The Name Game." In the early 1950s there probably wasn't a jukebox in a black neighborhood bar in America that didn't have at least one of those Liggins discs on it.

It was never one of my favorite genres. I always felt as if something was missing from the mix, a sense of some resistance in the scheme of things. In blues, for example, the singer was almost always restless and pushing against an oppressive situation, whether social, economic, or romantic. In early rock the subtext was always miscegenation—the breaking of racial barriers and taboos, black music often for white audiences. With the bebop of Parker and Gillespie the resistance was encoded in the music itself, a steeplechase reflecting the complexity of postwar social change. Jump blues didn't have that sense of resistance in it; it was, generally speaking, satisfied with its own assumptions.

"Going Back to New Orleans" is a big exception. Liggins's arrangements tended to be tight, smooth, functional, little-big-band arrangements. But something got loose with the N.O. record. First of all, it is set mostly in a minor key, which imparts a mysterious atmosphere at odds with Liggins's standard jolly boogie-woogie optimism. The intro smacks into the listener with bold rhythmic displacements influenced, I would guess, by what Dizzy Gillespie's big band was doing on songs like "Ow!" and "Jumpin' with Symphony Sid." Liggins slides into gear singing Walsh's excellent site-specific lyrics.

Goin' back home, tee-nah-nay,
To the land of the beautiful queen;
I'm goin' back home, to my bay-bee,
I'm goin' back to New Orleans.

The middle section goes briefly into a major key, but it is played over a rhumba beat as Liggins sings about having been to Cuba and South America and France but how he likes the women in New Orleans better; the rhumba is a knowing reference to the Latin flavor that always inflects New Orleans music, what Jelly Roll Morton called the Spanish Tinge.

And then, after the tune slides back into minor for eight more bars and Liggins declares New Orleans his home, the tenor saxophone, probably played by Maxwell Davis, begins a solo. It starts with eight bars of more or less regulation R&B tenor, but in the second eight bars, the tenor is joined by the clarinet, or soprano sax, probably played by Little Willie Jackson, and suddenly things are in a different neighborhood; the heat gets ratcheted way up and the record starts to sweat heavily. The bridge comes in the next eight bars, with the tenor playing alone again, and then the clarinet joins him again for the final eight and they pull and wail against each other until Liggins's rolling, insouciant piano comes in to smooth things out for a little before a reprise of the vocal. After a restatement of the beginning's jagged rhythmic intro, we are set back down in the day-to-day.

After all those relentlessly simple records, all that bubble-gum R&B, what happened to Joe Liggins for those three minutes?

Going back home, always a big theme in American music, took on a new resonance in the postwar years, especially after a few of those years had gone by. Usually the direction proposed was from north to south, with the singer tired of the big city and longing for family and the simple life he or she once knew. The theme was especially big in country music, with songs like "The Fields Have Turned Brown" and "Detroit City." It was perhaps slightly less prominent in blues, since down home, despite the fact that the weather suited your clothes, was a place where you could get lynched pretty easily. Still, there are plenty of blues about country people being taken advantage of in the city and hoping, like Muddy Waters, to get lucky and make "Train Fare Home." Years later, Bob Dylan turned the convention on its head in "Just Like Tom Thumb's Blues," in which the singer declares he has had enough and is going back to New York City.

In any case, Liggins's narrator is going back home for a straight-forward reason—to see his bay-bee. But that quickly gets mixed up with a desire to see the rest of the family—his cousins, his *parrain*, and Ma and Pa. The family stuff is also mixed up with all the other elements of New Orleans culture: music and a sense of place (he wants to "pat his feet on Rampart Street"), Mardi Gras, and, especially, food—crawfish, jambalaya, red beans, gumbo filé, and pralines (he even throws in dessert). In New Orleans, all these elements are of a piece, and Liggins's record is directly about all the sensual, tactile tension and gratification that most of his other records keep on a short leash. Maybe for Liggins, as for so many, New Orleans was a place where he could connect all the different parts of himself, for three minutes at least. His record has that sense of resistance overcome—in this case, maybe, his own resistance to letting the wilder part of himself out for a little air. Maybe for Joe Liggins, as for so many, past and present, the Crescent City provided an opportunity to change personas and dance. And in that minor-key agitation, maybe just a prescient hint of storms, social and meteorological, to come.

From the Oxford American *Music Issue, Summer 2006*

What follows are four pieces about New Orleans written in the five years following Katrina. As mentioned, the publication of Why New Orleans Matters *turned me, for a while at least, into an instant talking head on all topics relating to New Orleans. It also brought e-mails and letters from people who loved what I wrote and people who hated what I wrote.*

The first of these is an edited version of an online chat I conducted for the Washington Post *in February 2006, and it gives a fair idea of the elements that made up my standard responses to the questions I encountered about the city's prospects. Mary and I had moved into my just-repaired apartment from temporary quarters at a friend's house on Kerlerec Street. Repairs on Mary's house would not be finished for another six months. The editing is only to comb out pointless repetitions that cropped up here and there.*

The second, from May 2006, is something different: an exchange of letters about the future of New Orleans. The letter I received is typical of a certain narrow vein of response to my book. Such letters would invariably start out politely, even courtly, and would be written by someone with impeccable credentials as a lady or gentleman, always oozing with solicitude for the "underclass" while espousing a program for the future of the city that would effectively eliminate the "underclass" from New Orleans. The courtly manner was a perfume to disguise a familiar scent. My response to this particular letter sums up my feelings about the subtext of these communiqués. I had to do extensive plastic surgery on the reader's letter to disguise any trace of his or her identity; Harper lawyers have assured me that this was necessary.

After that summer of 2006, I became deeply involved in writing the novel that became City of Refuge, *and except for "Charlie Chan in New Orleans!" I did very little discretionary writing between the fall of 2006 and the fall of 2008, when the novel was published. During that period, though, there were many developments in the city, on both the positive and negative sides of the ledger. Essentially, the city came back to life, haltingly at first, and then with a vengeance, culminating in the extraordinary first half of 2010, when we got (at last) a new mayor, the Saints won the Super Bowl, and* Treme *debuted on HBO. That was quite a time to be in the city.*

On the down side, various cadres of influence had been at work trying as quietly as possible to engineer controversial changes in the city that became public knowledge only through the efforts of a handful of concerned citizens. "Other People's Houses" addresses one of these schemes: the effort to keep Charity Hospital closed and raze seventy acres of historic homes in the heart of the city to build a sprawling new hospital complex under the combined auspices of Louisiana State University and the U.S. Department of Veterans Affairs. Charity Hospital was the city's main venue for treating poor and indigent populations, and was ready to reopen within weeks after Katrina; it was kept closed through the enormous influence of LSU. This isn't the place for a rundown of post-Katrina New Orleans politics, but it is worth saying that the opponents of the plan (I was, obviously, one) agreed on the need for a hospital but argued for rehabbing Charity and utilizing the more vertical space available in the already-existing downtown medical district, much of which was vacant and begging for development, instead of expropriating the homes of hundreds of people who had sunk the previous several years and much of their life savings into returning to their homes. Guess who won the fight. The piece appeared as an op-ed in the New Orleans Times-Picayune.

Finally, an amuse-bouche that appeared in The Huffington Post *in September 2010, discussing the five-year Katrina anniversary in light of the infamous BP oil spill in the Gulf of Mexico. I wonder if anyone will remember that disaster in ten years, aside from historians and the thousands of people who had their lives upended, businesses destroyed, and sense of continuity terminated. Seemed pretty important at the time. The BP spill was treated in the media as a regional disaster, but if "Incontinental Drift" has a point, it is that there is no such thing, anymore, as a regional disaster.*

SEER AND SEEN: AN ONLINE CHAT ABOUT NEW ORLEANS

In February 2006 I was asked by the *Washington Post* to do an online chat about my book *Why New Orleans Matters* and the questions raised by the need to rebuild New Orleans. Here are some excerpts from that chat. In the introduction, the editor quoted something I had said in a previous interview, and it might illuminate the first exchange:

> In a recent interview Piazza stated that, in his eyes, 'New Orleans is . . . a small model of all the best of America. You have a truly multicultural city, in which all social and ethnic and economic levels of society have somehow managed to fashion a distinct and beautiful culture out of the tensions among their differences. . . . In a larger sense that is the story of United States culture as a whole, but in New Orleans the expressions of that culture have included jazz, rhythm and blues, a distinctive cuisine, and so much more. And an attitude towards life that includes a spiritual resilience which has spoken to people around the world—for a couple of hundred years.

Tom Piazza: I'm answering these questions from my New Orleans apartment, which is finally habitable after six months. During these months I have spent about half my time in New Orleans, and the rest on the road, speaking in Missouri, Connecticut, New York State, Vermont, Florida, San Francisco, and many other places. The intense concern for New Orleans on the part of so many people has been very moving, and it makes me hopeful about the future of my city. I had a number of questions waiting for me when I logged on, so I will just dive in with the first one in the queue.

New Braunfels, Texas: Why do you call New Orleans the "best of America?" To me, it is the worst of America—I lived there twenty-five years. It is the murder capital of the United States, witchcraft and voodoo thrive there as well as prostitution and gambling. If this city is the best I hate to think of the worst city. Mardi Gras is a pagan celebration and I think the Lord has had about enough of New Orleans.

Thanks for letting me sound off.

Tom Piazza: Thanks for your question. I'll try to answer as well as I can.

First of all, you lived in New Orleans for twenty-five years and all you remember is witchcraft, voodoo, prostitution, and gambling? It sounds as if you were hanging out with the wrong crowd.

I called New Orleans "a small model of all the best of America" because I have found here a vivid expression of my conception of what the United States can be at its best—a truly multicultural place, in which all social, ethnic, and economic elements of the society have somehow managed to fashion a distinct and vibrant culture out of the tensions among their differences. This embrace of diversity is a beautiful thing, when you can find it.

In the eleven and a half years that I have lived here, I have seen most of the downside aspects that you mention, along with horrible racism, corruption, official incompetence, crumbling public schools, and so on—much of which, be it said, you can find in most urban areas of the U.S. to some degree. I have also seen human beauty, generosity of spirit, humor, astonishing grace in adversity, and a heroic affirmation of life itself through music, cuisine, dance, and fellowship unequaled anywhere else in my experience.

If New Orleans's particular mix of good and bad is not to your taste, that's fine. But I think we need to be careful about seeing the Hand Of God at work in events that confirm our own ideas, tastes, or prejudices. As we know from the Book of Job, if not from our own experience in daily life, the hard rain falls on the good and the bad, the just and the unjust alike. If there is in fact a God, it is the height of hubris to think that you can fathom His reasons for doing what He does on this earth, and near-blasphemy to imagine that He is serving your own ideas of who needs correction or punishment.

By the way, I notice from the lead story in the online edition of today's [February 24] New Braunfels *Herald-Zeitung* [the city website calls the town "a little bit of old Germany"] that a local custodian at Smithson Valley Middle School in nearby Spring Branch has been arrested for allegedly possessing large amounts of child pornography. That's only twenty-five miles from you; you might want to bring an umbrella later if you are going out.

One more thing in the Acts Of God department: the catastrophe in New Orleans is the result of human incompetence and error—not, so far as I can tell, divine malice. The Hurricane Katrina winds and rain were disastrous, there is no question. But the massive and, again, catastrophic destruction that we have seen in the city is mainly the result of the flooding that took place—from the failure of the levees. And the primary responsibility for that tragic turn of events, and for fixing it, lies directly with the U.S. Army Corps of Engineers, and they have admitted as much. And we need to hold them, and those whose job it is to oversee them, responsible until they have repaired the levees and made a good start on restoring the coastal wetlands that protect the entire Gulf Coast from the worst effects of these storms.

Washington, D.C.: It's been eight years ago since me and a girlfriend of mine attended the *Essence* Magazine Fest in New Orleans and I will never forget that little city. The people, the food, the music was great. We had a wonderful time at the Superdome and the French Quarters. I am certainly glad that I got the chance to see and experience New Orleans before Katrina hit.

I had no clue how poor New Orleans was in its certain "wards" of the city, and now that it is 95 percent white due to those who were not affected by the "mysterious" breaking of the levees in the mostly black populated areas of the city—what should we expect to see now? Does the government have plans to bulldoze those "poor" areas and make way for moneymaking entertainment, or will there be plans to rebuild better homes and bring back the people who made New Orleans the city it once was?

TP: As you can imagine, there is a huge and complicated arm-wrestle going on right now over these exact questions. It is my view that the city needs, in every sense, to actively encourage the return of its citizens from all economic and ethnic backgrounds, and from all of its neighborhoods. There have been enormous problems involved in doing this, which have amounted to a kind of logistical gridlock.

Here is an example of what I mean: The trailers promised by FEMA as temporary housing for displaced people have been slow to arrive, when they have arrived at all. Those fortunate enough to have a trailer delivered have often found that there is no electricity to serve the trailer. The best estimate I have heard is that about three quarters of the city is still without electricity. This includes areas in which there is no electricity restored at all, as well as areas in which there is electricity in principle but houses are unable to get hooked up to it. The local power utility, Entergy New Orleans, has declared bankruptcy and is operating on what could generously be called a skeleton crew—hence drastically insufficient personnel to perform the hookups, not to mention all the other necessary public electrical work. By the way, the parent company of Entergy made something like $800 million in profits last year, and yet will not bail out Entergy New Orleans. Problems of this general sort exist in almost every area of the rebuilding process.

In any case, people who want to come back and rebuild their lives and property even in areas that have not been seriously compromised are having trouble finding places to live while they rebuild. Rents and property values have gone up astronomically in the areas that did not flood. Obviously this is going to weigh most heavily on the people with the fewest resources.

You suggest, correctly I think, that there is a racial dimension to the way some of these problems are being approached. The politics and economics of race in New Orleans, as elsewhere, are enormously complex. It is easy both to overstate and to understate the significance of race in this process. By the way, the rough division of black and white population in the city now is more like 65 percent white to 35 percent black, roughly the mirror image of the pre-Katrina ratio.

Here is my feeling about this. There is no question but that the heaviest weight of this catastrophe has fallen on the poorest citizens of New Orleans. The heaviest weight of any catastrophe usually falls on the poorest citizens. In New Orleans, the poor are overwhelmingly African-American. As I said in *Why New Orleans Matters*, most of those poor are people who work, or were working, very, very hard at low-paying jobs just to make ends meet. All of them were and are members of our community, in New Orleans and as Americans.

The question of their return sits at the moral and spiritual center of the discussion of post-Katrina New Orleans. But it is not a straightforward question, partly because until we have a clear picture of viable, rebuilt levee protection, it is close to murder to invite people to rebuild and reoccupy areas that could flood again. These areas, by the way, include not just the largely poor and African-American Lower Ninth Ward but the largely white, upper-middle-class neighborhood Lakeview, the upper-middle-class, mostly African-American New Orleans East, and mixed areas such as Gentilly, not to mention the overwhelmingly white, working-class St. Bernard and Chalmette.

So it is not a straightforward issue of race, but it is plainly inflected by racial politics. Some, for example, have raised the above-mentioned flooding concerns as a way of saying, in code, that it is better that the residents of the overwhelmingly African-American neighborhoods not return. I would raise it to say, straightforwardly, that it is a national disgrace that the federal government has not moved more aggressively to do what is necessary to rebuild the levees and, just as importantly, restore the coastal wetlands that weaken hurricanes and absorb much of their impact as they approach land. Everyone in New Orleans, and everyone who wants to return to New Orleans, has a major case of the jitters right now because nobody knows what will happen during the next hurricane season.

There are other major questions on the topic. Many of the evacuees in the post-Katrina shelters had school-age children with them. Most public schools in New Orleans are closed indefinitely. If these evacuees return, where will their children attend school? Most of the evacuees had no health insurance; presently, Charity Hospital, which was the main public source of health care for the poor, is closed indefinitely, and the number of beds in the hospitals that have reopened is down sharply. How will they get health care if they return? Where will they work? How will they care for sick or elderly family members?

It is not enough to use these questions to say, "Sorry—too bad about your old life, and good luck in your new one, as long as it is someplace else." That is just a way of not answering the questions in the first place. We need to use them to take a look at our priorities as a nation—a good, hard look at what we see in the mirror, and not just on the television screen.

One more thing that I do need to say before moving on to the next question: Your quotes around the word "mysterious" are misleading. There was nothing mysterious about it. Engineers have been telling us for years exactly what would happen to the levees sooner or later, under certain conditions, and they have also told us how much it would cost to fix them. Nobody wanted to hear it, especially the second part. Some people, additionally, have suggested that the levees were blown up during the hurricane to intentionally flood the largely African-American areas you mention. I have seen absolutely no evidence of this, and neither has anyone else. I am not saying that it is inconceivable that that kind of thing could happen, only that I don't believe it happened this time. The levees crumbled on black and white alike, poor and well-off alike. The outrage should be directed at the miserable and ineffectual response at the local, state, and federal levels alike.

Medford, Massachusetts: Tom, whether or not New Orleans is the type of town you say (and the view from the outside certainly matches the description in your first question), why should we rebuild it? Why, up here on a hill in Medford, Massachusetts, should we be paying to rebuild a city that is below sea level and that, except for human efforts, would not exist in its current form? It's politically unpopular to say, but I can't think of a good reason.

TP: Hi, Medford, and thank you for the question. I hear this question a lot, and I will answer it as well as I can. First of all, no city we know of would exist "in its current form," or any other form, if it weren't for "human efforts." I don't mean that to sound flip. I mean it to say that everything worthwhile that humankind has achieved involves a rear-guard action against entropy. And without continual effort it would all quickly revert to weeds and waste. Anyone who owns a house, tends a garden, raises children, shaves, or does just about anything else knows this to be true.

So our initial stance has to accept the fact that we are always, in this sense, pushing back against nature. Secondly, the sad fact of the matter is that many of the major cities in America are improbable, to say the least. Where are we going to make a stand and say that, as Americans, all of our country needs the efforts of all of us, whether up on a hill in Medford, Massachusetts, or down home in Tuscaloosa or way out west in Texas?

If we say we don't help New Orleans, then what do we do when those silly people in San Francisco get destroyed again by an earthquake? Do we tell them, "Sorry, you were pretty dumb to build on a fault line"? Do we say the same thing to St. Louis and Memphis, both of which are on or near the New Madrid fault? What do we say when Los Angeles is hit by an earthquake, or is ravaged by wildfires and mudslides? Or when Mississippi and Missouri and Iowa flood again the way they did in 1993? Or to Florida, when hurricanes strike there, or to New York and Washington, D.C., if, God forbid, they or some other city becomes a target for a terrorist attack. Do we say, "Too bad for you—you were too stupid to live in Medford"?

I know this sounds sarcastic, and I guess it is, but I have heard far too many people advance this attitude, which to me sounds as if they are just writing off the "United" part of the United States. To paraphrase Ben Franklin (I think)—we must all hang together or we will certainly hang separately. Plus, New Orleans is one of the most important American cities, culturally, historically, and economically—the site of the signing

of the Louisiana Purchase, birthplace of jazz music, location of one of the great treasure houses of vernacular
American architecture . . . We go to great lengths, or we
used to, to protect our cultural patrimony. We need to
continue to do that, it seems to me, and New Orleans is
the main place we should be focusing our efforts right
now.

Arlington, Virginia: Certainly, it is the poor and disad-
vantaged segment of New Orleans's population that has
suffered worst thanks to Katrina. Are they best served,
however, by efforts to rebuild and return, rather than
resettling where they are? Are they more likely to escape poverty in a new community than if they return to
N.O., which will certainly be in difficult circumstances
through the near future, no matter how much renovation
is undertaken? Should we be directing our public resources to help the resettlement effort rather than hoping
for rebuilding?

TP: This is a very important question, with profound
implications. The starting place for an answer is this: We
need to begin by asking the displaced residents themselves
what they need, and what they want. We need to have a
much better and more honest and more open dialogue
with New Orleans's scattered population than we have
managed to have so far.

    Many of those who are displaced may well decide
that they have found themselves in a better situation
than that in which they had lived before the storm.
Many others may decide that the most important thing
to them is to return to New Orleans, to the traditions
and culture that they knew, to whatever extent that culture and those traditions can be revived. In either case,

the effort should be aimed at listening, with respect, to
what they say, and then helping them, within reasonable
bounds, to achieve their goals, rather than imposing a
kind of abstract decision on them from above, arrived
at by experts who have no true understanding of the
residents' original milieu.

It seems to me that this is the necessary starting
point for any conversation about this question, and the
only way for people who have already suffered close to the
worst things that a human can suffer to be able to rebuild
their lives with dignity.

And one more thing in response to that question.
My strong feeling is that all people who want to return
to New Orleans, no matter who they are, should be able
to come back, and a place actively made for them. At the
same time, the questioner has a point: The fate of those
who were displaced needs to be addressed more seriously as
well. As most of you probably know, those with the fewest
resources are in many cases hanging on by the skin of their
thumbs in hotels across the country, waiting for FEMA to
pull the plug on them. I don't know what the answer is to
this situation, but the fact that no one else seems to know,
either, scares me.

Washington, D.C.: I'm prone to agreeing with you
that "New Orleans is one of the most important American cities, culturally, historically, and economically,"
but I'd like to hear your thoughts on why this is so.
Thank you.

TP: Anyone who is affected by the import and export
of grain, textiles, hard or dry goods of any sort, elec-
tronics, automobiles—which is to say anyone in the
U.S.—depends on the health of New Orleans as a port.

Likewise seafood, especially shellfish. For that matter, anyone who uses petroleum products should recognize the importance of New Orleans, and Louisiana in general, to the supply of oil on which we depend for heat and mobility—not just imports through the Port of New Orleans but the offshore rigs miles out that are supported by New Orleans's economic and technical infrastructure.

From a cultural standpoint . . . it is hard for me to get that into a small space. It took me more than one hundred and sixty pages to get it into *Why New Orleans Matters*! But I will say this: Beyond just being the birthplace of jazz, which is, after all, a fact of its past, New Orleans is today, still, one of the most remarkable cultural ecosystems in the world. The interaction, not just historically but in real time, in the present, between the deep cultural strains of France, Spain, Africa, the Caribbean, Italy, Germany, Croatia, Cape Verde, Ireland, and so many other cultures, has produced a music— many musics, as I say in the book—a cuisine, a style of dance, of architecture, of humor, of celebration, and of mourning that, taken collectively, is one of the glories of human history.

The side of New Orleans seen by the casual tourist during a weekend spent on Bourbon Street is not New Orleans, although it is a face of New Orleans. New Orleans is deep, and it must live, or something truly irreplaceable will be lost forever.

Omaha, Nebraska: I hear some people say things like, "They shouldn't live there; it's not our problem. Why should we pay?" Can you help me with a concise response to this?

TP: Hi, Omaha. I hope I addressed this in a previous answer. Basically it boils down to the Golden Rule, I suppose.

From the Washington Post *online, February 2006*

AN EXCHANGE OF LETTERS ABOUT *WHY NEW ORLEANS MATTERS*

Here, as promised earlier, is an exchange of letters from May 2006, about the state of New Orleans. It was, like many others I received, occasioned by the publication of my book *Why New Orleans Matters*. For legal reasons, I am able to print only the gist of my correspondent's remarks, with a handful of quotes included to give a flavor of the letter's tone.

My correspondent was a physician who had relocated from New Orleans to another state well before Hurricane Katrina. He was apparently a cultured and affluent man, articulate and even at times eloquent in his remarks. He began the letter by giving me his own personal background, which included medical work with some of the New Orleans's poorest residents when he lived in the city, his frequent post-Katrina visits to New Orleans, the fact that he continues to ride in one of the city's most prestigious Mardi Gras krewes, and his taste for Southern music, fine cuisine, and the many "architectural gems" to be found in New Orleans. After telling me how much he enjoyed my descriptions of the city's "sights, sounds, and smells," he got down to business by claiming, in essence, that he found my book naïve and wrongheaded.

"I think it is inappropriate," he began,

and a bit condescending, primarily to the black underclass, to suggest that the best thing for the city would be if everything and everyone came back the way it was. Do you realize the level of poverty that existed in New Orleans? Do you realize the misery that created? Generations of people were stuck in places like the Lower Ninth Ward with no idea how or if they could ever get out. Many barely knew that there was a better existence available.

He inventoried many causes of the city's pre-Katrina problems, as he saw them: a "relaxed work ethic"; prejudice; malfeasance; political manipulation carried out first by white city officials and then, "after 1960 or so," by mainly black city officials; a notoriously bad public school system; systemic inefficiency and corruption at all levels; population loss; and economic depression.

He went on to criticize my book's criticism of the governmental response to the disaster, including my insistence that strong efforts be made to bring back as many of the city's residents, including the poorest ones, as wanted to return. Tens of thousands of those poorer residents were stuck hundreds or thousands of miles away from home in strange surroundings among people with whom they had little or nothing in common. Some did not want to return to New Orleans; many others were desperate to come back.

When the images of thousands of mostly black citizens stranded and suffering in New Orleans were shown over and over on TV in the days after the storm, and then in the months afterward the absence of rebuilding efforts by the government, what did you see? I suspect you saw a government that had broken its promises. What people in most other parts of the country saw was a group of people who were for the most part physically capable of evacuating before the storm, but had not done so. They then saw those people evacuated at government expense to situations that were usually safer and more comfortable than the homes they had previously been living in. And they saw a local government that was inept at best, if not truly making things worse. In other words, what was seen was a group of people who refused to take responsibility for themselves, and a local government that encouraged that.

He acknowledged that many of the city's poorest residents took pleasure in "simple expressions of life—food, music, etc.," and that the rest of society enjoyed the "expressions" that often originated at the bottom of the city's social ladder. And yet . . .

Is it not condescending to suggest that those people would be better off returning to the poverty of a permanent urban underclass so they can continue to try to "amuse" themselves for our benefit? Would it not be better for them to finally have the opportunity to make a better life for themselves and their children in another location that didn't celebrate corruption and irresponsibility?

On this apparently optimistic note, he sketched out his vision of the silver lining that Katrina offered, if only we would recognize it and act on it.

Perhaps local government in New Orleans will improve without the burden of the underclass to deal with. New Orleans could become not another Las Vegas or Atlantic City, but perhaps Charleston, Jamestown, or Savannah? In other words, perhaps

New Orleans will become a kind of "museum" town, featuring a world-class university in Tulane, lots of great architecture in Uptown and the French Quarter, and not much else. Would that be so bad?

He closed by reaffirming how much he really did enjoy reading *Why New Orleans Matters*, promising to look for more of my writing, expressing optimism about New Orleans's future, and wishing me good luck.

On its face, it may seem a perfectly reasonable letter, and yet it was not the first time I had seen a number of the rhetorical moves this writer had made. They were, in fact, all too familiar, even at that early date, and I wrote the response that follows.

. . .

Dear Mr. ———,

Thank you for your letter and for your kind words about my writing. It's always good to hear from a reader whose musical tastes "wander between Memphis and New Orleans." Of course mine do, too; sometimes they even end up in Nashville for a while.

I will try and respond to your points as candidly as possible, since you have felt free to be candid with me about your take on the questions you raise. I'll take the time because you like music and because you wished me good luck. But I do not like your letter, and I will do my best to tell you why.

I get a lot of mail from all over the place, and I talk to a lot of people. I notice that those who want to see New Orleans turn into another Savannah or Charleston almost always present this desire as being for the good of the poor who are being displaced from their homes. They realize there is something not quite right, certainly not Christian, about the desire to get rid of the inconvenient, problematic poor (or the "burden of the underclass," as you put it in your note), so they need to cloak their agenda in the guise of generosity. Years ago, I remember that David Duke advocated euthanizing severely handicapped people, claiming that it was for their own good, and that they themselves would have wanted it that way. Worlds apart, maybe, but still this doesn't feel all that different to me.

Not, of course, that I see your thinking as having anything in common with David Duke's—not with your defense of the "black underclass" against my "condescension" and your implication that I am ignorant of the poverty and ignorance in which the faceless members of the underclass dwell. But I'm afraid that in your zeal to defend the underclass you may have forgotten about large parts of my book (I hope you didn't skip them!). You ask whether I "realize the level of poverty that existed in New Orleans . . . the misery that created"; I would point you to pages seventy-five to ninety-five of *Why New Orleans Matters*, in which I discuss it, along with the official corruption and other urban ills you raise in your letter. I never suggest that "the best thing for the city would be if everything and everyone came back the way it was," nor did I suggest that "those people would be better off returning to the poverty of a permanent urban underclass so they can continue to try to 'amuse' themselves for our benefit." This is a distortion of my argument. I would like them to be able to return, if they choose to do so, to a city capable of making a commitment to addressing these problems instead of just wanting them to disappear.

I have lived in New Orleans for eleven and a half years. I have spent a lot of time at street level, in many different neighborhoods of the city. I've been in houses with no doors, in conditions that I had previously seen only in San Juan and Dakar. I have seen things that I never could have imagined. I have also been in houses in the poorest neighborhoods where the owners have made warm, inviting, and soulful lives and environments for themselves and their families. I have known people who have been killed over nothing, and I know people who spend their lives helping others, even though they themselves have very few material resources. As you must know from your medical work among the city's poor, the people not just of the Ninth Ward but the Seventh Ward and Central City and all the rest represent the full range of humanity—intelligent, not intelligent, generous, selfish, well-read, illiterate, thoughtful, impulsive, devious, straightforward, lazy, and hardworking. They are not susceptible of easy generalization.

So, an axiom: We are talking about human beings. Although neither I nor any decent person can look on the kind of poverty that has existed in some parts of New Orleans and think it is a good thing, anybody who actually spends time in those neighborhoods will see that they are not simply pits of misery. The Lower Ninth Ward, since that is the example you use, consisted mainly of working people. This is a fact, not an opinion. Poor for the most part, yes, but in most cases hardworking, mostly homeowners, and also people who, as I say in the book, have found a way to express an extraordinarily vibrant sense of life in music, cuisine, humor, speech, and other less tangible ways. Crime? Yes. Illiteracy? Tell me about it. Are these problems to work on? Surely, and people have been saying this for years. But the point is that being poor and born into a partly hostile environment with diminished opportunity does not disqualify anyone from being a complex human being with a connection to their home and neighborhood, and not just a figure in a set of statistics.

Secondly, and stemming from this: Since these people are recognizably human, even if they are operating under tremendous disadvantages, then presumably they should be granted the dignity of making decisions for themselves. At least their desires and aspirations and preferences should be taken into account in the decisions others make about their lives. Those displaced New Orleanians who feel that they will have a better chance at a new life, more opportunity, better schools for their children, etc., outside New Orleans should be helped in their decision to try and better their lot in that way. But those who decide that the culture and the life that they have known, in many cases, for generations— their house that they or their father built and furnished, their neighborhood, the familiar food and surroundings— is important to them should be helped in their attempt to come back and build a better life here in New Orleans. They surely have as much right to be here as the developers who would like to turn the city into another Charleston.

You raise the question, as many have, of why so many people did not evacuate. You front-load it with the notion that most of them were "physically capable" of doing so, and then claim that this is evidence that they "refused to take responsibility for themselves." The extraordinarily complex and multifarious reasons why all kinds of people—white, black, brown, poor, working-class, and otherwise—did not leave town for the storm have been well documented and discussed at great length and are, in any case, not all that hard to figure out.

I realize that it is not automatic for people who have money and at least one car to imagine that it might be difficult for people who don't own a car and who rely on public transportation—who barely make enough money to survive and who are often taking care of disabled or elderly family members as well as children—to pack up the whole gang a couple of times every hurricane season, find their way out of town, pay for a hotel room for a couple of nights, pay for the family to eat every meal out someplace, pay for gas (if they do have a car), and all the rest—especially when it turns out to be a false alarm 95 percent of the time. There is simply no excuse for not trying to imagine just how difficult that is for people before calling them irresponsible. It doesn't take all that much effort.

You say you suspect that when I watched these people's lives fall apart around them that I saw a government that had broken its promises. Yeah, in fact, I did. By "promises" I assume you mean things like the assumption that the federally mandated and constructed levee system would be built to reasonable specifications and then maintained? Or like the promise that there would be fallback plans for communications for police and fire departments in the case of a repeatedly predicted disaster? Or do you mean like the promise that there would be transportation provided for people who couldn't otherwise get to the shelters of last resort? Or the quaint notion that, once they got there, United States citizens would not have to sit in unspeakably filthy conditions with no water or food or medical care or other supplies for five days in the sweltering heat in a disaster area while the president of the United States sat around with his thumb up his ass? You ask what I saw—what, exactly, did you see when you looked at all this?

You say that legions of nameless "people around the country" took the televised images as evidence of the affected people's irresponsibility, and if you don't agree with them, you certainly didn't make much of a case for the other side. If that is how you yourself feel, you ought to have the courage to come out and say it. Don't put it off on others, or try to camouflage it with remarks about my "condescension." Don't try to preserve your view of yourself as being more objective than you really are. I am well aware of the ways in which many people in other parts of the country interpreted the very processed and selected images they saw on television and in magazines during the time that the media's attention was focused on New Orleans and Katrina. I am aware because for the past year, as a result of the publication of my book, I have traveled all over the country talking with people about the future of the city and its citizens. I have been to New York City, Boston, San Francisco, Rochester, Tallahassee, Austin, Houston, Princeton, and many other smaller towns in Ohio, Vermont, New Hampshire, Virginia, Tennessee, Missouri, Connecticut, and elsewhere. Except for a small, scattered handful of hardened bigots, people raised these questions as genuine questions. They wanted to understand. They had no experience with New Orleans. You pretend to raise questions, but your questions are only rhetorical.

Is the lot of New Orleans's poor people their own fault, or the fault of their environment? Probably some of both. But if it is largely their own fault, if the poor people of New Orleans are, as you imply, lazy and ignorant and parasitic, then they will be that way anywhere, and your claims that relocation will offer a new start with more opportunity is disingenuous at best. Perhaps it would be better for you to be honest and admit that the agenda is not really the improvement of their lot; the agenda is to get rid of the "burden of the underclass" by sending them someplace—anyplace—else, so that New Orleans can become a "museum city" as you call it.

Where, after all, was all this solicitude for the poor, this desire for them to have a better life, when we had a chance to do something for them in the place where they had built lives and community for themselves over decades? Where was the community effort on the part of leaders black and white to improve public schools and provide good jobs and day care and training? So many of those who could have lent their resources to an effort to really help their less fortunate and less sophisticated and less resourceful brothers and sisters instead fled the city, stuck their children in private schools, and let public education and the city's tax base go to hell around the ears of the poor. Then they blamed and blame the situation on the people who had the least power to affect it in the first place. Instead of lobbying now to displace hundreds of thousands of people permanently from the only homes they have ever known under the dishonest guise of offering them more opportunity elsewhere, wouldn't it be more decent and honest to try and increase the quality of the opportunity and education available to them wherever they choose to be, even if it is New Orleans?

Of course, that takes a lot of hard, tedious, unrewarding work, and among people whom one would never invite to the ———— Ball. Easier to get out the leaf blower. Send the stuff someplace else. Let it be someone else's problem. Look how nice my showplace looks. The idea of turning one of the great, thriving, complex living cultural centers of the world—with all its problems—into a manicured jewel box like Savannah or Charleston, a "museum town" with "a world-class university in Tulane, lots of great architecture in Uptown and the French Quarter, and not much else" is nauseating and despicable. It doesn't have to come from an actively evil motive. All it needs is the turning of the back in the manner of Pontius Pilate, who washed his hands before the multitude and proclaimed his own innocence.

Tom Piazza

OTHER PEOPLE'S HOUSES

My house was finally broken into, after fifteen years of waiting for it to happen. It used to happen to other people. Now it has happened to me. Luckily, I own more or less nothing of any value to a thief, except for a handful of small items, which they took. They also managed to ransack the place pretty well. "Trashed" would be the word.

The break-in happened the day before the Katrina anniversary. On that same day, our governor signed an agreement that would allow marshals and bulldozers to come in and seize hundreds of people's homes in lower Mid-City to make room for a hospital complex that could easily be built on a different site.

Yes, I am upset that a thief broke in. But nobody is coming to take a house that I rebuilt with four years of hard labor after the levee failures. The city that I fought to come back to has not decided to summarily wipe away all my hard work and faith. That is happening to other people.

Four years after Katrina, New Orleans is at a crossroads—not just a logistical crossroads, but a moral one, and one might as well say a spiritual one. We are all rightly concerned about crime— violent crime, like the kind that took the lives of Dinerral Shavers and Helen Hill, and nonviolent crime like the house break-ins that might now fairly be called an epidemic.

But there is a different kind of crime about to happen in our city, and in some ways it is more ominous because it travels under the cloak of the law. With a stroke of a pen, an elected official, serving the interests of a cadre of greedy and selfish developers, has just wiped away the hopes, the work, and the dreams not just of a single victim, but of hundreds of hardworking people who trusted and loved this city and worked to rebuild it.

Would I like to get my hands on the thief who broke into my house? You bet. But he (she?) probably lives a wretched existence, sneaking around and stealing. Probably not being very highly rewarded for it either.

The people who will profit from the rape of Mid-City are already well-off. They sit on the boards of LSU and Tulane; they stroll the halls of the State Capitol, City Hall, and the Governor's Mansion. They won't hear the sound of the house they rebuilt being crushed by bulldozers. It will happen to other people.

Charity Hospital sits empty. Most of downtown, for that matter, sits empty. Instead of spreading out into Mid-City, the badly needed medical facilities could be built much more quickly, much less expensively, and much more humanely by updating and using Charity and the surrounding medical district. It would give downtown a badly needed revitalizing mechanism, and it would save people's homes, and it would get medical care to the city more quickly.

Why isn't it being done? Because a handful of greedy bastards want a shiny monument to their own power and ego. It's not about getting health care to the people of New Orleans. It's about money and power.

If you live somewhere else in the city, as I do, you can tell yourself that it's happening to other people. But if we learned one thing from Katrina, it is that we are part of an integrated social and geographical and spiritual ecosystem. We can turn our heads as long as it is going on somewhere else and happening to someone else. Or we can get mad now, and make a stand for human dignity and fairness against greed and power lust.

In his song about the bank robber Pretty Boy Floyd, written seventy years ago, the singer-songwriter Woody Guthrie sang,

> *As through this world I've wandered, I've met lots of funny*
> *   men.*
> *Some will rob you with a six-gun, and some with a fountain*
> *   pen.*

He could turn a phrase, that Woody Guthrie. He ended the song thus:

> *But as through this world you travel, and as through this*
> *   world you roam,*
> *You will never see an outlaw drive a family from their home.*

A crime doesn't stop being a crime just because the law is on its side. And Judas Iscariot was paid handsomely by the law for his services. There's still time, but not much, to rescue the soul of this city before the bulldozers crank up.

From the New Orleans Times-Picayune, *September 5, 2009*

INCONTINENTAL DRIFT

Already the Captains and Kings have departed, along with their attendant media grandees. It was nice of them to stop by New Orleans for the anniversary and give everybody around the country, and the world, a look from what must seem a comfortable distance.

Just five years ago, water was cascading into the Lower Ninth Ward, into Lakeview, into Gentilly and Mid-City and Broadmoor and St. Bernard. It would take a day or two, but the entire world was about to see what was possible in America, circa 2005.

At first it looked as if New Orleans had been smacked by a hurricane, which, of course, it had. It would take a while longer for people to understand that the images that halted the coffee cup en route to the mouth, or that kept their eyes open and fixed on the news past bedtime, were the result not of a natural disaster, bad as the hurricane was, but of a catastrophic planning and engineering failure on the part of the Army Corps of Engineers. Many still don't realize it. Of course, many also think that Iraq planned the 9/11 attacks.

And then, this summer, BP. It became a mantra: "You poor guys down there . . . First Katrina flooded your city, and now this . . ."

All this spillage. It was getting kind of . . . embarrassing. To be an American, I mean. We had had some dicey moments before Katrina, to be sure. The savings and loan scandal. Then Enron, then WorldCom. They proved relatively easy to contain and, importantly, they offered no searing visual images to disturb the sleep of the republic. By the time Katrina hit, we had been hemorrhaging money, human blood, and credibility in Iraq for two years, but we had a story to cover that: We had been attacked. The mainstream media mostly went along with that particular narrative, even though it had nothing to do with the war in question.

Katrina, however, was different. Katrina exposed something rotten at the root. The federally built levees were weak as a wino's teeth, and the governmental response to their failure was worse than inept. The federal government suddenly, glaringly, resembled a drunk who had all too publicly lost control of his, shall we say, faculties.

Three years later, in 2008, at least partly as a result of the previous losses of financial control, Wall Street and the housing market sheepishly said, "We've had a little accident . . ." and a massive dose of antidiarrheals in the form of endless debt for future generations was required to keep the body politic from draining out completely.

Two years later, another manifestation of the Great Incontinence, an oil well that ruptured and could not stop, millions (billions? who's counting?) of gallons of oil billowing out into some of the most ecologically sensitive waters on the planet. The government stood by, wringing its hands, as BP lunged at a series of ill-considered and untested solutions, one after another, falling repeatedly on their faces like country boys trying to catch a greased pig.

As their veins become less forthcoming, junkies, old-timers who have been shooting for years, are known to look for a place to hit anywhere—between their toes, in their groins. Well, we

Americans were famously "addicted" to oil. And with the Deep-water Horizon blowup, the needle had broken off and the earth itself seemed to be bleeding uncontrollably.

It was an image from the darkest wells of the collective psyche, a nightmare. They tell us that dreams exist to bring to light material that we are having trouble facing directly when conscious. What are these bad dreams telling us?

The result of uncontrolled indulgence is, ultimately, a lack of control when you need it most. Americans don't want to hear it. But we're not kids anymore, no matter how hard we try to act like it. There is an incontinence at our center now that is the result of years—decades—of telling ourselves that our destiny was manifest, our entitlement endless. We could spend uncountable amounts of money on a foreign war and offer tax cuts to the wealthy at the same time. We could consume energy without giving it a second thought—after all, we would be dead by the time the account ran dry. We could toss the regulatory chains from the shoulders of the oppressed banking and investment industries—sorry, *industry*. The regulations were, after all, so 1933. We could cut corners on crucial infrastructure projects since the odds were that the levees and bridges and pipelines and dams wouldn't fail anytime soon. As a result we are finding new orifices from which to bleed and drain at an ever-accelerating rate.

How is New Orleans doing? We are doing all right. We have a new mayor, we are strong. But how are you doing? The levee failures, the BP spill, the financial meltdown, all share the same root. Somewhere the nation lost the commonsense understanding that corporations and government agencies can't be expected to regulate themselves. Or perhaps we have only lost the will to act on the understanding.

The levees have been repaired, yes. In the places where they broke. The oil well has, finally, been capped, and all the oil has either evaporated or been eaten by microbes (you believe that?).

The too-big-to-fail financial institutions have had their bad gambling debts paid by Big Daddy. Sleep well.

It may be comforting to imagine that Katrina and this year's BP disaster happened "down there," but from down here they appear to be happening right in the middle of everything. On the day of the anniversary, the president for whom I voted so proudly not even two years ago, spoke in New Orleans, promising, as did his predecessor, a Full Recovery. But on the larger stage he is, dare I say it, pissing away his chance to articulate that oh-so-crucial sense of urgency, summon the necessary will to address a flawed underlying logic, rather than merely cleaning up the mess afterward. I know he doesn't want to be called a socialist. But if we can't figure out a way to grow up, and fast, there will be no diaper in the world big enough for us.

From The Huffington Post, *August 31, 2010*

It was my great good fortune to get to know my first literary hero when I was still young enough for it to feel like magic. "Norman Mailer: A Remembrance," published in the 2008 memorial issue of The Mailer Review, *tells the story of how I met Norman in 1981; he remained a close friend until his death in 2007. The companion piece here appeared in the* Columbia Journalism Review, *as part of its Second Read series, in which an author revisits a book that was important in his or her development. It makes the case as well as I am able for what I consider to be the heart of Mailer's value as a writer and intellectual.*

CITIZEN MAILER

Early in Norman Mailer's *The Armies of the Night: History as a Novel, the Novel as History*, the poet Robert Lowell tells Mailer that he thinks of him as "the finest journalist in America." One writer's compliment is plainly another's backhanded insult. Mailer had a lifelong ambivalence about his reportorial, as opposed to his novelistic, work, considering fiction to be a higher calling. "There are days," Mailer responds, tartly, "when I think of myself as being the best writer in America."

A year after Mailer's death in November 2007, at eighty-four, maybe we can begin to be grateful that he worked both sides of the yard. He was always an interesting and ambitious novelist, yet Mailer's loyalties were divided between his fictive imagination and his fascination with the way society works. At his best, the two merged, and the results made for some of the most extraordinary writing of the postwar era.

When Mailer died, commentators lined up to bemoan the dearth of serious writers who, like Mailer, were willing to match their own egos, their own perceptions and sensibilities, against large contemporary events. We suffer from no shortage of gutsy reporters eager to cover trouble spots around the world. But rarely does that kind of journalistic impulse coexist with a personally distinct literary style, an ability to use one's own point of view as an entry into the reality of a subject. For Mailer, that subjectivity was not just a stylistic trait but a kind of ethical tenet, the door into a larger—he would call it novelistic—truth.

Mailer brought this approach to its peak in *The Armies of the Night*. His journalistic mock epic of the 1967 March on the Pentagon first appeared in *Harper's*, occupying the cover and taking up practically the entire issue, and came out in book form in the spring of 1968. By that time, the so-called New Journalism was in full bloom; Tom Wolfe, Gay Talese, Hunter S. Thompson, Joan Didion, George Plimpton, Truman Capote, and others had already done significant work, bringing highly individual styles and sensibilities to a form that had stubbornly held to its conventions of objectivity.

The Armies of the Night stood out from all their work in some important ways. Most New Journalism focused on a subculture—motorcycle gangs, hippies, a football team, Hollywood celebrity—and, by rendering it vividly, attempted to make inductive points about the larger culture. Mailer had a different approach. He got as close as he could to the gears of power and then used his own sensibilities as a set of coordinates by which to measure the dimensions of people and events on the national stage: presidents and astronauts, championship fights and political conventions.

He had shown this predilection before writing *Armies*. There was his *Esquire* article about John F. Kennedy at the 1960 Democratic convention, "Superman Comes to the Supermarket," and "In the Red Light," a piece on the 1964 Republican convention. There was also the audacious interstitial writing, addressed directly to Kennedy, the new president of the United States, in one of his most interesting and neglected books, *The Presidential Papers*. But in *Armies*, Mailer upped the ante by placing himself at the center of the narrative, turning himself into a self-dramatizing (in the purest sense of the phrase) protagonist. He gave his consciousness not just eyes but a face.

The book presents Mailer as a reluctant participant in a mass protest against the Vietnam War that took place in October 1967. A cast of extraordinary characters populates the stage—Robert Lowell, Dwight Macdonald, Paul Goodman, Ed de Grazia—along with a secondary crew of protesters, marshals, homegrown Nazis, police, court bailiffs, and Mailer's fourth wife back in New York. The author also manages to cram a lot of action into the short span of the narrative. He delivers a drunken speech on the eve of the march, attends a party full of liberal academics, consorts with Lowell, Macdonald, William Sloane Coffin Jr., and other notables gathered for the march, participates in the protest itself, gets arrested, and spends the night in jail.

The publication of the first part of the book in *Harper's* created a sensation. A month later, the book's second part, a shorter and more formal account of the planning and execution of the march, was published in *Commentary*. They were combined in the finished volume, to which Mailer appended his subtitle, "History as a Novel, the Novel as History." It was immediately and almost universally recognized as a "triumph," to use Dwight Macdonald's word, and went on to win both the National Book Award and the Pulitzer Prize.

Mailer's most significant discovery in *Armies* was the technique of writing about himself in the third person, as if he were a character in a novel. "Norman Mailer," the character, is treated as a mock-heroic protagonist making his way through a complex network of competing interests and sensibilities during that weekend in Washington. Because we get a vivid sense of him early on, we gladly accept the topspin he puts on his perceptions as he serves them up.

He earns a powerful narrative leverage, starting with the very first sentence. "From the outset," he writes, "let us bring you news of your protagonist." This lone sentence is followed by an extended excerpt from *Time*'s snarky report on Mailer's pre-protest monologue at the Ambassador Theater.

It is a shrewd and effective opening gambit. There is a clearly stated "us" and "you," so an immediate dramatic relation is set up between the narrative voice and the reader. The voice is bringing us "news"—we love news!—and it is about "your" protagonist, drawing us into a subliminal complicity. Within a page we learn that the "us" who is bringing the news is, in fact, our protagonist himself, a man of many parts, apparently, perhaps containing Whitmanesque multitudes.

The *Time* excerpt is studded with value judgments masquerading as straight reporting: The upcoming march is referred to as "Saturday's capers," and Dwight Macdonald, who shared the stage with Mailer, is "the bearded literary critic." When the excerpt is done, Mailer quits this curtain-raiser with a single sentence, "Now we may leave *Time* in order to find out what happened." We are hooked. And we have been introduced to the book's underlying principle: the notion that a reporter who is willing to characterize events without first characterizing himself or herself is inherently suspect. One can't approach the truth without first turning an eye on one's own subjectivity.

The second chapter, the book's official beginning, puts this principle into practice immediately. "On a day somewhat early in September," the narrative begins, "the year of the first March on the Pentagon, 1967, the phone rang one morning and Norman Mailer, operating on his own principle of war games and random play, picked it up. This was not characteristic of Mailer. Like most people whose nerves are sufficiently sensitive to keep them well-covered with flesh, he detested the telephone. Taken in excess, it drove some psychic equivalent of static into the privacies of the brain."

Since we know that we are hearing this from Mailer himself, we are, again, complicit in the narrative; a game is in progress, and we are being shown the rules. We are going to get our events via a mind that is nothing if not subjective, and yet paradoxically objective about its own subjectivity. We will get descriptions of action (he picks up the ringing phone), background context for the action (it was not characteristic), observations delivered from an unexpected angle with a Mark-of-Zorro flourish (the oversensitive nerves with their sheathing of flesh), and an insistence on sharp detail in metaphor (the static being driven into "the privacies of the brain"). The author will juggle these ingredients in quick succession, always with huge linguistic gusto.

Mailer's prose obsessively amends its own perceptions, makes parenthetical observations, qualifies, anticipates, demurs, constantly tries to stand outside itself. He was, in fact, a species of performance artist, discovering metaphors en route and mingling them with dazzling audacity. Here he is, riffing on his discomfort at a party thrown by some liberal backers of the march: "The architecture of his personality bore resemblance to some provincial cathedral which warring orders of the church might have designed separately over several centuries. . . . Boldness, attacks of shyness, rude assertion, and circumlocutions tortured as arthritic fingers working at lace, all took their turn with him, and these shuttlings of mood became most pronounced in their resemblance to the banging and shunting of freight cars when he was with liberal academics." If your sensibilities are ruffled by a mixed metaphor, comic grandiosity, or long sentences, steer clear of Mailer.

Through it all, Mailer is crucially aware not just of his own motivations, but of how they might play to the public. "Mailer," he writes, "had the most developed sense of image; if not, he would have been a figure of deficiency, for people had been regarding him by his public image since he was twenty-five years old. He had, in fact, learned to live in the sarcophagus of his image—at night, in his sleep, he might dart out, and paint improvements on the sarcophagus. During the day, while he was helpless, newspapermen and other assorted bravos of the media and literary world would carve ugly pictures on the living tomb of his legend."

One would be tempted to find a new name for this point of view—"first person third," perhaps—and think of it as a technical innovation, but for two facts. Mailer winks at the first of these facts upon awakening in his hotel, the Hay-Adams, on the morning of the march, then never mentions it again. "One may wonder," he writes, "if the Adams in the name of his hotel bore any relation to Henry." Yes, one may, but nobody need wonder afterward where Mailer got the idea of writing about himself in the third person. By alluding to the author of *The Education of Henry Adams*, Mailer tips his hat, and his hand, to his fellow Harvard alumnus and consummate insider/outsider. The *Education*, published in 1918, may lack Mailer's bravado and sheer joy in language, but it does use the same first-person-third technique to locate its author in an ambiguous social and historical position. (Adams's book, by the way, also won a Pulitzer, presented posthumously in 1919.)

The other fact is that innovations, if they are indeed innovations, usually spawn techniques useful to succeeding practitioners of the form. But the technique of *The Armies of the Night* is so completely suffused with Mailer's personality, his peculiar mix of ego and charm, of self-regard and self-deprecation, his intelligence and occasional clumsiness, that subsequent attempts by other writers to use the first person third have inevitably read as embarrassing, inadvertent homages.

Mailer recognized early on, before a lot of writers, that politics—most of contemporary public life, in fact—was turning into a kind of theater. Actions on the political stage had a symbolic weight that often outbalanced what might previously have been thought of as their practical consequences. This development was the wedge that eventually drove an unbridgeable divide between the Old Left, with its programmatic preoccupations and endless appetite for dogma, and the New Left, with its vivid sense of the theatrical. It was also the subtext of the 1967 march. The real dynamics of public life were shifting away from the old tabulations of political give-and-take. Instead, the cut of a candidate's suit, or the unfortunate presence of his five o'clock shadow, would travel out over the television sets of the nation and affect people's perceptions on a level that bypassed any substantial argument.

The media, to use Mailer's terminology, was driving public events deeper and deeper into the "privacies" of every citizen's brain, short-circuiting linear thinking in favor of image-driven manipulation. And this was precisely why traditional reportage had become ill-equipped for locating the truth of "what happened." What we needed, insisted Mailer, was a different approach: "The novel must replace history at precisely that point where experience is sufficiently emotional, spiritual, psychical, moral, existential, or supernatural to expose the fact that the historian in pursuing the experience would be obliged to quit the clearly demarcated limits of historic inquiry."

Needless to say, this development dovetailed perfectly with Mailer's own impulses. And yet (and this is perhaps Mailer's most important saving grace), he was deeply ambivalent about it. Highly sensitive to the theater of events and personae, Mailer was alive to the ways in which the manipulation of surfaces could, and would, be used to deaden the public's ability to think, to sift and evaluate information. Writers, public officials, advertising people, politicians, speechwriters—all were in possession of a dangerous weapon, and they were obliged to use it with singular care. "Style," Mailer wrote, much later, in an introduction to a book by former SDS member Carl Oglesby about the JFK assassination, "is not the servant of our desire to inform others how to think, but the precise instrument by which we attempt to locate the truth."

In the light of today's endemic spin, such a sentiment would seem a touching artifact of a simpler time, if it weren't so achievable by any individual sitting alone in a room trying to locate the truth. The prerequisite is the sense that it is both possible and desirable. Citizen Mailer turns the act of seeing, the workings of consciousness itself, into the ultimate civic act—a responsibility shared by everyone in the privacies of his or her brain. There is something profoundly democratic in his insistence that the individual's sensibility could meet the largest events on equal terms, with one's own centering and irreducible humanity as the common denominator.

As a writer and as a man, Mailer was always in a state of tension. His mind and heart were planted in a wholly American flux—improvisatory, protean, deeply ambiguous in intention, supremely egotistical and supremely civic-minded. These tensions give his work its deepest dynamism, turning it into a theater of opposing psychic forces. At the same time, Mailer was not quite a wholly American spirit. Or say that his Americanness existed in extraordinary tension with his respect for European intellectual and artistic traditions. When, toward the end of *Advertisements for Myself*, he promises to write a novel worthy of being read by "Dostoevsky and Marx; Joyce and Freud; Stendhal, Tolstoy, Proust and Spengler; Faulkner, and even old moldering Hemingway," 80 percent of the honor roll has been read before an American is mentioned.

Mailer retained an almost sentimental attachment to the novel form, yet his major gift was not the ability to imagine living, three-dimensional fictional characters. What he did have a genius for was dramatized dialectic. He loved to interview himself; his 1966 collection *Cannibals and Christians* contains three self-interviews, and more followed through the years. The form of *Armies* is itself a kind of dialogue, in two halves, between two different modes of discourse.

In every sense—stylistic, cultural, political—he was stretched between two worlds. Never programmatic enough for the Old Left, neither was he ever anarchic enough to fully sign on to the New Left's Grand Guignol. Although at times Mailer liked to characterize himself as the Devil (or at least *a* devil) while criticizing America's "Faustian" ambitions, he was far from Goethe's "spirit that negates." Rather, he found in his own Hebraic, and specifically Talmudic, tradition (his grandfather was a rabbi) perhaps his deepest conviction: the sense that there is something central, necessary, and even sacred in doubt, in the nuanced weighing of competing intellectual and moral and spiritual claims. And this allowed him to put his own ego, his outsized talents, his brilliance and narcissism, in the service of a higher calling. Because of that, *The Armies of the Night* remains one of the most enlivening, and most deeply American, testaments ever written.

From the Columbia Journalism Review,
November/December 2008

NORMAN MAILER: A REMEMBRANCE

Norman Mailer was the writer who made me want to be a writer. And when he died, I lost a friend of nearly twenty-seven years. The transformation of a hero into a friend with strengths and failings, and shared memories, is not always easy or natural, but Norman insisted upon it. Famously aware of his fame, of the reputation that preceded him and created a perimeter around him, he always did what he could in an individual encounter to dismantle the unreality that such preconditioning tends to generate.

Norman was, for me as for so many others, an essential presence, a psychic fact. He was a mind and a spirit in action in the world, a protagonist, and he made sentences and entire books that are themselves protagonists of a sort. *The Naked and the Dead, The Armies of the Night, The Executioner's Song, Miami and the Siege of Chicago, Advertisements for Myself, An American Dream,* not to mention everything else he wrote . . . These books act upon you, whether you like them or not. There was nothing passive about the act of writing for their author, and there is nothing passive about the result. Several decades ago, I spent some weeks in a college aesthetics course examining the question of whether a work of art can be said to be a physical object. Whatever the answer turned out to be in the abstract, Mailer's works are not objects—they are subjects. Mailer's work helped me see that part of the activity of an artist is to transform objects into subjects.

I encountered that work for the first time in 1977. I was just out of college, living in New York and playing jazz piano in bars and nightclubs here and there. I had taken a job as a clerk at the Barnes and Noble Sale Annex, now defunct, on Eighteenth Street and Fifth Avenue in New York City. After a lackluster career as an English major, reading Sir Philip Sidney and Edmund Spenser, I had begun to think that literature wasn't really my thing. Jazz music was alive in every line—it depended for its rationale on being alive in every line, the sense of bets being entered, and antes increased, as the soloist's thought was spun out. Literature, I thought, couldn't compete. Then one day, bored shelving books, I picked up a hardback copy of *An American Dream*. I recognized the author's name—I had seen him on TV once or twice. The cover didn't look like your standard literary book—it had loud colors and a picture of a beautiful woman implanted in the design. I turned it over and there was his face—the shag rug of tangled curls, and the look in the eye, as if he had been caught in the middle of something, a weird, violent, charming, slightly crazed light in those eyes.

Reading the book was like stepping on a land mine. Mailer brought you where he was—he didn't just describe the sights and sounds and smells but supercharged those sense realities with the narrator's extreme emotional states. You encountered lust and murderous rage, shrewdness and naïveté, charm and clumsiness, close observation and paranoid projection, all mixed in together, stirred with a willingness, a manic desire, a *need*, to take risks. Wild foreshortenings of language and combinations of unlikely imagery set up constantly shifting holograms of mood. I didn't know it was possible to get that kind of intensity in narrative prose. I started reading everything by him, and about him, that I could get my hands on.

Before long, I began taking walks in the warm months, across the Brooklyn Bridge to Brooklyn Heights, in hopes of running into him. It's a slightly embarrassing admission, but I was cheered later to find that one of Norman's favorite musicians, the saxophonist Sonny Rollins, had done something similar as a young man in the 1940s in Harlem, hoping to catch a glimpse of his hero, the saxophone patriarch Coleman Hawkins. And anyway, just the walk across the bridge was inspiring—the harplike cables rising on both sides of you, the wooden boardwalk, the echoes of Hart Crane and Whitman, old iron and steel New York, the harbor muscle and movement and glinting sun off the water below.

In the late spring of 1980, I went for one of my walks on a bright Saturday. After poking around Montague Street, grabbing a slice of pizza and walking down Hicks Street and back up Henry Street, looking out at the harbor and the downtown skyline across the water, I started to head back to the bridge, along Columbia Heights from Montague. That was when I saw him from a block away, crossing Columbia Heights toward the row of brownstones that backed up against the view of the harbor. He was unmistakable—silver-grey hair, denim shirt, looking at the ground as he walked with a rolling gait, plainly deep in thought.

It was a shock. I'm not sure that I ever truly expected to encounter him, but there he was. I had no idea what I would say, but I assumed I'd think of something. I quickened my steps to catch up with him and, as I drew nearer to him, and then abreast of him, I could see that he was indeed looking at the ground, following some idea along some deep corridor of thought. I felt instantly unqualified to interrupt him. Yet what was I there for, if not to interrupt him? My heart was pounding. As I started to walk past him, I looked at him, with the moment sliding through my fingers, and at that moment, from the depths of wherever he was, he looked up at me, like someone briefly assessing a possibly developing situation through a pair of binoculars, and gave me a short, preemptive nod of acknowledgment. Stunned, I could do no more than nod back and say, "Hi." That provoked a secondary, smaller nod, and he descended back into his thoughts, and I continued walking.

Do I need to say that I kicked myself all the way home to the West Village? I consoled myself with the notion that I truly did not want to interrupt him if he was working something out in his head, and this may even have been partly true. In any case, I wrote him a letter that afternoon, the kind of letter you can only write when you are in your early twenties, telling him about what had just happened, and that I hadn't wanted to interrupt him but had been kicking myself anyway, that I had read his books and was trying to write fiction, that I had written about jazz but I wanted to write novels, that I had taken a job as a messenger at *The New Yorker*, and that I was writing a long nonfiction account of a jazz festival I'd attended in Senegal—the letter must have been three pages long—and I closed by telling him that I wanted him to know how much his work meant to me and that I was going to be a writer and I wanted him to know about me. I mailed the letter to him at his address on Columbia Heights, which I had somehow found out.

A month later I received an answer—brief, but not too brief, and full of characteristic flourishes. He told me he had "of course" enjoyed reading my letter, and that he appreciated the fact that I hadn't interrupted him, that he probably was in fact in the middle of a thought. He wrote that answering mail was a periodic "comedy," that it all went into a bag to be answered at regular intervals. He said that he would look forward to reading my article and would write to me about it then. No piece of mail, before or since, has ever made me as happy.

Over that summer I finished writing the article about the jazz festival in Senegal, and William Shawn himself bought it for *The New Yorker* in October of that year, paying what I thought was an astonishing sum, and then never published it, and that is a story for some other occasion. In any case, I sent the manuscript to Norman, reminding him of our exchange of letters earlier in the year. I never heard back from him.

Winter came, and went, and in the spring of 1981, as luck would have it, I met Peter Alson, Norman's nephew, at a party. I had started work on a novel and was planning to use my *New Yorker* money to move to New Orleans and write the book. Peter was writing his first novel, too, and we became instant best friends. After we had known each other for a few weeks, he invited me to the house of his mother, Barbara Wasserman, on West Eleventh Street for a family gathering. Norman was there, and when Peter introduced us, Norman's face opened up and his eyes focused in, simultaneously.

"Oh . . . Tom, hey . . ." he said, slapping himself lightly on his stomach and then chopping the air with his hand. "Listen, I haven't had a chance to read your piece yet." Crinkles formed around the sides of his eyes as he looked up at me with a serio-comic, faintly appraising look. "But my assistant has. And she liked it. And her pride would be that she doesn't suffer fools gladly." On that last sentence he kind of arched his eyebrows, holding my gaze and nodding slightly and deliberately toward me to let me know this was no small compliment. Later, when I met Judith McNally, I knew it was not. But at the time I wondered how in the world he had remembered that envelope that he got in the mail nearly six months earlier. Yet another smoke signal from yet another Young Writer In The Wilderness, among all the similar letters and manuscripts he received . . . But there it was. Norman took it all seriously, and the list of writers who can report similar experiences is long.

That afternoon he invited me to join him and Peter and José Torres and the rest of the gang at the Gramercy Gym the next Saturday morning for their boxing club, which I did, and which I kept doing for three years. And if I were to start telling the stories, detailing the kindnesses, the laughs, the visits to Maine and P-town, the insights and, later, the help I received from Norman, there would be room for nothing else in this issue of *The Mailer Review*. I will say that because of that meeting I did not move to New Orleans as planned. I stayed in NYC for another ten years, until I left town in 1991 for the Iowa Writers' Workshop (with a recommendation from Norman). In 1994 I finally did move to New Orleans.

Norman was a profoundly generous friend. He read my early stories and articles and discussed them with me seriously. He wrote letters of recommendation, to Iowa and to arts colonies. Eventually he wrote a beautiful and heartfelt cover quote for my first book of fiction. He counseled me about literary agents and editors and reviewers, and once—most wisely and comfortingly— about a lost love that was tearing my life up two decades ago. He took me out for a drink in the late afternoon, and he listened to me talk about it, and he didn't give me direction or advice, merely let me know, by an anecdote here, a metaphor there, that he had been through it too, and had (obviously) survived, and that one's work was, ultimately, what got one through.

After I moved out of New York I saw him less frequently, but we would usually manage to have lunch at the Chinese restaurant by the St. George Hotel in Brooklyn Heights on my visits back from Iowa or New Orleans. After my novel *My Cold War* was published, in 2003, Norman invited me to visit in Provincetown. There were some things he wanted to say to me about being a novelist. Of course I went, and in January 2004 we spent three days talking, talking, talking, once well past midnight—about novels, about the war in Iraq, about the nature of God and whether He existed, about Tolstoy and Chekhov, but mainly about what it means to be a novelist and what one should strive for. It was a gift beyond measure, really. I visited Norman and Norris again in P-town several times, and it always counted. Even when he must have known there wasn't a lot of road left, Norman was brilliant, funny, cranky, unself-pitying, generous, and utterly committed to the craft at which he had spent his life.

When Norman was in the hospital for the last time, I was at the MacDowell Colony, in New Hampshire, trying feverishly to finish the first draft of my novel *City of Refuge*. My editor at HarperCollins was audibly drumming his fingers on his desk, and I was riding the novel through the chutes and rapids of its final playing-out. I wrestled with the question of whether to drive down from MacDowell and visit him in the hospital. If I had been able to ask him directly, my guess was that he would have told me to stay where I was and finish my fucking book. I was hearing guarded optimism from some family members, even the possibility that he might be discharged, and I let myself believe it. I sketched out a day-to-day schedule of work for two weeks, ending on November 10, the date on which I would write the book's final scene. Then I would go wherever Norman was and visit him.

I worked like a demon in those weeks, and I thought about Norman every day, about the terrible deadline pressure under which he so often wrote, about many of the things I had learned from him about work, about what was necessary when you were up against the wall and needed to call on your reserves. I worked harder than I had ever worked in my life. The two weeks went by and I was all but done. The morning of November 10 arrived, and I went to my studio to write the final scene of the book. By this time I knew essentially how this scene was going to go, and I was ready. I got to the desk around seven a.m., and for some reason I checked my e-mail before starting work, which is something I never do, and there, in my in-box, was the short e-mail from Norris, telling me that Norman had died and that she thought I'd want to hear it from her before I heard it on the news.

I left the studio and walked around the beautiful grounds of MacDowell, trying to digest this indigestible fact, and realizing that it would be a long time, if ever, before I could. I thought about whether I should have gone to see him instead of pushing to finish the novel. And maybe I should have. But what would I have said? "Good-bye?" That would have been intolerable. "Thank you?" Norman had once told me, "Friends don't say thanks." I didn't agree with him then, and I think I told him so, but anyway I'd already said "thank you" in a lot of ways, and he knew what I thought. I knew he was surrounded toward the end by a lot of love from family and friends, and he hated overly dramatic or demonstrative scenes. I walked around MacDowell for an hour or so, then went back to my studio and finished my novel.

I did go to see him, several days later, in Provincetown. Along with Larry Schiller, Dick and Doris Kearns Goodwin, Peter Alson, Mike Lennon, Doug Brinkley, and several of Norman's children, I was honored to speak at the small graveside ceremony; I read a brief passage from *The Armies of the Night*, the extraordinary description of his night journey on a bus through the Virginia countryside en route to his brief jail stay after the 1967 March on the Pentagon. The passage is so full of his sense of mystery, his love for the poetry of the landscape of the United States, his tenderness. He was off, now, on a journey about which he had been very curious, where awaited, perhaps, some answers to the questions he lived with, about God and karma and the afterlife. Or maybe, knowing Norman, not answers but more extraordinary questions.

I miss him, badly, and I miss him every day.

Sometime in 2010 I was asked to contribute something of my own devising to an anthology titled The Late American Novel: Writers on the Future of Books. *After the gracious invitation I took a couple of running jumps at the topic, but everything I wrote felt very talky and stale and I got busy with other things. Then, months later, with the deadline approaching, a call from editor Jeff Martin reminded me that I had promised a piece. I took one more shot at a conventional essay, scrapped it, and then found myself engaged in this little dramatic scenario, which pretty much accurately reflects how I was feeling at the time. Not that I mess around with guns or anything like that, y'unnerstand . . .*

AN INTERVIEW WITH TOM PIAZZA ON THE FUTURE OF THE BOOK

The Questioner arrives at room 204 of the London Lodge, on the outskirts of New Orleans, the motel room where he is scheduled to meet with Tom Piazza, author of the novels *City of Refuge* and *My Cold War* and the nonfiction collection *Devil Sent the Rain*, and a writer for the HBO series *Treme*, to discuss the future of the book. Knocking once, twice, he receives no answer. The Questioner tries the door and finds it unlocked. Walking into the room he finds Piazza asleep in his street clothes on an unmade bed, with books stacked on the floor, on the couch, on the coffee table, and a small child's record player emitting a ticking sound as the needle goes around the inner spiral of a long-finished LP. The Questioner replaces the record player's tone arm on its perch and shuts the machine off. Pulling the desk chair up to the side of the bed, the Questioner tentatively reaches out to shake the sleeping figure by the shoulder.

Tom Piazza: [*still asleep; shifting slightly in bed*] Three bucks's too much . . .

Questioner: Mr. Piazza . . .

TP: [*shifts more, frowns, groans*]

Q: We're here to talk about the future of the book.

TP: [*waking up*] . . . huh?

Q: The future of the book . . . your thoughts . . . ?

TP: What the fuck are you talking about?

Q: Uh . . . we discussed this . . . ? You were going to . . .

TP: What do you mean by "book"? Where are my glasses . . . ?

Q: We can come back some other time, if this . . .

TP: Here they are. How did my glasses get on the floor? [*picks up an envelope from the nightstand, shakes it slightly, plucks out two small pieces of what appears to be rock candy, and places them under his tongue*] Okay—which book are you talking about, now?

Q: You were going to give us a few words about the future of the book. For a . . . book.

TP: Right, right. [*sits up; opens nightstand drawer; pulls out a .38 pistol*] I assume I can define the word "book" any way I want to, since you won't define it for me?

Q: [*alarmed, staring at gun*] Yes, certainly . . .

TP: Okay. [*significantly more alert*] I'll skip all the usual drainage about electronic books and the death of publishing and how many cookbooks get published and how hard it is to sell midlist fiction. And how important literature is, and how we tell ourselves stories to make sense of our lives, or how in the future we'll all be able to write our own endings to books, as if we can't do that already, or whether backlit screens will replace regular LCDs on the new Zorro e-reader . . . You don't need me for that crap. I really don't care anyway. I'm old-school.

Q: [*still staring at the .38*] Meaning . . . ?

TP: Meaning first of all that I like books that I can hold in my hand. Made of paper. I don't need to plug them in, and I don't have to buy batteries for them. They look different from each other, and I like that. I like looking at *Bleak House* and being able to tell that it embodies a different sense of life than *Jesus' Son* does. I like carrying the fuckers around with me. One weighs more than the other. If you like to read your books on an Etch A Sketch, that's fine with me. Especially if you're reading my books. But it's like looking at a book of paintings where *Guernica* is the same size as a Holbein portrait. You get no sense of the scale of things, of the nature of the artist's ambition.

Q: Isn't ambition a little . . . corny?

TP: [*raises .38; cocks hammer*] I'm sorry; would you care to repeat that?

Q: I said, "Ambition makes me horny."

TP: [*lowering .38*] Yeah, me too. Listen, I want to talk about novels right now, because that's what I write.

Q: You're also writing for TV, aren't you?

TP: [*angrily; defensively*] Yeah—so what? Besides—it's not TV; it's HBO . . .

Q: [*holding up hands*] Nothing wrong with that. Just checking.

TP: Computers and e-books and smartphones all basically look alike. They are strictly vehicles; you pick them up to step through them into some consensus reality; you're wired in. Everything is leveled out. When everything has equal weight, everything is weightless. The world they offer is one of infinitely diverse information with a common denominator—the screen. The computer is neutral in that it gives you access to limitless amounts of information, but the one requirement is that you have to get it on the computer. The information has no smell, no weight, no texture. Nothing that seriously impinges on your reality. People think it represents some kind of democratizing of information because everything's the same size. But democracy is when things of different sizes get a chance to mix it up and work it out, measure themselves in their respective strengths. If everything is the same size, there's no perspective. Perspective, as in, you know, painting. Everything becomes two-dimensional, flat . . .

Q: Isn't perspective an illusion? A person's face looming close to the viewer might appear larger than a skyscraper in the distance . . .

TP: Exactly. But that tells you something about reality. Whereas if you had a little chart where you could see everything rendered in exact relative scale but boiled down to a fifteen-inch frame, it might tell you something factual, but you wouldn't have an experience. You wouldn't learn something about the reality that something small near at hand can have a much larger impact than something large far away . . .

Q: Well . . . whatever . . . So what about the novel?

TP: I'm coming to that. A novel makes a world from one writer's perspective. It offers point of view, in the specialized literary sense, which is to say that it places point of view in a contrasting context. The writer makes the point of view, maybe multiple points of view, and also makes the context for those points of view. You make a world. A computer is a competing kind of world; it's an anti-world. The computer's ambition is to transcend point of view entirely.

Q: [*gaining confidence*] But what about all the chat rooms and discussion boards and social networking sites? There are a lot of points of view offered there.

TP: There are a lot of points of view being offered right now down in a dozen bars outside on Airline Highway, but very little perspective. Their dynamic is about letting off steam. If you want to cook something you have to keep the oven closed for a while, otherwise it will be half-baked. Nobody really works anything out at the corner bar. They just confirm their own assumptions. They think they have a point of view because they're arguing with somebody. But perspective means arguing with yourself. Two eyes, set in different locations on your face, make 3-D. Thelonious Monk used to say, "Two is one." That's what he meant.

Q: I'm having trouble following you.

TP: Yeah . . . right . . . well . . . I guess it boils down to some people like books and some people don't.

Q: But you're making a case for one over the other.

TP: I'm not, really. I'm just saying they're different.

Q: I mean, why is that important? Why is it important whether you get your information from a computer of some sort or from a physical book?

TP: [*regarding the questioner appraisingly*] The information is qualitatively different, isn't it? Isn't there some sort of meta-information in the weight of a book, in the effort and time it takes to produce it, as opposed to just hitting a button and sending your latest notion off into the Internet? There's a resonance. Somebody else might have held the book, and valued it. Maybe they made notes in the margin, and kept it and handed it down to their children . . . I mean, you can give somebody a book; it has weight, it's a gesture of faith in the future. The message of the Internet is that the moment is what matters; the closer you can get to that virtual moment, the closer you are to reality. But a novel offers perspective; it says time curves and things change, and what looks big now might really be small, and vice-versa, and here's a model of how that works . . . I mean, if there's no future for books, there's no future. People who are interested in time, and have a taste for the individual consciousness up against mass con-sensus, will always have a taste for books.

Q: So that's your prediction about the future of books?

TP: [*annoyed*] Look, I don't know about the fucking future. Nobody knows what's going to happen in ten seconds.

Q: [*exasperated*] Oh, that is ridiculous; everybody is obsessed with it. There are tens of thousands of websites dedicated to making guesses about the future . . . [*gasping*] Dear God . . . what are you doing?

TP: [*points the .38 at the questioner and tightens his index finger on the trigger*] I've just about had it with this conversation.

Q: Please . . . Don't shoot . . .

TP: [*pulls trigger; flame sprouts from the tip of the gun. It is a gag-store cigarette lighter*]

Q: [*shaking, wiping forehead with a kerchief*] Jesus . . . What is wrong with you?

TP: Oh, come on . . . You saw that coming, didn't you?

> *From* The Late American Novel: Writers on the
> Future of Books, *Jeff Martin and C. Max Magee, editors*

Three

Hurricane Katrina and its aftermath changed everything for me. It knocked over the tables, emptied the drawers, and changed the locks. For five years it became the gravitational center of my life, as I dug out, and as New Orleans dug out. Like most other New Orleanians, by the time the five-year anniversary rolled around, I was ready for a new chapter.

After City of Refuge was completed, in 2008, I began work on a new novel, set before Katrina and having nothing to do with New Orleans. It was a relief to be thinking about something else. As I worked, though, I found that I wasn't the same writer I was before the disaster. A lot of new information—not just socioeconomic, but emotional and spiritual—had entered the picture, and I needed to sift through it and do some thinking about what mattered to me in my writing as I went ahead with the new novel. The essay that follows is one gesture in the direction of that stock-taking—by no means the final word.

Before writing the essay, I went back to read, or reread, some of the recent and semi-recent manifestos dealing with the question of how writers should write and readers should read, and I found myself getting more and more depressed the more I read. Tom Wolfe's 1989 Harper's piece "Stalking the Billion-Footed Beast: A Literary Manifesto for the New Social Novel"; B. R. Myers's grouchy 2001 Atlantic diatribe "A Reader's Manifesto: An Attack on the Growing Pretentiousness of American Literary Prose"; Jonathan Franzen's 1996 Harper's piece "Perchance to Dream: In the Age of Images, a Reason to Write Novels" and his subsequent New Yorker article "Mr. Difficult," an anxiety-of-influence manifesto against novelist William Gaddis and literary difficulty in general; Ben Marcus's Harper's attack on Franzen's perceived attack on William Gaddis ("Why Experimental Fiction Threatens to Destroy Publishing, Jonathan Franzen, and Life As We Know It: A Correction"); Cynthia Ozick's 2007 Harper's attack on Franzen's and Marcus's attacks on one another ("Literary Entrails: The Boys in the Alley, the Disappearing Readers, and the Novel's Ghostly Twin"); and David Shields's 2010 book Reality Hunger: A Manifesto, as well as essays and letters and rants by Zola, Flaubert, Nabokov, Proust, and a dim torchlight procession of other axe-grinders. The process of reading all this advocacy for one or another approach to an activity that can really only be worthwhile if you figure out your own approach was so oppressive that I put the essay aside for nine months. I almost gouged out my own eyeballs with a rusty melon-ball scoop I found in William Dean Howells's attic. I mean, look at this paragraph. It made you tired just to read it, right?

Anyway. The net effect was to make me sick at even the suggestion that there was a right or wrong way to write or read. In a 1990 lecture at Iowa, asked about the Tom Wolfe Harper's essay, which had only recently been published, Norman Mailer said that when writers talk about how other writers should write, what they are usually really saying is, "This is how I can write." Words of wisdom.

So the following essay is my little farewell to all that manifestology. It is followed by one last column from the Oxford American. It's about record collecting, but it's also about grace, in the theological sense. And that is it for this collection. If you want to find me, I'll be working on my next novel.

THE DEVIL AND
GUSTAVE FLAUBERT

Along time ago, when I was getting started as a writer, I got a note from an editor at one of the big magazines—a rejection note, naturally—bestowing some faint ritual praise on the story under rejection, in the course of which the editor wrote that my story was "about evil—the best subject, really."

Aside from the dissonance involved in hearing work praised as it is being rejected—most writers get used to that—the remark confused me. I didn't think the story was about evil, for one thing, and his claim that evil was the "best" subject raised its own questions. What were the other contenders for best subject? Were they ranked in any particular order? Does a story always have a "subject"? And, anyway, what did he mean by "evil," and why was it the best of all possible subjects? The editor in question was a clean-cut, affable fellow with lovely manners, a family man, and a skilled operator in the switchy waters of the New York lit biz. I wondered how much evil he had had in his life, and why he had such need of it in the fiction he read.

Years later, in the spring of 2010, during a residency at the Virginia Center for the Creative Arts, I was sitting around before dinner with a couple of writers, talking about favorite short stories. Some usual suspects were mentioned—Chekhov, Flannery O'Connor, John Cheever, Raymond Carver, Alice Munro, Isaac Babel—and along the way I expressed my admiration for Carver's story "Cathedral," with its extraordinary moment of unlikely communion between two characters at the story's end. One of the other writers winced and said that he found the story sentimental and had never liked it.

I think the story is Carver's finest, so I pressed him on this. Why didn't he like it?

"I don't like stories that tell me what I want to hear," he said. If a story ended well, he went on, he felt that it was playing to his wish fulfillment. He wanted to hear things, in other words, that he didn't want to hear.

This writer is a nice guy in middle age, with several books of fiction to his credit, a comfortable teaching position, a marriage of several decades, and a grown son with whom he has what appears to be an excellent relationship. We're not close, but I assume he has had his share of love and human connection, along with bad luck and loss. Why would he want to disqualify a significant part of his experience from a place in fiction?

He went on to say that all human experience was essentially fraudulent, and that love itself was an elaborate form of fraudulence. At that point I decided that I knew him well enough to tell him that I thought this was ridiculous, and that his own experience proved it. "Talk about fraudulence," I said. "You don't even believe what you're saying right now." To his credit, his face turned bright red and he laughed guiltily, conceding the point. He didn't believe it. So why was he saying it?

Literary modernism, beginning with *Madame Bovary*, gave writers an array of sharp tools with which to probe the relations between appearance and underlying truth. Flaubert's willingness to illuminate his characters' flaws and self-deceptions with pitiless clarity, his unmatched eye for the telling detail and the precise metaphor, his insistence on style as salvation, on the correct word, on prose itself as the bulwark against what T. S. Eliot called the "general mess of imprecision of feeling," created such seductively holographic mimetic effects that his method began to seem more than merely a highly evolved and sophisticated tool for getting at a larger truth. Style itself became truth.

If any paradigm of writing were designed to flatter the writer's opinion of himself, it would be Flaubert's. Outside, all around, swirls a universe of shit and sham, against which stands style, technique itself, in the person of the writer. Everyone in the fictional world of *Madame Bovary* stinks—Charles Bovary, Homais, Emma herself. They stink of terminal naïveté, of bourgeois venality, of self-satisfaction, of provincialism, of outright stupidity, of romantic self-delusion. There is only one agency in the book that doesn't stink, and that is the writing itself—and, by extension, the author. Pitiless, fearless, the wounded surgeon plies the steel, a paradigm of intelligence, courage, skill, and . . . well, authority, in a kind of extended revenge upon the world under description. For the ambitious writer, who more often than not begins as an oversensitive outsider trying desperately to avoid the sins of sentimentality, of not being smart enough, of betrayal by one's own failings or feelings, Flaubert's sentences, in their lapidary focus, their intelligence, their immaculate cool, are there to insist that only the most rigorous syntactical and lexicographical prophylaxis can ward off that stink.

Flaubert's approach was partly a reaction to a time of revolution in Europe, of grand rhetoric that sooner or later betrayed every ideal it advertised. His method became crucial in the aftermath of World War One, with Europe again fallen to pieces amid its summonses to glory. An insistence on clarity, intelligence, and skepticism became the necessary antidote to the empty pomposity of the slogans that helped steer Europe (and much of the rest

of the world) into the ditch. The techniques that Flaubert pioneered, and which his modernist offspring, especially Joyce and
Hemingway, brought into general use, picked up a philosophical,
and even a political, valence that lent aestheticism a dimension
that reached beyond the strictly aesthetic.

Today we are learning, again, the ways in which reflexive piety
and patriotism lead to disaster. The examples are so obvious that
there is no point in listing them. The detached, precise, cool, and
intelligent analysis, the articulate nuance, the heightened wari-
ness of the sentimental and the tumescently advocatory, are necessary virtues. But we are also learning—again—that a lack of
any conviction is as corrosive as its inverse, and reflexive cynicism
is as bad as reflexive credulity. Each, in fact, feeds the other.

In an essay published forty-five years after the appearance of *Madame Bovary*, Henry James noted that Flaubert had pulled off the
trick of fathering both the naturalist and the aestheticist streams
of the novel. On the one hand, literary courage was equated with
facing into and depicting the worst of society and human life with
clinical detachment; anything less would constitute a failure of
nerve. On the other hand, literary intelligence was equated with
style itself—the *mot juste*, the perfect sentence. In Flaubert, truth
and beauty existed in a kind of tragic relation to one another; the
beauty of the execution was there in opposition to the wasteland of
the subject matter.

Any writer will admire a good sentence. Sentences can lilt,
and drift, and settle lightly down. Sentences punch. Sentences
thrust, and parry. Sentences can extend out past the point at
which they might reasonably have been expected to end, bend-
ing under the weight of first one dependent clause, then another,
tiring the reader out, making her wonder when the line will end,
but not, perhaps, without hope that the exercise will deliver some
point, however small—some perception or image that will arrive,

at the very end, like, say, a caramel apple. Who would argue that the form of the sentence should not help deliver the sentence's meaning? But in all hermeneutical humility one is entitled to ask, "What is the meaning of this meaning?" Or, as Barry Hannah once said in response to an Iowa student who claimed to like a story's "drive": "Yes, but what is it driving *at*?"

It is entirely possible to have a breathtakingly realized technique and use it in the service of something trivial, or ill-considered, or even evil. (Susan Sontag's essay "Fascinating Fascism," on the career of filmmaker Leni Riefenstahl, is a most useful examination of this phenomenon.) A finely honed technique can be used to lie, to flatter, to seduce. An admiration for the technique itself can override or anesthetize an ability to evaluate or even to see the human dimension of what the artist is saying. A supremely skilled artist may use a great technique to hide something from himself, just as a wily analysand can construct subterfuges to elude the purpose of psychoanalysis. To focus on the surface of sentences at the expense of the meaning toward which the sentences build is a way of evading the most important questions one can ask of a text. Some claim that the surface of a sentence is its meaning, but that's like saying the design of a chainsaw is its meaning. You can use a chainsaw to clear a road or to cut somebody to pieces.

Sainte-Beuve, after praising Flaubert's literary virtues in his 1857 review of *Madame Bovary*, wrote, "there is one reproach which I must make against his book. It is that the good is too much absent; not a single character represents it. . . . If truth alone is sought, it is not entirely and necessarily to be found only on the side of evil, on the side of human stupidity and perversity. In provincial lives, where there are so many vexations, persecutions, sickly ambitions, and petty annoyances, there are also good and beautiful souls. . . . Why not show them, too?"

Henry James, who practically hyperventilated in admiration of *Madame Bovary*, voices a similar reservation about its characters, which he also applies to *Sentimental Education*'s Frédéric Moreau.

Why did Flaubert choose, as special conduits of the life he proposed to depict, such inferior and in the case of Frédéric such abject human specimens? . . . He wished in each case to make a picture of experience—middling experience, it is true—and of the world close to him; but if he imagined nothing better for his purpose than such a heroine and such a hero, both such limited reflectors and registers, we are forced to believe it to have been by a defect of his mind. And that sign of weakness remains even if it be objected that the images in question were addressed to his purpose better than others would have been: the purpose itself then shows as inferior.

We can grant the author his material—we have to—and her genius, and still feel that it is possible to write about such "abject human specimens" with something like empathy and compassion, rather than revulsion at humanity. The effort to understand, to empathize, leads, finally, to humility. If it leads only to pride in one's sentences, something is wrong.

In the weeks and the months following Hurricane Katrina, one had a recurring experience. Sitting down to eat at a restaurant, or waiting in line at a grocery store, one asked the server, or the person standing next in line, how they did in the storm. I do not know how many times I heard some variation on the following, stated matter-of-factly: "We lost everything, but we're blessed. We got Mama into a facility in Houston, and we've been staying by my cousin in Boutte." Or their brother in McComb, or Baton Rouge. Or maybe their Mama didn't make it but they got Daddy into an assisted-living facility in Atlanta, where their cousin could look after him, "praise God." They were *blessed*—because they had a bed to sleep in, or because they were still alive even though every plate had been broken, every family photo lost, every piece of clothing and every piece of furniture ruined beyond repair, every toy, and every memento. They would say this without a shred or a shadow of irony, and they had earned the right to be taken at their word.

This is a literary essay, and I'm sorry to drag in exhibits from what people once referred to as real life. My justification in doing so is that as long as we use terms such as "evil," "fraudulence," "love," "goodness," "perversity," "sentimentality," and the rest, the airtight shrink-wrap around questions of style and language has already been fatally punctured. To the extent that writing has any reference at all to the phenomena of life outside the circle of our reading experience, the evidence is admissible. To the extent that we are talking about the kind of writing that concerns itself with characters whom we allow ourselves to think of as "real" for at least the duration of the book, it is not just admissible but necessary, and central.

Allow me to draw uncomfortably close, here. It wasn't just triumph-over-adversity stuff, heart-of-gold stuff. One person I knew hanged herself, and another shot himself, because they couldn't take it. One woman, a mother I had known for years, jumped off of a bridge after spending a lovely Mardi Gras Day with friends and family. Just parked her car and jumped off the fucking bridge during the morning rush hour. A bookstore owner broke down crying in her store while we talked, with customers browsing around her, as she told me how her father had died in a makeshift triage unit on the floor of the airport. Dozens of people who spent years, and most of their life savings, rebuilding their houses after the disaster had those houses expropriated in the name of a real estate scheme that will profit some of the worst scum in and out of the city. How someone in that position could find the strength to go on, let alone to make an occasional joke or enjoy a meal, is a mystery. But it's also a fact. And after such knowledge, what forgiveness for the easy, lazy cynicism of the privileged and insulated who flatter themselves that they know the last word about human emotions and it is "shit"?

I hate to poke a hole in the tissue of my otherwise modulated sentences. I'm not being self-righteous, or priding myself on my oh-so-precious wounds. I got off relatively easy, as Katrina trauma goes. Out of my house for six months, a little touch of PTSD, nothing too bad. You can read about it elsewhere, if you want to. But it did make me impatient with shallow nihilism delivered from a safe, tenured perch. And it raised questions about choice, literary and nonliterary, that I might not have had to think about otherwise.

A refined style, or a fine style, at least, comes out of a sense of continuity not just between past and future but between the author and the reader, the sense that the reader shares the same reference points and the same developed antennae for tone, diction, pace, and the other elements that animate prose. Just as one needs the equivalent of a particular background to understand what is going on at a debutante ball, or at certain cocktail parties, a mandarin literary style presumes a shared social milieu stable enough to act as a norm against which the finest overtones may create their delicate moiré patterns.

In this sense, at least, style has always been a problem in American art, because the essence of the social reality is not stability and continuity but transformation and mobility. There is no guarantee that the reader, or even the various characters, will speak the same language. Characters wear masks; they come out of nowhere; they change shape. That, itself, is the common fact. American music, which is constantly combining and recombining elements from diverse sources, has provided a kind of subterranean ligature that embodied American ideals even while those ideals were being kicked to death in the civic, political, and economic arenas. But since Melville, Twain, and Whitman, our literature has struggled to find a form equal to the kaleidoscopic, protean nature of the national life.

Hurricane Katrina wasn't a regional event, although it was treated as such in the media; it was a national one. People who had never been off their New Orleans block landed in Arizona; white Connecticut families suddenly had African-American houseguests, and on and on. And into full national view erupted a painful reality of poverty, race, and social disproportion that had been there, hidden in plain sight, all along—not just in New Orleans but deeply embedded in the weave of the national reality, acknowledged or unacknowledged.

In writing my novel *City of Refuge*, which followed characters through the events of Katrina, this became partly a technical problem of composition. The book demanded to be written in a couple of different styles; a single, consistent style would telegraph a continuity to the events, and there was no continuity. And certainly a fine mandarin literary style would run counter to the reality in the book—the variety of the characters, and the disjunctive, harsh, chaotic nature of their experience. There are times when good taste is in bad taste. And I felt that readers shouldn't come out of a book about such a disaster feeling as if they had just spent a day at a spa having their assumptions manicured and their complacencies flattered.

In the aftermath, a small handful of readers expressed discomfort, even embarrassment, that the book contained no evil characters. An evil character, in life as in fiction, can act as a grounding wire to discharge the currents of guilt, anxiety, and shame evoked by individual or collective failure. In Katrina, the facts pointed toward a collective failure of government and, by extension, of the society represented by that government. Against that collective failure, and in light of the collective responsibility for it, hundreds of thousands of individual characters struggled to rebuild broken lives. With Katrina, the finger pointed unavoidably at the witness—each citizen, each viewer, each reader—rather than at an Other who could embody the guilt and carry it away.

• • •

"Though I have never suffered, thank God, at the hands of man . . . still I detest my fellow-beings and do not feel that I am their fellow at all." That's Flaubert, in a letter to Victor Hugo composed at the time of *Madame Bovary*'s writing. Also to Hugo, around the same time, he wrote, "What is best in art will always elude mediocre natures, that is to say, seven eighths of the human race. So why denature truth for the benefit of the vulgar?"

It may be one of the underrecognized tragedies of literary history that the intelligence and talent that resulted in all of Flaubert's exquisite observation and fine prose was coupled in him with an inability to experience a degree of humility in the face of the kinds of sacrifices and strengths that those mediocre natures exhibit in caring for their families, in making it through the day. It is the great weakness of Flaubert's otherwise sublime art, and of his legacy to literature—the message that the truth about humans is one-sidedly ugly, and that the writer (and the adequate reader) stands outside and above, redeemed only by style.

After the conversation with my friend who hates "Cathedral," I found myself wondering what the psychic benefit might be in telling yourself that, while you want to hear good things, you instead make the brave choice to face the bad. Fiction writers pride themselves on getting underneath characters' ostensible motives and finding the true motive structure underneath. If we can do this with characters, the author ought to be eligible for the same questioning.

The flip side of brutality and evil is, dependably, sentimentality. The hit man kissing the picture of his sainted mother before he exterminates a mark, the mawkish evocations of home and youth in Nazi propaganda, the image of the pristine Southern belle under siege that propelled so many lynchings, the need for cleansing, cleansing . . . Sentimentality is the perfume that disguises, and even justifies, this lust for brutal cleansing and killing.

But the inverse is also true: that an attitude, or a pose, of cool and bracing willingness to face evil and brutality, and to dismiss its opposite as wish fulfillment, might function as a seawall against a tide of shame and grief so heavy that it can't be faced directly. The stink of mistakes made, or possibilities lost, can make an image of the good intolerable. If it is too expensive to look at what might have been and realize that one may just not have been good enough, it can be a comfort to think that it was never possible in the first place. This evasion is possible on a societal level, as well as in the private hearts of individuals. The novel is still the best tool we have for understanding the one level in terms of the other.

An insistence that seven eighths of the human race is basically dispensable, and that we inhabit a doomed, shrinking island of the elite, is the quintessence of the sentimental. Flaubert, the begetter of our sharpest tools and our most brilliant mistakes, paid dearly, for his cynicism, and for the right to express it. He realized it in prose that changed the way people wrote and perceived. He was a titan. But that is never the end of discussion. Flaubert's weaknesses as a writer were weaknesses of character. It takes nothing away from his literary genius to say that his human weakness left a wound in the writing. Maybe it left a wound in all of us who followed him. It hardened our hearts and, in the process, broke them. But maybe we don't need to sit up with that ghost anymore.

Anyway, for me, for the length of the story "Cathedral," Raymond Carver was a greater writer than Flaubert, because he was able to get past that tired old jive.

NOTE IN A BOTTLE

*[The pattern] imposed by a circular image of this kind compensates
the disorder and confusion of the psychic state—namely, through the
construction of a central point to which everything is related, or by
a concentric arrangement of the disordered multiplicity and of contradictory and irreconcilable elements. This is evidently an* attempt
at self-healing *on the part of Nature, which does not spring from
conscious reflection but from an instinctive impulse.*

—C. G. Jung, *Mandala Symbolism*

Sunday afternoon along the river road heading west from
New Orleans; low clouds over the levee. I was in the passenger seat, for once, as we passed under the giant, rickety
Huey P. Long Bridge and out through Harahan, where the housing subdivisions creep outward, like a fungus, from Metairie. I
always expect to see a billboard reading, TIRED OF SURPRISES?
LIVE HERE. A wasteland of time and space spreading out in all
directions.

That day I had been feeling edgy for no reason I could name,
and I was no fun to be around. I remembered the feeling all too
well from when I was a kid, returning home from church on a grey
afternoon, watching the leaves tossing fitfully along the curbs, the

feeling of being in exile, somehow, from someplace I had never
seen, and which would have been a lot better than where I was.

So we decided to take a ride, a time-honored way to put the
blues off for a few hours. We had made it out into Kenner, passing
modest brick houses built on cement slabs with lawns that were
turning brown, dogs in groups of two and three, when the car
slowed sharply and pulled to the shoulder.

"What happened?" I said, jolted out of wherever I was in my
head.

"You want me to prove I love you?" she said. It wasn't an entirely
rhetorical question, but she was smiling mischievously, looking
into the side view, waiting for the car behind us to pass. Then she
made a U-turn and started back toward where we'd come from,
slowed immediately, and I saw the sign, tiny, stuck into somebody's
lawn: FLEA MARKET, with an arrow pointing down the side street,
away from the levee. Usually I am the one who notices these signs.
I must, I thought, be slipping. She pulled into the street, and we
made our way along, guided by more tiny signs that took us over
the railroad tracks and along behind some giant Quonset huts.

Eventually we found it, a permanent building the size of an
airplane hangar. It would have been hard to imagine a more out-
of-the-way location. We parked and strolled in together through
an open garage door beneath the dim fluorescent lights high up
under the corrugated metal roof, through the aisles and alleys of
forgotten junk.

You train yourself not to get optimistic in these circumstances.
Flea markets often mean factory-second clothes, cheap, shrink-
wrapped tools. But this place had a promising mix of older furniture, display cases with military medals and advertising pens,
stacks of sheet music along with hideous ashtrays and baby stroll-
ers, computer equipment from the late 1980s, ancient boom
boxes.

And then I saw the 78s and felt the immediate surge in my
pulse that they always elicit. There were several stacks of the

shellac discs in bins, next to some LPs and eight-track tapes. I squeezed Mary's hand and walked over to the bins. The old 78s have fascinated me for as long as I can remember. Each one is a little world of its own, a ten-inch-wide mandala in which the grooves spiral gradually inward to the central point, which is the ending, a disappearing center consisting of the hole through which the turntable spindle fits.

The 78s contain about three minutes of recorded sound on each side, three minutes in which every detail counts, as in good fiction. For the three minutes between the recording's beginning and its ending, the blues singers and jazz bands and old-time string bands cast their thoughts, their whole style of approaching reality, out into the world without being able to know exactly where it would all land. Such wit, such intensity, such heartbreak, such style, such care with the expressive detail. Each record is like a note in a bottle. They made the records, and the records landed in places no one could predict, and they added oxygen to the world. Finding a good one is like experiencing grace itself descending upon you. Time itself is redeemed, to live again and again, expanding infinitely.

Now, standing on the cement floor under the high, dim lights, I looked through maybe a hundred records in various small stacks squirreled away under tables and on shelves. While they were from the period that I favored—the late 1920s and early 1930s—most of the records offered more or less inconsequential dance or pop music of the time, by performers like Jesse Crawford, Seger Ellis, Art Gillham, Nat Shilkret—the now-forgotten artists who were the Bee Gees and Ricky Martins of their period. I found one or two things that were marginally interesting, but the search was basically a washout. As a formality, I asked the proprietress if she had any more 78s lying around anywhere.

She gave a short, almost derisive laugh. "Sure," she said. "Come on over here." I frowned and followed her around a corner, and stacked up against a wall were at least thirty boxes big enough to hold fifty records each.

"Holy smokes," I said.

"Yeah, well, when you get finished smoking there's just as many boxes up front."

Mary was standing nearby when this exchange took place. I looked at her, and she said, "I'll be outside. Don't worry. I have the paper. Have fun." She gave me a reassuring smile and headed out. I sat on a stool and started looking.

Quantity, in Engels's famous remark, changes quality. But not to a shellac collector. Each new record you pull from the stack is a potential New Beginning, as fresh as the pull of the lever on a slot machine to a confirmed gambler. The records were grouped together in the boxes roughly by label—Victor, Brunswick, Columbia, OKeh. Again most were from that late '20s to early '30s period. There were multiple copies of certain titles, which suggested, along with the extraordinary quantity, that they came from a store stock. But store stock tends to be found in new or nearly new condition. Many of these had clearly been played repeatedly. A puzzle.

It took about forty-five minutes to go through every box. The proprietress loaned me a red marker so that I could check off the boxes I'd looked through. I turned up nothing. Some of the records were tantalizingly close—duds by pop singers who occasionally recorded with jazz accompaniments, items by well-known personalities like Maurice Chevalier or Fanny Brice, which might have interested another collector but not me. Still, the time frame was right. I could almost smell the scent of what I was looking for. But the fact that there was almost nothing was discouraging; it suggested that someone else had gone through the boxes already and beaten me to the good stuff.

When I was finished in back I stood up and made my way around front ("You didn't find *anything*?" the lady asked as she pointed me in a new direction), where I was now confronted by a small mountain, an Aztec pyramid, of similar boxes, at least forty of them. The prospect of looking through all of them and again turning up nothing was momentarily demoralizing. Yet there was always the possibility. The possibility. Guiltily, I peeked out the door toward the car, where Mary was engrossed in the newspaper. I sat down on a stool with the marker and opened the first box.

It wasn't long before I pulled up a record that sent a jolt through me—"The Only Girl I Ever Loved" by Charlie Poole with the North Carolina Ramblers—Columbia 15711-D, from 1930, one of his last records, one side of which is not even available on CD. This one was in almost new condition. I fought the impulse to yell out. It's like catching a good trout. You don't want to spook the whole river. You unhook the fish, place it in your pack, and keep fishing. I quietly set the disc to one side and kept looking. Before long I pulled the next good one: a fine copy of "Nehi Mamma Blues" by the Memphis blues singer Frank Stokes, a very rare record. Breathing deeply through my nose I set it on top of the Poole record. A few records later I turned up a copy of "Got the Jake Leg Too" by the Ray Brothers, a Mississippi string band, a rare Victor 23500 series from the bottom of the Depression, also in fine condition.

Now I was getting excited; this had the markings of a major haul. I went out to tell Mary that I might be a while. She had moved the car into the shade of a tree and was reading the paper with the door open. She nodded indulgently. I told her, sotto voce, that I'd found a copy of "Got the Jake Leg Too." "That's good, honey," she said, reading.

I felt like Walter Huston in *The Treasure of the Sierra Madre*, setting up his scaffolding and sluice gates, concentrating feverishly, separating the gold from the bulk of the rock and clay. I went through every single disc, and before I was finished I'd also found a beautiful 1932 blues record on Columbia by Lonnie Johnson under the pseudonym Jimmy Jordan, a Depression-era Carter Family on Victor ("The Dying Soldier"), something by the old-time guitarist Henry Whitter on the Broadway label, entitled "There Was an Old Tramp," which turned out not even to be listed in any of my discographies, and several records by Gid Tanner and His Skillet Lickers, Riley Puckett, Kelly Harrell, and Fiddlin' John Carson.

By the time I finished, I had looked through at least three thousand discs and had whittled down my stack to thirty-five. I paid two dollars apiece for them ("They always find some good ones," the proprietress said as she counted out my change from a wad of bills she kept in the pocket of her housedress), and I walked out slightly overstimulated, a little toasted around the edges, but with a sense of satisfaction and even of gratitude for being able to retrieve these records from the mountain of chaos where they had languished. That my own emotional cloud cover seemed to have evaporated was not lost on me, either.

Mary had been reduced to reading the automotive supplement of the *Times-Picayune* and I felt a little sheepish. She looked tired, and I didn't blame her. She had, after all, been sitting there for almost two hours. Between the lines, her smile said, "Love costs." I didn't go into much detail about my finds. She understands and she doesn't understand. The important thing is that where understanding leaves off, she has the faith to hang with me anyway. Grace, I thought as we drove off, is not something anyone has a right to expect in this life. But when you find it, you can at least say thank you. Which I did.

From the Oxford American, *January/February 2001*

About the author

About the book

Insights,
Interviews
& More . . .

Read on

Meet Tom Piazza

Tom Piazza is the author of ten books of fiction and nonfiction, including the Willie Morris Award–winning novel *City of Refuge* and the post-Katrina classic *Why New Orleans Matters*. His other books include the novel *My Cold War*, which won the Faulkner Society Award for the Novel, and the short story collection *Blues And Trouble*, which won the James Michener Award for Fiction. He currently writes for the HBO drama series *Treme*, created by David Simon and set in post-Katrina New Orleans.

No less a literary critic than Bob Dylan has said, "Tom Piazza's writing pulsates with nervous electrical tension—reveals the emotions that we can't define." Piazza's work has

Rick Gargiulo

been praised by writers as different as Norman Mailer, Mary Gaitskill, Richard Ford, Monica Ali, Barry Hannah, Ann Beattie, Richard Russo, Douglas Brinkley, James Alan McPherson, and Elvis Costello. Piazza is a graduate of the Iowa Writers' Workshop.

Piazza is a well-known writer on American music as well. He won a Grammy Award for his album notes to *Martin Scorsese Presents The Blues: A Musical Journey* and is a three-time winner of the ASCAP Deems Taylor Award for Music Writing, for his books *Understanding Jazz* and *The Guide to Classic Recorded Jazz*, as well as for his *Oxford American* article "Note in a Bottle," which appears in *Devil Sent the Rain*. His writing on music and American culture has appeared in the *New York Times*, *The Atlantic*, *The New Republic*, the *Village Voice*, *Bookforum*, *Columbia Journalism Review*, and many other places. He lives in New Orleans. You can visit him at www.tompiazza.com, or at his author page on Facebook. ∿

A Conversation with Tom Piazza

Tom Piazza and his editor, Cal Morgan, have worked together on six works of fiction and nonfiction, dating back to the early 1990s. They talked about Devil Sent the Rain *in the spring of 2011.*

Cal Morgan: Some readers may be surprised to find Gustave Flaubert, Jelly Roll Morton, and Bob Dylan all sharing mental space (and cover space) in this collection. What was going through your mind as you pulled these figures together? What do such diverse figures have in common for you?

Tom Piazza: Real artists are all mutants. That's the main thing artists have in common. None of the people in the book takes anyone else's word for how reality looks. If anything connects them, it's the idea that the individual sensibility is what you have to assert against a basically hostile or entropic world. Of course it takes a lot of hard work to convert that individual sensibility into something other people can use. Obviously a lot of ego is involved. . . .

I think there's a real affinity between imaginative writers and creative musicians. You have to stand at the microphone, actual or virtual, and deliver something that's worth someone else's time, and that people can't find anywhere else. My favorite writers all have a strong performative aspect to what they do—where you can feel their minds working between the lines. I like a little sense of struggle in there, a little trace of the improvisation that is always involved in coming up with the scenes and ideas.

Morgan: I can see that in the work of Norman Mailer, whom you write about, but didn't Flaubert try to erase any evidence of his own effort in his prose?

Piazza: He tried, but at the same time he was absolutely obsessed with his own process. He wrote about it constantly in his letters, especially the ones he wrote when he was composing *Madame Bovary*.

Morgan: There is a lot of tension in the book around the question of what role an artist's persona plays in his or her art. In your essay on the singer-songwriter Gillian Welch, you claim to "trust the song, not the singer." Yet elsewhere you spend a lot of time thinking about the public faces of Dylan, Jimmie Rodgers, Mailer, and other artists. Are the personal qualities of artists a meaningful aspect of their work, or a distraction from it?

Piazza: Both. Artistic creation has always attracted speculation and fascination with the person who makes the art. The activity is recognized as ▶

> **❝** None of the people in the book takes anyone else's word for how reality looks. **❞**

being different in kind from other human activity, and yet it also feels familiar. That simultaneous sense of familiarity and strangeness is the essence of attraction.

Beginning in the twentieth century, with the rise of sound recording, film, and broadcast media, that fascination has grown exponentially. It has also coarsened in the process. One of the reasons artists are a little strange is that most of them simultaneously invite that fascination and are at least a little disgusted by it. That ambivalence itself is very interesting.

Morgan: In the 1980s and early '90s, you wrote a great deal about jazz. In the years since, your focus has shifted to what some might consider more "vernacular" music—country, blues, bluegrass, folk. Was this a conscious choice?

Piazza: In 1991 I left New York City, after years of living there, to attend the Iowa Writers' Workshop. Before I left, a friend made up a whole library of cassette tapes for me—like thirty or forty; he just ran them off. Some of the artists I had heard of, most I hadn't. Everything from Jimmie Rodgers and the Carter Family to Uncle Dave Macon, Mac Wiseman, Hobart Smith, Almeda Riddle, the Monroe Brothers, Mike Seeger, the New Lost City

Ramblers, Ewan MacCool, Hedy West, Hank Thompson, Jimmy Martin, Dock Boggs. Some blues in there, too: Crying Sam Collins, the Memphis Jug Band, Frank Stokes, the Mississippi Sheiks. . . . It went on and on.

I listened to those tapes as I drove to Iowa, and that mix of sound got fused, for me, with the experience of leaving New York and moving into the heart of the country. I listened to those tapes the whole three years I was in Iowa. It was like having a giant ham in the refrigerator. You'd just go in and cut yourself another slice. Eventually I started playing and singing, as well. There were a lot of good players and singers in Iowa City and still are— Greg Brown, Dave Moore, Bo Ramsey, Dave Zollo, Al Murphy.

Iowa City is a cosmopolitan bubble in the middle of endless farm country. If you drive for ten minutes, you're out in the rolling cornfields. Everything about it was so different from New York that it demanded a different soundtrack. Jazz is very urban music. The subtext is always the fusion of disparate cultures in a hothouse environment. All the folk music I was listening to also had that syncretic aspect to it—all American music does—but it was under less pressure, in a sense. The elements exist in a different relation to one another. The musical structures are usually ▶

7

simpler than those found in most jazz, and the expression is a little more straightforward. That's not to say that the result is any less profound.

I think most writers' experience of something isn't complete until they have written about it. The writing is a way of processing experience. I always wrote about music. One of the dangers of writing about art is that you can become a specialist. You get known for writing about a subject, and so you get asked to write about it more, and pretty soon you start repeating yourself, and then your experience begins to grow dull. At a certain point I felt that I had said what I had to say about jazz, and I was interested in all these other kinds of music, too, so I started thinking about them in print. But I've never stopped listening to jazz. I just went through a big Sonny Rollins phase, in fact.

Morgan: The essays in *Devil Sent the Rain* always seem to circle back to the context that America provides, which informs these artists and against which they work. Do you think our country recognizes its artists for what they actually create?

Piazza: I'm not sure what you mean by "our country." Are you talking about the state apparatus, or the citizens?

> 66 I think most writers' experience of something isn't complete until they have written about it. 99

I don't love the idea of the state getting too involved in "recognizing" artists.

Morgan: I was thinking about citizens—about what meaning artists really have to the audiences who follow them. As you point out, Jimmie Rodgers embodied the new promises and dangers of America in the 1920s. A decade or two later, the character of Charlie Chan offered moviegoers an example of sly rationality in the face of an increasingly crazy geopolitical landscape. Do you think these effects were key reasons for their success in their time, or were they more like dividends that have paid off in retrospect?

Piazza: Important artists are usually important because they articulate something of which the audience is not yet fully conscious. Even the artists themselves may not be fully conscious of it. The theme, or the concern, or the subject, is there under the surface, but it can't yet be seen directly. An artist gives it some kind of tangible symbolic embodiment through image and sound, in the same way that dreams express elements in the psyche that haven't yet reached the dreamer's conscious mind.

I don't mean necessarily in terms of subject matter. Someone who says to ▶

> " Important artists are usually important because they articulate something of which the audience is not yet fully conscious. "

himself, "I will now write a novel about climate change, because it is an Important Issue . . ." is likely to deliver something dead on arrival. Creative artistic work isn't primarily a linear, rational process. At some point the rational mind comes in and works with that dreamlike mind; otherwise you can end up with something unintelligible. It's a partnership, or a dance, involving both parts. But, for me, the intuitive part has to lead the way.

Obviously, if that is how you work, elements enter the picture that will surprise you, and that even run counter to what you think you want to say. You have to recognize the need for that and create a space where that can happen. The will can't dominate the process, or control the results in advance.

Generally speaking, I think this has become a harder thing for people to recognize and understand, in America at least. There's even a degree of hostility toward it. In any case, people who have no feeling for imaginative expression have seemed freer in the past few years to express that hostility. People are anxious about everything— the economy, the environment, the political process itself. Images of domination and control become attractive in proportion to the degree that elements of unpredictability and

vulnerability feel threatening.
Art constantly reminds us of
unpredictability and vulnerability,
so it is a logical target.

Morgan: As you mention in your
introduction, *Devil Sent the Rain*
changes course in Part Two, after
the impact of Katrina shifted your
compass. For me, though, the most
surprising moment comes just before
that—in your 2004 essay "World Gone
Wrong Again," with its wild, arresting
parade of images and questions. At
the time, did you recognize that your
writing was leading you in a new, more
urgent direction—in terms of both
style and content?

Piazza: Not really. That was the way
I had to write that particular piece.
I wasn't thinking about any new
direction. I'm not sure that it did
represent a new direction. I mean,
I did write more conventional pieces
again after that. But things were headed
straight toward a brick wall in America
right around when I wrote that piece.
We had invaded Iraq, a disastrous
decision for every reason you can think
of, and the media were still giving the
Bush administration a free ride, and
like many people I found the situation
sickening. Maybe the sound in that
piece reflected some sense of
foreboding. Like a preemptive ▶

impatience with a certain kind of polite rhetorical strategy. Ironically enough, it was the administration's botched response to Katrina that ended their free ride in the media.

Morgan: In *Why New Orleans Matters*, you asked readers to consider what we had to lose, as Americans, if the city were allowed to fail after Katrina. Your post-Katrina pieces in this book suggest that the city remains both vital and vulnerable. What have we learned from these six years? And what are we still overlooking?

Piazza: One of the main things that give individuals the strength to come back from a disaster like Katrina is the love of a shared culture, attached to a sense of place. This is a lot of what we have been writing about in HBO's *Treme*, and my books *Why New Orleans Matters* and *City of Refuge* deal with it, too. Of course, the aftermath of a disaster like Katrina also brings huge opportunities for hustlers, con men, and real estate developers with no interest in the development of community, and everything to gain from wiping out any connection to the past or to place. But that's an old story, and certainly not specific to New Orleans. I offer some thoughts about it in "Other People's Houses" and "Incontinental Drift."

Morgan: From the very first piece in the collection, your profile of Jimmie Rodgers, through the new essay "The Devil and Gustave Flaubert," you return several times to the idea of sentimentality and its temptations. Why do you think the power of the sentimental persists—attracting both great artists (like Rodgers or Jimmy Martin) and callous politicians?

Piazza: Sentimentality involves the exaggeration of the emotionally obvious for a short-term gain, at the expense of the more subtle and ambiguous truth that usually lies underneath human relations. It's like a sugar high—you get an immediate rush of what feels like empathy, but eventually the body grows fat and slack.

You can also have the opposite problem. A certain kind of sensibility can easily mistake real emotion for sentimentality. Some people are fundamentally embarrassed by human connection. The embarrassment, or shame, translates into an active distaste, and they want to eliminate it from literature, make it only about language, or form. In extreme cases— someone like Robbe-Grillet, or Michel Butor—they are like people who starve themselves to eliminate every last ounce of fat from their body. The demand for utter rigor and purity suggests a degree of self-loathing, ▶

> " Sentimentality involves the exaggeration of the emotionally obvious for a short-term gain, at the expense of the more subtle and ambiguous truth. "

a deep shame in the body, even shame at being human in the first place. You need what Philip Roth called the "human stain." Obviously, without delight in language, intellectual surprise, formal satisfaction, literature wouldn't be literature. But without a tangible sense of the human it's a dead end—or I find it so, at least. Of course, Robbe-Grillet and Butor seem fatally dated now, like the serial composers who rigorously eliminated any trace of tonality from their music. I mean, apologies if you still dig that stuff. . . .

But all this talk is making me hungry. Let's go eat.

Morgan: One more question: Of all the people you write about here, who would you most like to have dinner with? Spend a lost weekend carousing with? Be marooned on a desert island with?

Piazza: Seriously? Same answer to all three—my better half, Mary, about whom I write in the final piece, "Note in a Bottle." Hope that doesn't sound sentimental; too bad if it does.

Now can we eat? ∽

Further Listening and Reading

DEVIL SENT THE RAIN has a Facebook page, for all who catch the connections between music, literature, food, and place. Visit it for film clips of musical performances and literary interviews, tips for further reading, and images of rare records, interesting places, and fried chicken. Charley Patton, James Joyce, Jimmy Martin, Bob Dylan, Norman Mailer, Furry Lewis, and their associates pop up on a regular basis. Be sure to "like" *Devil Sent the Rain*, and you'll be notified as new items are added.

In the meantime, you can't go wrong with the following:

Jimmie Rodgers

For the complete recordings: *Jimmie Rodgers: The Singing Brakeman* (six CDs, Bear Family).

Nearly complete, at a much lower price: *Recordings 1927–1933* (five CDs, JSP).

Single CD: *The Essential Jimmie Rodgers* (RCA).

Also worth hearing: Merle Haggard's *Same Train, a Different Time*, available online.

Charley Patton

For the complete recordings: *Screamin' and Hollerin' the Blues: The Worlds of Charley Patton* (seven CDs, Revenant). ▸

Nearly complete, at a much lower price: *Complete Recordings, 1929–34* (five CDs, JSP).

Single CD: *The Best of Charlie Patton* (Yazoo).

The Blues: A Musical Journey

Martin Scorsese Presents The Blues: A Musical Journey (five CDs, Hip-O Records).

Rev. Willie Morganfield

Several of Rev. Morganfield's gospel albums, including *Serving the Lord, The All-Powerful Name,* and *The Bible,* are available online.

Jimmy Martin

The Music of Bill Monroe from 1936–1994 (four CDs, MCA Nashville) includes many of Martin's classic recordings with Monroe and the Blue Grass Boys.

Songs of a Free Born Man (CMH Records) collects twenty-five of Martin's recordings as a leader between 1959 and 1992.

Will the Circle Be Unbroken includes Martin's unforgettable performance on "Sunny Side of the Mountain." In 2002, it was reissued in a 30th Anniversary edition (two CDs, Capitol).

Carl Perkins

For his complete recordings, 1954–1965: *The Classic Carl Perkins* (five CDs, Bear Family) collects his work for Sun, Columbia, and Decca.

Double CD: *The Essential Sun Collection* (two CDs, Recall Records).

Perkins's 1996 comeback CD was *Go Cat Go* (Dinosaur).

Gillian Welch

The essay "Trust the Song" was occasioned by Welch's first two CDs, *Revival* and *Hell Among the Yearlings* (both on Acony). Her later work includes *Time (The Revelator)*, *Soul Journey,* and *The Harrow & the Harvest.*

Bob Dylan

If you don't yet know Bob Dylan's work, you have a lot to look forward to. His catalog as of this writing runs to more than fifty albums, not counting best-of compilations. Even a top-ten list involves very painful omissions. But you could never leave out the following discs and sets: *The Freewheelin' Bob Dylan, Bringing It All Back Home, Highway 61 Revisited, Live 1966, Blonde on Blonde, Blood on the Tracks, Slow Train Coming, Infidels, Time Out Of Mind, Love and Theft,* and *The Bootleg Series, Vol. 1–3.* Oh— was that eleven? Sorry about that. Did I mention *The Basement Tapes*?

The Other Side of the Mirror: Bob Dylan Live at Newport Folk Festival 1963–1965, Murray Lerner's ▶

documentary, is available on DVD (Sony).

Gotta Serve Somebody: The Gospel Songs of Bob Dylan, with performances by Shirley Caesar, Aaron Neville, Rance Allen, the Fairfield Four, Mavis Staples, and Dylan himself, is available on CD (Sony).

The essay "World Gone Wrong Again" discusses Dylan's albums *Good As I Been to You* (1992) and *World Gone Wrong* (1993, both Sony). The albums that followed, *Time Out of Mind* and *Love and Theft*, are among the best work he has ever done.

Charlie Chan

Charlie Chan Collection, Vol. 1 (four DVDs, 20th Century Fox) collects five films featuring Warner Oland, including *Charlie Chan in London*, *Charlie Chan in Paris*, *Charlie Chan in Egypt*, *Charlie Chan in Shanghai*, and *Eran Trece*, the Spanish-language version of *Charlie Chan Carries On*. *The Charlie Chan Collection* went on to comprise five volumes, all of them necessary for the connoisseur.

The Charlie Chan Chanthology (six DVDs, MGM) picks up where the 20th Century Fox series leaves off, collecting Chan films featuring Sidney Toler, including *The Secret Service*, *The Chinese Cat*, *The Jade Mask*, *Meeting at Midnight*, *The*

Scarlet Clue, and *The Shanghai Cobra*.

Jelly Roll Morton

Complete Library of Congress Recordings (eight CDs, Rounder) is the definitive collection of Morton's recordings for Alan Lomax, featuring both spoken-word and musical performances.

Joe Liggins

"Going Back to New Orleans" can be found on *The Shuffle Boogie King: Joe Liggins and his Honeydrippers* (two CDs, Proper).

Dr. John's CD *Goin' Back to New Orleans* (Warner Bros.) closes with his own version.

Norman Mailer

Mailer wrote more than thirty books of wildly varying quality, almost all of which have something interesting going on that nobody else would have come up with. If you haven't read him, the five that I would recommend to begin with are *The Naked and the Dead* (his first book, a World War II novel that made him an instant celebrity at age twenty-five), *The Armies of the Night* (a journalistic piece on the 1967 March on the Pentagon, which won both the Pulitzer Prize and the National Book Award), *The Executioner's Song* (his stunning "nonfiction novel" about the crime ▶

and punishment of Gary Gilmore, which won him his second Pulitzer Prize), *Miami and the Siege of Chicago* (a classic of political reportage, on the 1968 Democratic and Republican conventions), and *Advertisements for Myself*, a seminal collection of essays in which Mailer first found his own distinctive voice.

If you want another five, try the novel *An American Dream*; the essay collections *The Presidential Papers* and *Cannibals and Christians*; his fantastic *The Fight*, about the 1974 Ali-Foreman championship bout; and his slim, brilliant polemic against the Iraq invasion, *Why Are We at War?*. The last title is also available as an audio book from Random House Audible through iTunes, read aloud by Mailer himself. It is well worth getting.

Gustave Flaubert

Madame Bovary is available in several translations, including a new one by Lydia Davis (Viking, 2010). My own reading is based on the translation I am most familiar with, by Francis Steegmuller (currently available as a Vintage paperback or Everyman's Library hardcover). Steegmuller also wrote *Flaubert and Madame Bovary*, one of the great literary biographies, newly reissued by NYRB Classics.

D on't miss the next book by your favorite author. Sign up now for AuthorTracker by visiting www.AuthorTracker.com.